AL CAPONE AND THE
1933 WORLD'S FAIR

Aerial view of the 1933 World's Fair (*Source:* Library of Congress)

AL CAPONE AND THE 1933 WORLD'S FAIR

The End of the Gangster Era in Chicago

WILLIAM ELLIOTT HAZELGROVE

ROWMAN & LITTLEFIELD
Lanham • Boulder • New York • London

Published by Rowman & Littlefield
A wholly owned subsidary of The Rowman & Littlefield Publishing Group, Inc.
4501 Forbes Boulevard, Suite 200, Lanham, Maryland 20706
www.rowman.com

Unit A, Whitacre Mews, 26-34 Stannary Street, London SE11 4AB

British Library Cataloguing in Publication Information Available

Library of Congress Cataloging-in-Publication Data
Names: Hazelgrove, William Elliott, 1959– author.
Title: Al Capone and the 1933 World's Fair : the end of the gangster era in
    Chicago / William Elliott Hazelgrove.
Description: Lanham : Rowman & Littlefield, [2017] | Includes bibliographical
    references and index.
Identifiers: LCCN 2017006093 (print) | LCCN 2017023717 (ebook) | ISBN
    9781442272279 (electronic) | ISBN 9781442272262 (cloth : alk. paper)
Subjects: LCSH: Chicago (Ill.)—History—20th century. | Chicago
    (Ill.)—Civilization—20th century. | Chicago (Ill.)—Social
    conditions—20th century. | Century of Progress International Exposition
    (1933–1934 : Chicago, Ill.)
Classification: LCC F548.5 (ebook) | LCC F548.5 .H39 2017 (print) | DDC
    977.3/11—dc23
LC record available at https://lccn.loc.gov/2017006093

For Kitty, Clay, Callie, and Careen

A smile can get you far, but a smile with a gun can get you further.
—AL CAPONE

I haven't been out of work since the day I took off my pants.
—SALLY RAND

CONTENTS

CONTENTS

Forty Years Later

Forty years after the Columbian Exposition and Dr. H. H. Holmes's macabre, psychopathic murders in 1893, Chicago decided it was time to have another world's fair. The times and the reasons differed, though. Orville and Wilber Wright had left the earth for twelve seconds in Kitty Hawk, North Carolina, in 1903. The *Titanic* had met black ice in the Atlantic and already been resting on the bottom of the ocean for two decades. The beau arts tradition of 1893 had been left in the dust for a modernist vision of the world promoted by industry, architecture, and advertising.

The intervening years had rendered Holmes's crimes quaint by comparison with the mechanized slaughter of World War I and gangsters duking it out over the fruits of Prohibition in the streets of Chicago. Humanism was dead. Technology and materialism had taken its place—a very different God indeed. The secular world was using Thompson submachine guns and offering sex through peep holes and in back rooms. The 1933 World's Fair would hold its breath and hope Al Capone didn't pull the whole thing under.

When the Great Depression came crashing down, many thought people would never spend money on a fair in the bleakest times America had ever known. In 1933, when the fair opened, 15 million people were unemployed, and one-third of the banks had failed. Men from the J. P. Morgan and DuPont empires had plans to overthrow the government and replace Franklin D. Roosevelt with a fascist government modeled on that of Italy. Only when General Smedley Butler revealed the plans to Congress was the coup thwarted.

While the Columbian Exposition of 1893 showed that Chicago had arrived, the 1933 World's Fair declared that the city and the nation would survive. But a party had been going on. Bathtub gin and speculation and America's insatiable appetite for modern conveniences and getting rich quick had fueled the 1920s. F. Scott Fitzgerald christened it the "jazz age" and said the "gaudiest spending spree in history was beginning."[1] Fitzgerald was right. Sleek wooden rumrunners bumped off the shores of Lake Michigan with men bringing in the booze that made its way to the speakeasies on every corner of the city of Chicago. People simply wanted to drink, and Alfonse Capone was there to make sure they could.

For a price.

That price was murder and an ongoing war between the Italian from Brooklyn and anyone who challenged his rule. Men in long coats carrying machine guns rode crouched down on the running boards of black Cadillacs and held the city in their grip. The whole country watched in fascination as gangland culture appeared in movies, fashion, and common slang while gun-toting men habitually wiped each other out with .45 Automatic Colt Pistol slugs.

The mayor of Chicago, William Thompson, owed his election to Al Capone and men who threw grenades at opposing polling stations. Another mayor, Anton Cermak, tried to clean up Chicago until an assassin supposedly hired by Capone shot him dead. The government had erred badly in legislating American morality, and Al Capone had moved in to fill the resulting demand with murder on a scale that would have shaken even a psychopath like Dr. Holmes.

In 1933, Adolf Hitler had just become chancellor of Germany, and Benito Mussolini had risen to power in Italy. The hubris of holding a world's fair during these times seemed to invite disaster. President Roosevelt had just told the country it had nothing to fear but fear itself; then he passed the Banking Act of 1933, essentially closing banks to stop people from withdrawing their money. Charles Lindbergh's baby had been kidnapped and murdered just the year before. But Chicago saw the 1933 World's Fair as a way to rehabilitate its sagging reputation as a Wild West town of gangsters and also as a catalyst for economic recovery. If the city could pull off *A Century of Progress*, then maybe it could get rid of Al Capone and the awful darkness of the Great Depression. This was the thinking after the worst gangland shooting in American history, ironically named for a holiday of love.

When people left the fair, they wondered why Chicago was so dingy compared to the shimmering metropolis on the lake. Coal burners that dropped soot down from on high still fired the city. The Union Stockyards slaughtered over a million hogs a year, with the smell wafting into Chicago when the wind blew from the south. Steam locomotives still lumbered into the city and killed pedestrians. The trains had yet to be confined to Union Station, and the soot from their coal-burning engines contributed to the brown dense fog that sometimes enveloped the city.

Many buildings manufactured their own electricity in boiler-fired dynamos tucked away below ground. The Chicago River had been reversed, but in bad storms it spewed sewage into Lake Michigan. A book published to promote the 1933 World's Fair gives a snapshot of the best statistics the organizers could offer up: 3.475 million people lived in Chicago in some 400,000 dwellings; they drove 396,533 automobiles along 226 miles of parklike boulevards; they attended 1,800 churches and sent their children to 360 public schools.

Only 11 percent of the population owned a car in 1933. Horses delivered milk, blacksmiths dotted city blocks, and carriages competed for space. Few people had flown in a plane. Yet the city had come a long way: from a dot on a map drawn by Antoine Charles Louis Lasalle, it had become an Indian trail, a trading post, a US government agency, and then a sprawling town of log cabins. When the Illinois and Michigan Canal opened in 1848, Chicago began to grow quickly, and three years later the village of Chicago became the city of Chicago. A reason for a world's fair nearly a hundred years later was born.

Even the Civil War would do little to slow Chicago's expansion. By 1870 the city was growing at a clip of 500,000 people per decade. It experienced a setback in October 1871 when Mrs. O'Leary's fabled cow kicked over a lantern; the Great Chicago Fire left the city built of wood a smoking ruin and 100,000 citizens without homes. The "I Will" spirit burst forth and Chicago roared back, surviving the financial panic of 1873 and labor troubles that culminated in the Haymarket riot, then breaking into the modern era with the world's first skyscraper, the Home Insurance Building.[2]

In 1893 the "Paris of the Prairies"[3] launched the World's Columbian Exposition, while the city's stockyards became meat supplier to the world, dispatching one million creatures each year. Alderman John J. Coughlin would be the only elected official in power during both world's fairs. In a black-and-white photo taken at the Rainbow City of 1933, he proudly wears his medal from the 1893 fair. His confident smile makes it clear that Chicago was ready to do it again.

ACKNOWLEDGMENTS

WRITING ABOUT THE WORLD'S FAIR OF 1933 AND AL CAPONE IS GOING over well-trod ground. So one has to be on the lookout for anything that might spark a different view, a different interpretation of historical events. I was fortunate enough to have the University of Chicago nearby, which has a lot of the papers related to the 1933 World's Fair, *A Century of Progress*. The Chicago History Museum just happened to have the papers of Sally Rand, which, for a person about whom there has not been much written, were an enormous help. The Chicago Public Library archives filled in the blanks with correspondence and many books. And since I live in Chicago, I was able to wander around and try to feel those people of 1933 and see what they saw. Much of Chicago during Capone's time is, amazingly, the same. And the lakefront is timeless. Many thanks to the good folks at Rowman & Littlefield for bringing out *Al Capone and the 1933 World's Fair*. And, of course, to my family for enduring.

CHAPTER ONE

Chicago, May 27, 1933

SALLY RAND LOOKED LIKE SOMETHING FROM THE HEAVENS ON HER white horse, her bare skin painted white. Holding onto a bridle, she sat bareback atop the skittish horse and glided across Lake Michigan toward the back of the fairgrounds. The lake whooshed softly against the gurgling motor as the pumping horse blood warmed her thighs. The fair's colored lights jumped in the cool, rushing water. Sally was pimply with goose bumps, even though it was late May.

The low-riding wooden Chris-Craft could barely contain the horse, and as water slapped up, she leaned close to his ear. "It's fine . . . it's fine, baby. We are almost there." She pulled the white velvet cape around her and felt the wind pass over her loins and breasts. Except for the ankle bracelet, her blond wig, some makeup, and the cape that barely covered her breasts, Sally Rand, a.k.a. Harriet Helen Beck from Missouri, was naked from her painted toes to her dimpled smile. Who would turn away this gliding nymph approaching the opening of the 1933 World's Fair?

The boat bumped the dock, and the horse stepped down from the low bow as if he had done so all his life. Sally Rand clamped his sides with her legs and dug her heels in. The horse jumped to life as her blond hair flew back. They raced down the deserted streets heading for the grand opening, where people gathered around the stage. *A Century of Progress*, the 1933 Chicago World's Fair, was about to open during the worst year of the Great Depression, with a gangster-ridden city at its back. It was a perfect setup for a naked woman on a charging white steed.

CHAPTER TWO

Valentine's Day, 1929

FEBRUARY 14, 1929, WAS COLD, ABOUT EIGHTEEN DEGREES, AND OVER-cast—a typical day in Chicago. George "Bugsy" Moran got off the phone. He had just been told to meet a stolen shipment of Canadian whiskey at his garage on Clark Street at about 10:30 a.m. He let his gang know, then walked outside and looked up. It might snow; it might not. Winter was long and dark, and if you couldn't handle the icy wind off Lake Michigan, you'd better move. Bugsy began walking toward the garage and then turned into a barbershop. He wanted a haircut.

The garage, the Moran gang's unofficial headquarters, was on Chicago's North Side in Lincoln Park at 2122 North Clark Street. "Machine Gun" Jack McGurn had selected it for the day's events and had previously survived a hail of bullets from Moran's two "torpedoes," the Gusenberg brothers. The projectiles had torn the phone booth in which McGurn stood to pieces, but the doctors had pulled the lead out of him, and he had survived.

He told his boss, Al Capone, that he wanted to eliminate the Moran gang once and for all and came up with a novel plan. He had a stolen police car and two uniforms and brought in assassins from out of town. This would be McGurn's opera of death, while Capone relaxed in the sun of Miami.

Seven men in long trench coats and fedoras walked into the garage and waited. A German shepherd, Highball, was tied to an oil pipe. Well dressed, with diamond stickpins and spats, each carried $1,000 to pay for the bootleg whiskey from Canada. Bugsy Moran was to meet them there, and they would transport the contraband. Lookouts in an apartment at 2119 North Clark Street had watched as they entered and sent word that Bugsy had arrived.

Moran's men had no reason to be suspicious. Moving bootleg whiskey had become much like any other job in Chicago. Prohibition had taken effect in 1919, and Chicago had paid off like a cash register ever since. People wanted booze, and Al Capone was the biggest supplier in Chicago, with mobsters like Bugs Moran fighting for a piece of the action. Everyone wanted to take down Capone.

Alfonse Capone had been born in Brooklyn, close to the Navy Yards on Navy Street, on January 17, 1899. The Capone family lived in a cold-water flat with a shack out back for an outhouse. His mother took in money as a seamstress, and his father cut hair. They spoke no English. Al liked to watch the soldiers march in the Navy Yard when he was ten years old and often taunted soldiers who got out of step. One day one of the soldiers went after the bigmouthed kid from southern Italy.

"Hey you! You long-legged number three! Get in step. You're holding 'em up," Al shouted through the fence.[1]

The soldier charged the gate where Capone stood, looking like he was going to kill the kid. A corporal stopped the soldier and pulled him away from the pudgy dark-haired boy. But Al hadn't moved a muscle and, to the amazement of the corporal, shouted at the soldier, "C'mon! Let him outside the gate, and I'll teach the big sonofabitch a lesson!"[2]

The corporal shook his head and later said that people would hear from the boy one day if some wiseguy got hold of him. Al didn't wait for the wiseguy or to finish school. In the sixth grade, a teacher hit him, seeing him as just another wop from Brooklyn. At this time, the nation was awash with immigrants, with more coming every day. Henry Cabot Lodge had said that the immigrant hoards, pouring into Ellis Island like a firehose spouting dirty water, were destroying American culture. The Italians and the Irish were the worst. And the southern Italians were seen as the laziest, the most lascivious, and the most violent.

Smacking Italian kids around was a common form of discipline, but this time the kid hit back. Young Capone punched his teacher in the nose, and blood spouted. The nun grabbed Alfonse by the hair and almost yanked his arm out as she dragged him down to the principal, a large, blue-eyed man with a red face who gave the mouthy wop a severe beating.

"I ain't never coming back to this dump," Al shouted afterward.

The principal was amazed. The kid never shed a tear, just swaggered down the hall and out the front door. Al Capone's education ended then. The school had already held him back a couple of times, and he was fourteen years old: it was time to go to work.

The family moved from the slums on Navy Street to a better apartment on Garfield Place. There Johnny Torrio entered Al Capone's life and completed his education. A small, well-dressed man, Torrio ran some small brothels from his apartment building and paid Al five bucks to run errands. He sized up the young Capone for membership in his gang and administered a simple test. He invited the boy to come to his headquarters and then didn't show, instead leaving a pile of money on the table. If Al took it, then he was out. Capone left the money on the table, and Torrio became his first mentor in the ways of racketeering.

Al joined the Five Points Gang but then went straight for a while. He worked in a box factory, got married, and had a child. Novelist Daniel Fuchs met the young Capone and was shocked when this gregarious, well-mannered, hardworking young man became the Al Capone who lived in ten rooms at the top of the Lexington Hotel in Chicago at 22nd Street and Michigan Avenue.

The adult Capone had taken the rooms at the Lexington Hotel under the name George Phillips and spread out until he took over the hotel. The Lexington was pretentious, with a Moorish and Italian facade and big "Chicago windows." From his office Capone surveyed the South Side from a chair with a bulletproof back; he went out in a ten-ton armor-plated Cadillac. The Lexington, along with places in Cicero and Chicago Heights, a winter retreat in Miami, and a summer hideout in Lansing, Michigan, completed the Capone empire, from which he ran a bootlegging operation that "reached from New York's Long Island to Lake Michigan."[3] Capone controlled the flow of illegal booze from Europe, Canada, and the Caribbean and made a hundred million untaxed dollars a year. Many simply referred to him as the mayor of Chicago.

Daniel Fuchs hadn't known that in New York Al liked to frequent the Adonis Social Club, where bullets flew and he met with prostitutes. There the young gangster also picked up syphilis, which at the time ran unchecked through the population. The draft of World War I brought to doctors the shocking realization that 10 percent of the population had venereal disease. Millions of Americans suffered from syphilis, and thousands died from this cagy illness, which hid away for twenty years before striking in the final stage with an Alzheimer's-like dementia. Capone was never treated, and many historians speculate that syphilis accounted for his murderous rages.

The public had become enamored of gangster culture by 1929, the bloodiest year yet, with sixty-four murders in Chicago since January 1. Prohibition was entering its tenth year, turning millions of Americans into outlaws. People just wanted a drink, and Capone saw himself as supplying a demand. Ultimately, gangsters had become part of American life. In 1925 F. Scott Fitzgerald had published his greatest work, *The Great Gatsby*, with two gangsters at the center of the tale: Gatsby was a bootlegger, and Meyer Wolfsheim had fixed the World Series. Movies had taken on gangster speak, and celebrities and public officials liked to have their pictures taken with Al Capone at ball games. Besides, Capone had officially gone straight and told everyone he was just a businessman giving people what they wanted.

In Capone's view, the logic of Prohibition was all semantics. If you poured a drink up on the North Shore on Lake Shore Drive, you were providing hospitality. If you poured a drink in a speakeasy, you were bootlegging. Most of the deaths in Chicago were the result of drinking denatured alcohol laced with antifreeze or straight wood alcohol. People had come to accept that this was the risk of taking a drink in the same way that they accepted speakeasies and bathtub gin. In Chicago, everyone was partaking.

The North Side garage, with its storefront window reading S. M. C. Cartage Company, was familiar to the armed men in suits and long coats who smoked and stamped their feet to keep warm. There, they would distribute Prohibition beer or just hang out. But Highball the German shepherd was getting restless, pulling at his chain, pacing back and forth. Someone said they were bringing the illegal whiskey from Canada through a contact of Capone's. This made the job even better. Stealing from that wop was just fine with the Gusenberg brothers, Frank and Peter, the very ones who had shot up the phone booth where Machine Gun McGurn was making a call.

Reinhardt Schwimmer smoked and stared at the grease-stained bricks. Not technically in the mob, he was an optician who had become involved in illegal horse betting and stopped fitting eyeglasses to hang around with gangsters. He liked to brag to his friends that he could have anyone murdered at any time. He had recently become more involved in the bootlegging operation and moved into a Chicago hotel. When he got the call to come to the garage, he probably felt like he was moving in the right direction. Dr. Schwimmer, as he called himself, liked to wear white carnations in the lapel of his suit. He wore one that morning for Valentine's Day.

He wasn't like John May, who had arrived first with Highball and worked on the trucks hauling bootleg whiskey. May knew nothing good would come of hanging out with the Moran gang. His wife wanted him to break away from the gangsters, but he had seven kids, and every time he tried to go straight, he ended up back with Moran to make some money. He found it strange that no trucks were waiting in the garage but reasoned the gangsters wanted him to work on them when the booze came in.

Albert Kachellek, Moran's second in command, was talking to Adam Heyer, the gang's bookkeeper and business manager. Then there was Albert Weinshank, who ran some cleaning and dying operations for Bugs and had the same height and build as his boss. The lookouts had mistaken Albert for Moran. He was smoking with the mechanic May and the optician. The garage was unheated, and the men kept moving to keep warm.

Bugs stayed at the Parkway Hotel, which wasn't far away. The Gusenbergs figured he would be there soon and would be driving the trucks and running protection. Everyone wore expensive suits, and all were armed except the mechanic John May and the optician. Three of the men had handkerchiefs in their top pockets. The door clicked open behind them, and they expected to see Bugs or Henry Gusenberg, another gang member. Two uniformed cops appeared with two other men in suits and long overcoats. The Moran gang shook their heads.

"What the hell?" Frank Gusenberg growled.

Someone had obviously dropped the ball. The gang had paid off Mayor William Thompson and the police, so the last thing they anticipated was a couple of beat cops and some detectives.

"Everyone against the wall!" the policemen shouted, holding shotguns.

The seven Moran men looked at each other, then shrugged and turned to the greasy brick wall. They would have put up a fight any other time, but the presence of the policemen had thrown them off. They would all be out in an hour anyway, even if the cops took them downtown. Mob lawyers were always on call. Still, there was something strange about the two men in suits. Gusenberg didn't think they looked like detectives. Their eyes had the glint of killers.

"C'mon, up against the wall!" the men in the suits shouted at him.

Frank turned slowly to the brick wall. Both of the Gusenbergs had seen a couple of Thompson submachine guns under the long coats of the two men in suits. One had a fifty-round canister and the other a twenty-round stick.

Wanting to upgrade the Browning automatic in World War I, General John T. Thompson had come up with a machine gun that used the force of the bullet to eject the shell and chamber up another one. You just had to pull back the bolt the first time. Once you pulled the trigger, the twenty-round clip or fifty-round barrel fed the bullets into the firing pin like a frenzied creature spewing fire and death. Thompson came up with the perfect name: the Annihilator.[4]

The general thought he would sell his machine gun to the army for "trench sweeping" in World War I.[5] But the war ended two days after Thompson had debugged the weapon. Armor-piercing .45 Automatic Colt Pistol (ACP) slugs were the only bullets that worked with it. Some soldiers felt the gun was too heavy and the fifty-round barrel hard to load. The British complained about the rattling noise of the trigger mechanism. But everyone loved the way it fired. Two men with Thompson submachine guns had the firepower of nine men with pistols. The US

Post Office bought some after a series of robberies. The tommy gun cost $200, at a time when a Model A Ford cost $400.

Gangsters loved the tommy gun. General Thompson had unwittingly provided outlaws with the perfect weapon. After Al Capone's car and driver were riddled with bullets as he sat inside a restaurant, he studied the holes and knew the game had changed. A man with a Thompson could decimate a couple of cops. A gangster could riddle a police car with holes in seconds, and if the cops weren't running for cover, they were dead. The gun was compact; you could keep it under your overcoat until you were ready. Then you pulled the bolt back and simply *annihilated* your target. The gun fit weirdly into a violin case, and many gangsters looked like they were going to a recital before they wiped somebody out.

The Thompson also was perfect for firing from a car into a liquor store that didn't pay or refused to sell your booze. It wasn't accurate, but that didn't matter: the Thompson literally sprayed bullets and commonly dealt its victims as many as fourteen bullet wounds. Hit men liked it because they could be sure their man was dead. Nobody could survive a Thompson onslaught; General Thompson's Annihilator always lived up to its name. And the $200 price tag wasn't an issue. The only drawback: the Thompson kicked back and bruised your ribs.

Now seven of Moran's men were staring at the wall, breathing the scent of cold motor oil; the mechanic May trembled and turned his head slowly. Highball was growling at the men and bearing his teeth. Not liking any of this, May was thinking of his kids when he saw the two cops nod to the men in suits. The Thompsons swung up from under their overcoats, and everyone heard the distinctive double click of the firing bolts being ripped back. Every man knew that sound. It meant that short little machine gun was about to turn into the Annihilator. Schwimmer the optometrist never saw the bullet that pierced his head. The other men felt the impact of .45 ACP bullets ripping into their bodies with dull thuds, like rounds fired into meat.

The two gangsters sprayed back and forth like men watering a lawn. The shooter on the right moved across at skull level, while the one on the left swept across just below the targets' necks. Then each dropped down and swept across again. Seventy bullets blasted out of the machine guns in a fiery torrent as the force of each bullet chambered up the next. The Thompsons grew hot as shells fell on the concrete in musical succession, and the two men felt the shake through their arms with the explosions echoing off the brick walls. Blue smoke filled the dim garage as Moran's men crumpled and grabbed their arms, chests, and stomachs, their heads exploding, their necks spouting arterial blood. The two Thompsons chewed like angry piranhas, still striking even though the men were dead or dying, until all seventy bullets had been ground up in that ferocious maw of destruction. Then a deafening quiet settled over the smoke-filled room.

The two cops walked over to the felled men. John May groaned. The first cop lowered a sawed-off shotgun and blew his face clean away. Peter Gusenberg made a sound, and the second shotgun obliterated his face. The brick wall had been chipped into the red dust, and pieces of brick lay among the dead men. A restaurant in Indiana would later purchase the bricks so that patrons could stare at the Thompson-chewed masonry as they dined.

The two cops turned, took the machine guns, and led the men in suits out with their hands up; all climbed into a police car and drove away. The people outside the garage who had heard the shots assumed the police already had the scene under control. But the assassins had left one witness: Frank Gusenberg. With twenty-two bullet holes, when the actual cops arrived and took him to a hospital, Gusenberg was just barely hanging on. Sergeant Clarence Sweeny wanted to know who the perpetrators had been.

"Who shot you?"

"No one . . . nobody shot me," Gusenberg groaned.

"What gang was it?"

Gusenberg turned pale. The sergeant had seen many gangsters die this way. They just faded away in front of you.

"You want a preacher, Frank?"

"No," Gusenberg whispered. "I'm cold . . . awful cold . . . Sarge . . . it's getting dark."[6]

Sweeny turned up the electric heater but knew it didn't matter now. He bent close to the dying gangster.

"Who was it, Frank?"

Gusenberg didn't say anything. His lips pressed tightly together, and then he shivered. Three hours after being gunned down by Thompson's Annihilator, he was dead. The only witness left now was the howling German shepherd inside the garage. And Highball wasn't talking either.

The press was slow to arrive. There had been so many gangland slayings that they just didn't spark the same interest anymore. Walter Trohan, a young reporter working for the Chicago City News Bureau, worked the coroner's office and was used to seeing men torn apart by tommy guns. Once he had to saw a corpse's head open to retrieve the bullets because his editor demanded to know if the bullets came from another gangster's pistol.

Valentine's Day had been a slow news day . . . so far.

"I was in the press room when the call came through that six men had been killed at 2122 North Clark Street," Trohan later recalled.[7] He thought about taking a taxi, but his editor told him to save the money. So Trohan took a streetcar to the scene after calling in a bulletin to several newspapers. A lot of times news came in erroneously, and the young reporter wasn't sure what he would find in the garage. He was there five minutes ahead of everybody except one or two cops. Highball was barking crazily, and Trohan heard the dog as he walked up.

A policeman looked up at the door, and Trohan muttered, "City press"; then he passed through a small office with a desk and phone but no other furniture. Trohan shivered as he pulled open the door to the garage and stopped. The iron scent of blood stopped him cold. He later wrote,

There were just pools of blood everywhere and the dead guys spread out as in the movies. I'd seen dead guys before—it was part of my job— but I'd never seen that many before. They were sprawled all over and there was blood all over and this crazy German shepherd was barking and crazy and lunging on a heavy chain. . . . I was impressed, but I was also interested in running to a phone. I did know that the victims were the Moran gang and I knew Moran wasn't among them. . . . I knew Capone was behind it because they were rival gangsters fighting for chunks of the rope.[8]

When questioned at his home in Florida, Al Capone said famously, "The only man I know who kills like that is Bugs Moran." Bugs Moran, who had seen a police car outside the garage that morning and ducked into a coffee shop, remarked later, "The only man I know that kills like that is Al Capone."[9]

The St. Valentine's Day Massacre raised the death toll even higher in what was already Chicago's bloodiest year yet. People were worried. The city would host a world's fair in three years. *A Century of Progress.* People had a hard time saying the name without laughing. Who were they kidding? Chicago was the Wild West, and the Federal Bureau of Investigation had neither the authority nor the will to stop the carnage. The cops and judges had been bought off. Al Capone lived in a penthouse in the nicest hotel in the city, while the mayor lived in Bridgeport. Who the hell would come to Chicago after machine-gun fire had ripped apart seven men in a garage?

Ironically, the fair was supposed to celebrate how far Chicago had come—its progress, if you will—since its incorporation as a town one hundred years before. Tell that to the glassy-eyed dead men—and to those who didn't even have eyes left. Somebody had to do something, or the 1933 World's Fair would be just as dead as Bugs Moran's seven men.

People really wanted to know who had come up with the bright idea in the first place. The city was broke and ridden with gangs, and the economy was beginning to make funny noises. Hadn't Chicago just had a fair back in 1893 and then a smaller one in 1921 on Navy Pier? Buildings left over from that fair were still standing. So who had dreamed up holding another one?

Chicago's Second World's Fair

RUFUS C. DAWES READ WALTER TROHAN'S PROSE AND WONDERED WHO
had come up with the idea to hold a world's fair. He stared at the headlines in his office in downtown Chicago. The slaughter shocked even
Chicago's hardened cops. "I tell you, I've never seen anything like it," one
detective lamented after staring at the twisted bodies.[1] Patrick Roche, a
federal investigator, went even further: "Never in all the history of feuds or
ganglands has Chicago or the nation seen anything like today's wholesale
slaughter. . . . [N]ever," he concluded, "has there been such a massacre."[2]

Newspapers across the country picked up the story and sold millions
of copies. The *New York Times* led the way: "7 Chicago Gangsters Slain
by Firing Squad of Rivals, Some in Police Uniforms."[3] Beyond the scope
of the massacre, people found the fact of police involvement doubly
shocking. The president of the 1933 Chicago World's Fair read the lead
in the *Chicago Tribune*:

> *Chicago ganglands leaders observed Valentine's Day with machine
> guns and a stream of bullets, and as a result seven members of the
> George (Bugs) Moran, Dion O'Banion North Side gang are dead
> in the most cold blooded gang massacre in the history of this city's
> underworld. . . . Gang warfare in Chicago began with the slaying of
> Dion O'Banion in November 1924. In the fifty months since then,
> thirty-eight murders, most of them attributed to the enmity between
> the North Side band founded by O'Banion and the West Side syndi-*

cate established by John Torrio and turned over to Al Capone have been recorded.[4]

Dawes dropped the paper and groaned. He didn't know it, but Machine Gun McGurn had done his work well. Not only was Capone off the hook because he was in Miami at the time, but now the police were suspect. On February 15, 1929, the *Wisconsin News*'s headline read, "Chicago Police Killers of Gangmen."[5] People felt anything was possible in Chicago where corruption was well known. Rufus Dawes wanted to be anywhere other than where he was. Outside his office on LaSalle Street the press clamored for a statement. He heard footsteps in the hallway and the building murmur of people waiting to ask how in the hell he planned to hold a world's fair in a city run by gangsters who destroyed each other with Thompson submachine guns. He couldn't deny the validity of the question as he stared at the bloody mess plastered on every major newspaper in the United States.

The truth was that Rufus didn't like the public aspect of his job. He wasn't his brother Charles Dawes, who was now vice president under President Calvin Coolidge. The brothers had been born in Marietta, Ohio, the sons of Civil War general Rufus Dawes and the great-grandsons of Revolutionary War fighter William Dawes. Their brothers, Berman and Henry, would distinguish themselves in business, but Charles Dawes was different. He had won the Nobel Prize in 1925 and helped settle World War I with a reparations plan that would go down in history as the Dawes Plan.

Charles had even penned a popular tune, "Melody in A Major." Rufus and Charles had no way of knowing that the song would be retitled "It's All in the Game" and become a number one hit in 1958 when Tommy Edwards recorded it with Carl Sigman's lyrics. Charles Dawes would be the only vice president in history to have a number one pop hit.

Charles Dawes had experienced down moments. His son had drowned in Lake Geneva in 1912, and Teddy Roosevelt had turned against his bid for a Senate seat in 1901. Even the Dawes Plan for Germany's economic revival had been deemed unworkable and replaced with the Young Plan, which made sure Germany would never recover. Charles had also let Rufus know that Coolidge and he didn't get along, and the sooner his term ended, the better.

Charles had thrown Rufus a bone after World War I and let him serve on the commissions to set up the staggered reparations outlined in the Dawes Plan and later the Young Plan. Before that Rufus had run the family gas and lighting business with his brothers and then become president of the Union Gas & Electric Company, Metropolitan Gas & Electric Company, and Dawes Brothers, Inc.

Rufus's civic career had been restricted to serving on the Illinois State Pension Laws Commission (1918–1919) after his selection as a delegate to the Illinois constitutional convention. Next he had enjoyed a short run as president of the Chicago Commerce Club, and then . . . the world's fair came along and changed his life forever.

For years Rufus had been walking a tightrope, pitching the fair as both a beacon of a future in which America was again prosperous and a way to clean up Chicago's image as a haven of machine-gun-toting gangsters. He had come up with the theme for *A Century of Progress* and oriented it toward science and industrial technology. Nobody wanted to see a bunch of moldy exhibits. The world had changed since the 1893 fair, and people needed to look forward to something. Let the corporations strut their stuff and show consumers their offerings. Getting Chicago back on track was of paramount importance, but right now, Dawes wished he had never heard of the world's fair.

The man really responsible for this mess was Captain Myron E. Adams, a minster and social service worker who came up with the bright idea in August 1923 in a letter to then mayor William Deaver. He proposed that the city sponsor a centennial exhibit to celebrate Chicago's incorporation as a village in 1833. Adams saw the need for many civic improvements, including implementation of Daniel Burnham Sr.'s languishing "City Beautiful" plans. He believed this scheme would bring worldwide attention to Chicago and push it along on its course to becoming a major US metropolis. He even suggested locating the fair on man-made land along the lakefront created by the bulldozing of charred buildings from the Great Chicago Fire.

In 1926 the Chicago City Council approved the idea, and Deaver appointed 150 citizens to a planning commission to celebrate the hundredth anniversary of Chicago's incorporation. Then William Hale Thompson was elected, and besides being the most corrupt mayor Chicago would ever have, he didn't believe the fair could make money. He pronounced the project officially dead in August 1927.

But the city treasurer, Charles Peterson, had a different take. He believed the fair *could* make money—and lots of it. At a contentious public meeting, he and others pointed out that Chicago had another problem: the gangland wars were turning people away from the city. The fair offered a way to reverse the slide of the city's reputation and bring people to Chicago to spend money.

Thompson changed gears and, on January 5, 1928, formed a not-for-profit corporation among the city's businessmen to hold a world's fair in Chicago in 1933. At this point Rufus was appointed president of the Chicago Second World's Fair Centennial Celebration Corporation. Daniel Burnham Jr. signed on as secretary—a good omen, as his father had overseen the Columbian Exposition of 1893; in Dawes's mind, this fact cemented the two ventures nicely. Charles S. Peterson was named vice president; George Woodruff, treasurer; and Arthur Anderson, comptroller.

Things were moving along nicely, and businesses began to make pledges to fund the fair. Charles Dawes secured a joint resolution from Congress authorizing the US president to invite nations from around the world to participate—a must if the fair were to succeed. Rufus knew they faced a hard road, even though the economy in 1928 was humming along. The Columbian Exposition had received almost $6 million from local, state, and national governments. The 1933 World's Fair would depend entirely on private-sector money, and that meant getting big business to pony up. Charles oversaw financing, but he couldn't ask the titans of business for money when Capone and his gangsters were mowing people down in the streets.

Rufus shifted in his chair and rubbed his chin. He stared at the newspaper again. He knew he would have to reckon with Al Capone and the gangsters creating terror in the city. If the city's business leaders didn't act fast, Chicago would cease to be a viable economic center for the nation.

The gangland wars had left hundreds dead in spectacular machine-gun slayings that the press pushed to the front pages to drive ratings. Now the worst gangland slaying of all time, with seven dead, had given the press more red meat. The FBI didn't have jurisdiction over Chicago, and J. Edgar Hoover wanted no part of the mess that became bloodier with each passing day. Capone was ensconced in the top of the Lexington Hotel and lived like a king, while the mayor and police chief paid him visits like serfs offering tribute to a benevolent landlord.

Rufus looked at the headlines again. Capone was in Florida, and Bugsy Moran wasn't among the dead. His retaliation would surely be brutal. Rufus stroked his small mustache, then flipped on the intercom.

"Sylvia, get me Robert Isham Randolph."

Dawes stood up, straightened his tie, and walked into the hallway, where the press blinded him with flashbulbs. He momentarily wavered, then smiled. Reporters fired questions in rapid succession. Rufus held up his hands and smiled.

"Gentlemen . . . I assure you Chicago will be safe and sound for the World's Fair of 1933. That I can assure you."

The press assaulted his sensibilities. Rufus would never get used to this part of the job. His brother was much better at public relations than he. Dawes answered the questions as best he could, but with each minute he felt more panicked. *How would he stop the gangsters?*

"How can you assure the world Chicago will be safe when Capone is gunning people down in garages?" a reporter from the *Chicago Tribune* barked.

Rufus smiled at the young man and realized he was in over his head.

"Well . . . young man. We have a plan and I can assure you the gangsters will be gone by the time the fair opens."

He then turned abruptly and walked back into his office, drenched with perspiration, his hands shaking.

"I have the president of the Chicago Association of Commerce, Mr. Dawes."

Rufus grabbed the phone like a man finding water in the desert. He didn't wait for the man who ran business in Chicago to start. He couldn't afford to wait. His brother would be asking for millions of dollars from the wealthiest businessmen in the country to fund the fair, and Al Capone was about to single-handedly destroy all his work.

"Robert, we have to do something."

The subsequent pause told him the man on the other end of the line was having the same black day. Rufus could still hear the press outside his door. The next two words were not an answer but a balm: "I know." Randolph couldn't put up with the shooting gallery that had become Chicago either.

Rufus squeezed the bridge of his nose. A real pounder of a headache was coming on, but at least the two men found themselves in the same lifeboat. He breathed heavily. Randolph paused. He had ties to every powerful businessman in Chicago. Nothing happened unless it passed through him. Randolph cleared his throat, and Dawes waited.

"I have a plan."

Dawes breathed again and stared at the commotion outside his office window.

"Thank God."

Chapter Four

WAMPAS Baby Star

Across town just off State Street, in an alley of trash and Model A Fords parked behind tenements, a garbage man picked up some folded boxes. The early morning was still cold as he began his route in the South Loop, heading slowly west. He hoisted up the boxes, and that's when he saw a woman's leg—well curved and white as a baby's bottom. It was too white, and he jumped back as the woman sat up like the dead risen and stared at him with the bluest eyes he had ever seen.

"Do ya' mind, I was trying to sleep, you know!"

The black man stared at her. Was she a ghost or an angel? An angel, he decided. The woman pushed off the other boxes and grabbed her cardboard suitcase. She wore a sparkly uniform that had reflected stage lights the week before, but when the vaudeville revue ended, the costume had become Sally Rand's clothing when she couldn't pay the rent on her Madison Street flat. Sally had become one of the thousands who slept in alleys, under bridges, or on lower Wacker Drive.

Sally grabbed up the newspaper she had used to keep herself warm and ignored the man's stare as she walked down the alley. She kept one page of the paper with her. It was her way out. The Paramount was holding auditions for exotic acts and dancers. The *Chicago Tribune* said the auditions were at 3 p.m. She had just enough time to find a cup of coffee and search the secondhand stores for a new costume for her audition.

The girl who would ride into the middle of the opening-day ceremonies of the 1933 World's Fair was probably a hillbilly. She craved fame. It is hard to gauge whether this burning desire had lessened by the year

1929, but she'd had it all her life. The nineteenth century was still an echo in 1904, when Harriet Helen Beck was born on Easter Sunday in the Ozark Mountains of Missouri.

The year she was born, Teddy Roosevelt won his first election after inheriting the presidency following William McKinley's assassination. Her father had placed her in Roosevelt's lap after riding with the big man up San Juan Hill. It would seem fate had marked her for greatness.

Her mother, Annette Mary Grove, was a teacher; her friends called her Nettie. A Pennsylvania Dutch Quaker, she had a lively mind and liked to discuss the politics of the day. She had met Corporal William Beck in Elkton, Missouri, and they had married. Beck, just back from the Spanish-American War, probably had the restlessness that Teddy Roosevelt demanded of his men. After riding up the hills of San Juan, settling down to family life was hard, and he did not take the time to get to know his daughter. Rescue came when war broke out with the Germans, and he took off for France in 1914, never to return.

Harriet discovered the theater when an aunt took her to see the great Anna Pavlova dance in *The Dying Swan*. Maybe it was the day a traveling carnival stopped in the Ozarks, but somewhere along the way the little girl fell in love with performing. The country was young, and so was the century, and Harriet managed rides in a horse and buggy to see dancing, get books, watch nickelodeons . . . anything to glimpse the bigger world. Horatio Alger novels of the rags-to-riches variety were not known to her, but they had seeped into American culture, and if America grew anything in abundance during the early part of the twentieth century, big dreams were the mightiest crop. The swarthy, smart-mouthed wop from the Bronx stealing fruit from stands and then fighting it out in the streets had a dream similar in scope, albeit in a different profession. These dreams drove the country and people to exceed themselves, and Sally Rand was destined in the same way as Al Capone.

But first she had to get out of her hometown. Her father had let his family know that he wasn't coming back from the war; he had married a French girl and would go on to have five sons. Harriet had been taking ballet lessons, but those went by the wayside, and the home in the Ozarks had become a prison. Escape came with a traveling carnival that pitched its tents just outside town. She wanted more than the carnival, but at least it was a way out for the five-foot teenager.

Like Dorothy in *The Wizard of Oz*, she would find salvation somewhere over the rainbow that would allow her dreams to come true. She did handstands and backflips and a few cartwheels for a cigar-chomping manager who was not impressed. She told him her age (sixteen) and pleaded. Her family was poor and needed money. She had to do something. His heart thawed. Maybe his motives were lascivious, maybe not. But she had a job when the carnival pulled out the next morning. The manager reminded the barefoot girl to bring her shoes.

And the scene played out that was happening all over the country as the culture of the city invaded the national consciousness. There was something bigger out there—if a girl could just get off this damn farm. People didn't live very long; life expectancy ran a little beyond sixty at the time, and there was not a moment to lose even for a sixteen-year-old named Harriet Helen Beck. Her mother sensed something was wrong when she dropped a dish in the kitchen and heard the sounds of packing in her daughter's bedroom.

"Harriet, are you all right? What's going on?"[1]

The clothes on the bed and the open suitcase, along with the red face, told the whole story, and then came the line stamped into Americana: "I've got a job with the carnival, Mom, and I'm going with them tonight."

This big rural nation was on the verge of becoming something else, something new, with kids running across farm fields toward a departing light. The carnival would take them to the city lights and beyond.

"No."

That was all Mrs. Beck could say. But Helen (who dropped Harriet like an old shoe just then) would not take no for an answer.

"Yes, Mother. It will be OK. The manager is a kindly person, and I'll be all right. Don't worry about me. If I don't like it, I'll come back and go to school. And when we get to Kansas City, I'm going to get a job in the Ballet Company."[2]

Retelling this story years later, Sally Rand probably didn't add much. It was a simpler time, and the sawdust dialogue has the ring of truth. She wanted to become somebody, and leaving was her only alternative. The carnival took her as far as Kanas City, where she took a job as a dancer at the Green Mill Café. She stayed in a back room until she had enough money for a hotel. Grandfather Beck found her there and brought her back to the Ozarks.

But she had escaped for a time, and like an astronaut who has sampled the outer layer of the atmosphere, she knew she would leave again. A year later she followed another carnival to Chicago. Her first job was with the Adolph Bohm Chicago Ballet Company, and when it closed, she ended up with the Ringling Brothers Circus as part of the "Flying Wards" trapeze act.[3] With each carnival she had been learning the ropes and developing her prowess as an athlete. Her size and compact muscular body made her a natural. In New York she left the circus.

She joined a theater company, and now the Great War had ended and the men were returning, and New York was the center of the world. At this moment Helen Beck had succeeded in escaping the Ozarks and the oblivion of country life. But she still had to eat.

Gus Edwards's theater company also boasted Eddie Cantor and Walter Winchell. Helen was beginning to make her way to the brighter life. She joined Will Seabury's Repertory Theatre Company and made a decision: she would be an actress. Years later Sally Rand claimed to have studied Chekov and Ibsen and other contemporary playwrights. Maybe she did. In 1925 she starred opposite a young Humphrey Bogart in *Reverend Davidson's Rain*.

That year, short stories in the *Saturday Evening Post* portrayed a life of jazz, booze, and gangsters. Everyone wanted to be in the movies, and the rights to F. Scott Fitzgerald's *The Great Gatsby* sold quickly. It seemed that movies would consume the entertainment landscape, and Will Seabury followed the tide west to Los Angeles. Then he fell ill, and the theater company folded. Sally was left with a small pay envelope and no prospects.

Helen became Billie Beck as she made the rounds of the studios. She took a room in Glendora, where a lot of silent movies were shot on location. The wide-open spaces allowed for the car chases and stunts that dominated the early Buster Keaton films. Without sound, the sight gags were essential. Her family joined her as Billie tried out for parts and ended up in a Mack Sennet film as a girl who dives from a ladder into a small tank.

At the very beginning she depended on her physicality to open doors for her. She was blond, pretty, and athletic, and she photographed well in the black-and-white pictures. Her break came when director Cecil B. DeMille noticed her.

DeMille liked the petite blond, and she was named a WAMPAS Baby Star in 1927. So what? Well, the 1926 stars had included Mary Astor, Mary Brian, Dolores Costello, Janet Gaynor, and Fay Wray. Loretta Young joined the young actresses in 1929. Harriet Helen Beck was about to turn the corner into stardom.

Then, one day on the set, DeMille decided he didn't like her name, spied an atlas, and changed it to Sally Rand. Apocryphal? Maybe. It does have the ring of Hollywood bull. But it probably happened. In the early days of Hollywood, you made it up as you went, and DeMille was probably just discovering the power of a name. And so Harriet Helen Beck, a.k.a. Billie Beck, vanished, and Sally Rand was born. It was the name of a star, and a string of films followed: *King of Kings* (appearing as Mary Magdalene's handmaiden), *Fighting Eagle*, *Man Bait*, *Night of Love*, *His Dog*, *Getting Gertie's Garter*, *Galloping Fury*, *Heroes in Blue*, *Girl in Every Port*, *Nameless Men*, *Golf Widows*, *Black Feather*.[4]

Sally shivered as she started to walk down State Street. Her costume was thin, and someone had stolen her coat at her last show; she hoped she might find another while searching for a new costume. Sally shook her head and thought of her horrible luck once again. She had worked for various studios, and her reputation grew. But those were all silent films. *The Jazz Singer* had put everyone on notice that the era of silent movies was over. After that, Sally's dream of movie stardom was extinguished. She had a lisp; her voice hissed and crashed on recordings. DeMille didn't have to tell his young star she was finished. Just like that.

While Humphrey Bogart and other Broadway actors hustled to Hollywood to feed the demand for actors who could enunciate (Bogart, in a great twist of irony, would make his career with a distinctive speech pattern), Sally Rand headed out of town for the vaudeville circuit. That circuit was not so different from a traveling carnival, and though she didn't know it, Sally Rand would never get off the road again.

Then the stock market crashed and changed everything once more. Sally ended up in New York in a snowstorm, broke, not knowing that in Chicago two seven-foot ostrich-feather fans were waiting to carry her aloft again. She spent her last dollars on a midnight train to the Windy City. A friend had told her of opportunities in the theater, and she remade herself again, dancing in burlesque revues for a while. The last one had ended abruptly, and now she was freezing and walking down State Street to the secondhand store that she hoped would provide a costume for her comeback.

Sally Rand never felt sorry for herself. She would be a star one way or another. She walked toward the gloomy store. A man in a worn hat slumped against the wall; he looked up, and Sally Rand broke into a quick soft-shoe. The tassels and glittering silver on her costume caught light as she tapped out a quick rhythm, her blond hair flying back in the wind. The man stared at her with rheumy eyes and smiled. Sally smiled back and winked. She loved the way men stared at her biggest asset, her body, and if she didn't take that to the bank, then her name wasn't Sally Rand.

Besides, everyone was talking about some big fair. The talk gave her a feeling of hope. A world's fair would bring the world to Chicago and also to Sally Rand. They said forty million people might come to the city for the event. She had promised herself she would be part of it somehow.

The man slumped against the wall clapped as Sally finished her soft-shoe.

"How'd you like that, honey?" she asked, opening the door to the dismal store of clothing that people had dumped so they could eat.

"You know, you should be in show business," the man rasped.

"I am," Sally Rand replied, going into the shop.

A woman behind a desk barely looked up as Sally perused the clothes. She would know it when she saw it. And it would have to cost less than a quarter. She walked and walked and found an off-white chemise that she could make into a robe. She liked that because she had a habit of doing things with clothes that they were never meant for. The chemise was twenty cents. Sally kept walking, with the old floorboards creaking. She hummed and absently clicked her tap shoe, which made the woman look up and frown.

She was about to pay for the chemise when she saw two large, pink ostrich-feather fans on top of some army coats from World War I. They were seven feet long, and each weighed forty pounds. Sally picked them up and swept them past her several times. She liked the way they flowed through the air and then across her body. They were like great moving dressing screens.

The burlesque shows were dying, and the striptease was coming in. People just wanted to see women take off their clothes, and Sally didn't mind that. The craze had really started with the 1893 Columbian Exposition and the "Little Egypt" exhibit. The "hoochie coochie" had made its appearance there when a scantily clad woman danced seductively, and it had never left. People didn't care about singing or dog acts anymore, with radio and movies giving them other options. You could dance with "pasties" on your nipples or in a "gadget" later named a G-string, and the cops wouldn't bother you. But Sally knew men really wanted to see a woman take it all off.

She clicked her tap shoes and spun around with one fan in front and the other behind. The woman looked up from her desk and saw a brilliant flash of light among the dingy secondhand clothes. Sally's blond hair shimmered, and her skin was opalescent and pure. The fans moved hypnotically while she twirled and dipped, keeping time with her taps. She vanished behind the pink ostrich feathers and then reappeared like a young nymph from another world. The feathers were very large—one covered her entire midsection. The vision held one fan over her breasts and the other over her loins. She switched them out and then swung one around to her rear end. She looked up and met the old woman's eyes, then twirled twice, bringing up the fans and spreading them like wings.

Sally Rand's blue eyes flashed with a smile that seduced the world.

"How much for these?"

CHAPTER FIVE

Public Enemy Number One

THE MAN SITTING ON THE PATIO OF 93 PALM AVENUE, BUILT BY ST. Louis brewer Clarence M. Busch, would appreciate Sally Rand. Al Capone liked women, especially young, beautiful ones. He wore a striped terry-cloth robe and smoked a cigar in a long, glass-enclosed sun porch. He was reading the Miami paper with news of the St. Valentine's Day Massacre plastered all over the front page. The Dade County prosecutor had already questioned him. No, he had been here in Florida. The prosecutor had shrugged, and Al went back to fishing and relaxing by the ocean.

But another article caught his attention and harkened all the way back to his childhood. Chicago was having a world's fair in 1933. Al Capone crossed his legs and felt the warm Florida sun on his right arm. He was having coffee in the "sunny Italy of the new world,"[1] as he had called Florida when he first rented a room from Mrs. Sterns during one Miami winter. She was a nice lady and loved the Capones after he and his wife, Mae, took care of a $700 phone bill to Chicago with a $1,000 note.

But he wanted his own place, and the "two story neo Spanish house of white stucco with the flat tiled green roof . . . shaded by twelve royal palm trees" on Palm Island in Biscayne Bay was perfect.[2] The mansion boasted fourteen rooms with patios and walks, a gatehouse, a long, graveled drive, and a dock that accommodated three yachts. The Florida hideaway offered escape from the cold hell of Chicago winters and only cost $40,000, which Capone paid in four installments.

Al sipped his coffee and parked his cigar. He was excited and licked his fat lips. A fair like the one they had in New York or like the fairs on Coney Island—the notion took him back to when he worked for that murdering racketeer Frankie Yale at the Harvard Inn Bar. You could smell the ocean all the time. The bar was close to the beach on Coney Island and full of whores and drunks. He was just eighteen and working as a bouncer behind the bar when he saw her.

She was a dark-haired Italian beauty with a great body, and he couldn't resist. Al walked over, picked up an empty beer glass to clear the table, and faced her.

"Honey, you have a nice ass, and I mean that as a compliment."[3]

A man with a pencil mustache and expensive suit jumped up and took a swing. Capone found out later he was the woman's brother, Frank Gallucio. Al punched back hard, and Gallucio pulled a four-inch blade. He slashed savagely at Capone's face—once, twice, three times. Capone felt the sharp blade slice his cheek like a hot wire as blood gushed over the table and the floor and streamed down his neck from his left cheek. Capone went crazy and punched even harder until Gallucio ran out with his sister.

Al absently fingered the three long scars on his cheek. They had been red and angry in the beginning but then finally faded to white lines. That didn't stop the public from forever tagging him "Scarface."[4] He rarely let anybody take his picture from then on and only from the right side. Sometimes he wore white powder to cover them. He had wanted to kill Gallucio then, but Frankie Yale and Salvatore Luciana said no. Years later, he put Gallucio on his payroll and had him run errands.

"You want some more coffee, Al?"

Capone turned to his wife of twenty years. Mae Capone was a stunning Irish blond with long legs and daring blue eyes. They had married at nineteen and had a son, Albert Francis "Sonny" Capone. Al liked family life and enjoyed nothing more than big meals with lots of family.

"Nah, I'm OK. You know, they're talking about having a world's fair in Chicago in '33."

Mae paused in her long, sweeping sequined robe.

"Yeah?"

"Yeah." Al shook his head. "They say forty million people will come." He leaned back and smiled broadly. "That's a lot of beer, baby."

Mae shrugged.

"You never know . . . Prohibition could be over by then."

Al frowned as if someone had just told him the sun wouldn't rise. He picked up his cigar and shook his head.

"Whadaya' crazy . . . not a chance."

Mae shrugged and pulled a cigarette from her robe.

"You never know," she said, walking back in with the coffee.

Al looked back at the paper and thought about the fair again. He wondered if they would have dancing girls or burlesque shows or maybe a Ferris wheel. It troubled him that this Randolph guy was saying he would clean up Chicago and get rid of the gangsters by the time the fair opened. They were even calling him public enemy number one now.[5] Randolph said he had a "secret plan" to get the job done in just three years.

"Secret plan," Al murmured and shook his head.

The hysteria would pass when everyone calmed down. As long as there was Prohibition and people wanted to drink, there would be gangsters. Who were they kidding? The mayor, the police commissioner, the senators—they all took a drink. They hadn't complained when he donated money to their charities or gave Mayor William Thompson 250,000 smackers for his 1927 campaign and then bombed the precincts of his opponent.

"Yeah . . . public enemy number one," he muttered.

Capone laid the paper down and puffed meditatively on his cigar. He thought about what Mae had said. Ending Prohibition would require a constitutional amendment. His lawyer said such an amendment would never pass because all the states had to ratify it. Besides, Prohibition wasn't keeping anyone from drinking.

Al leaned back and stared at the warm ocean sparkling in the morning sun. He frowned and puckered his fat lips.

"Not a chance," he murmured.

Chapter Six

The White City

Precedence is everything. The 1893 World's Fair, whose white-stucco buildings were dubbed "the White City," marked the four hundredth anniversary of Christopher Columbus's discovery of America. Chicago held the fair to announce to the world (and especially New York) that the city had arrived. And on the day of the fair, June 10, President Grover Cleveland, his bulbous fingers touching a gold key, proclaimed, "As by a touch the machinery that gives light to this vast exposition is set in motion, so at the same instant let our hopes and aspirations waken forces which in all time to come shall influence the welfare, the dignity, and the freedom of mankind."[1]

A giant 3,000-horsepower Allis steam engine kicked in and began pumping power into Daniel Burnham Sr., John Root, and Frederick Law Olmstead's dream of a fair to put Chicago on the map once and for all. As Eric Larson wrote in *The Devil in the White City*, "Immediately thirty other engines in the building began to thrum. At the fair's waterworks three huge Worthington pumps began stretching their shafts and pistons, like praying mantises shaking off the cold. Millions of gallons of water began surging through the fair's mains. Engines everywhere took steam until the ground trembled. . . . [W]ater pressurized by the Worthington pumps exploded from the MacMonnies fountain and soared a hundred feet into the sky."[2]

The Columbian Exposition was a hybrid. George Ferris's grand wheel turned ever so slowly and gave people a bird's-eye view of Jackson Park, where the fair covered one square mile and filled more than two hundred buildings. It would last just six months, with 27.5 million people attending overall and more than 700,000 people attending on a single day—at a time when the US population was barely 100 million. The fair was all electric lights, and a taste of the modern came with Shredded Wheat cereal and Cracker Jack snacks. But old America was just outside the gates.

Denied entry, William Cody and his Wild West show filled an 18,000-seat arena, displaying cowboys, Indians, and a woman named Annie Oakley, who could shoot the tip off a cigarette seen in a mirror. Buffalo Bill was decidedly not modern, and that was fine with the fair's planners. The Columbian Exposition's White City bespoke a beau arts tradition that really didn't exist in Chicago but pointed to the last gasp of nineteenth-century enlightenment riding on the heels of the Gilded Age.

Buffalo Bill's show celebrated a Wild West declared closed as recently as 1890. Yet people wanted to see men ride horses and shoot Indians and save women in distress, just as they wanted to see Burnham's skyscrapers (the Rookery) and the controversial Midway attraction, "Little Egypt," which featured an exotic belly dance by a woman with a bare midriff wearing a diaphanous skirt.[3] The "hoochie coochie" was thus born and would pave the way for a woman hiding behind feathers forty years later.

The great drama of the Columbian Exposition for Burnham, Root, and Olmstead involved time. They were running out of it, and their reach had exceeded their grasp. Essentially Burnham and Root had to build an entire city in three years, "not just any city, but one that would surpass the brilliance of the Paris exposition. The fair would also have to make a profit."[4] The pressure was enormous: more than a million tons of earth had to be excavated for the lagoons, and the soft gumbo of Chicago's soil made building by the lake in Jackson Park a nightmare.

Eric Larson's description of the park's preconstruction is telling in not only the geography but also the barrenness of the dream against the cold realities of Chicago in the 1890s: "Jackson Park was one square mile of desolation, mostly treeless, save for pockets of various kinds of oak—burr, pin, black, and scarlet—rising from a tangled growth of elder, wild plum, and willow. . . . One writer called the park 'remote and repulsive'; another, a 'sandy waste of unredeemed and desert land. It was ugly, a landscape of last resort.'"[5]

So the race was on, and there could be no failure. Too much was at stake. The city, just twenty-odd years past the Great Chicago Fire, had recently slipped into anarchy with the Haymarket riot, and now the Gilded Age economy was beginning to slip. And the modern age had brought evil with it as well. H. H. Holmes became Chicago's first serial killer, specializing in young women who had left home for the first time. This underpins Eric Larson's dual treatment of the fair: on the one hand, we have the drama of building the fair itself; on the other, we have Dr. Holmes and his nefarious, if not hideous, machinations, leaving skeletons in his wake.

Did the 1893 World's Fair inadvertently light the match and provide the perfect laboratory to produce the modern psychopath? It would seem so. As Burnham and company dealt with strikes and deaths on the construction site (eighteen before all was said and done), Holmes was building an empire of death, fueled by the anonymity enabled by the disruption that a world's fair produces in a city of the new urban world. The back-and-forth narrative of *The Devil in the White City* gives Holmes at least as much importance as Burnham living in a shanty in Grant Park while steam shovels excavated the old world for the new.

The evil on the edges of the 1893 fair would find modern echoes forty years later in men on the running boards of cars carrying Thompson submachine guns. And yet *A Century of Progress* was intended to prove that Chicago had moved beyond the Holmeses and Capones of the world. The 1933 fair would show the world that the city had solved its gangster problem and that it was time to start shopping again—or at least to visit the fair to see what was on offer. Holmes would not be apprehended and electrocuted until after the fair of 1893; more important, no one knew what he was up to until afterward.

Of course, novelty was the centerpiece of the Columbian Exposition. The Ferris wheel enthralled, as did a large gun from the Essen Works capable of firing a one-ton shell, presaging a different type of warfare for the twentieth century. George Washington Gale Ferris had written to Burnham, "I am going to build a vertically revolving wheel 250 feet in diameter."[6] Nowhere did he reveal that this wheel would "carry thirty-six cars, each about the size of a Pullman, each holding sixty people and equipped with its own lunch counter" or "how when filled to capacity the wheel would propel 2160 people at a time three hundred feet into the sky over Jackson Park, a bit higher than the crown of the now six-year-old Statue of Liberty."[7]

The straight line between the Ferris wheel of 1893 and the Sky Ride of 1933 could not be clearer. The fairs were different, but the similarities are striking. Each had impressive buildings—the Hall of Science for the 1933 fair and the Liberal Arts and Sciences Building for that of 1893—and each had a technical showstopper designed to give fairgoers a lasting overall impression—a tagline, if you will—at the end of their experience. While the Ferris wheel ruled in 1893, few could image the Sky Ride's eclipse by a five-foot, 115-pound blond hiding behind feathers and becoming the number one financial draw.

In the end, the White City closed much as the fair of 1933 would. Looters and vandals attacked first, and then fire finished off a lot of the buildings. The fair made virtually no money but did break even. A moment of triumph came when a check for $1.5 million, presented to the Illinois Trust and Savings Company, satisfied the last of the exposition debts. Buffalo Bill made a cool $1 million from the fair, or about $30 million today.

The 1893 fair prompted President Grover Cleveland to designate October 12 as Columbus Day. Every fair since has included a Ferris wheel and a Midway, which is essentially the concession and games area of any amusement park. The 1893 fair was one of architecture, Americanizing ancient Rome, and many banks, libraries, and post offices are the stylistic descendants of the White City. "Even the Lincoln Memorial can trace its heritage to the fair. In this way the Fair ultimately belonged to the architects who conceived and built it under incredible pressure and odds."[8]

And then, of course, many would point to their ride on that giant wheel that lofted them higher than most people had ever soared in 1893. The Ferris wheel was eventually shipped off to the Louisiana Purchase Exposition of 1904. There explosives brought it down for a final time, and it was hauled off for scrap. George Ferris himself died soon after the 1893 exposition, in 1896, with his estranged wife refusing his ashes, saying he had succumbed to the ravages of celebrity and prominence—a common aliment of those made famous by world's fairs.

Chapter Seven

Bootlegging

How could one man sitting in Florida, sipping a beer and smoking a cigar, hold an entire city hostage while orchestrating the killing of seven men in a garage on the North Side of Chicago? Rufus Dawes and other city fathers wondered much the same thing, but, of course, Al Capone held the keys to the kingdom—or at least the speakeasies. The term was derived from the admonishment to speak softly so that no one would know that the people of Chicago were hiding away and drinking as though their lives depended on it. Al Capone had all the beer and booze they needed, and they needed plenty.

Even as far back as 1839, Americans were known for imbibing. "I am sure the Americans can fix nothing without a drink,"[1] wrote Frederick Marryat in *A Diary in America*. "If you meet you drink, if you part you drink, if you make an acquaintance you drink, if you choose a bargain you drink, they quarrel in their drink, and they make it up in their drink. They drink because it is hot they drink because it is cold."[2] By 1830 adults were drinking seven gallons of pure alcohol each year, or the equivalent of 1.7 bottles of 80-proof liquor per person per week.

People liked to drink, and it was a shock almost inconceivable to our modern-day sensibilities that on January 16, 1920, the country ran dry. Franklin D. Roosevelt, as secretary of the navy, raised a final glass of champagne with members of Harvard's Class of 1904 and said good-bye to the freedom ever to take a drink again (or so they thought). The ban on alcohol would last from 1920 to 1933; the organized crime and black market it engendered would give Al Capone $100 million a year and allow him to buy every judge, politician, or cop during the Depression, when everyone needed money. It allowed Capone to open soup kitchens, hobnob with movie stars, own Mayor William Thompson, live a lavish lifestyle, and defeat democracy in Chicago, which knew only the rule of the Thompson submachine gun.

Prohibition would spawn more than Al Capone, however. The speakeasies disseminated jazz, popularized African American musicians, and got women into bars. Before this, drinking was a male-dominated avocation, but women started drinking bathtub gin, with the expected effect on sexual mores. Now men and women smoked and drank together in dark basements on Chicago street corners in illegal settings that made the behavior all the more taboo. The watchful eyes of society had given way to men in loud suits and fedoras with extra pockets sewn into their coats for .45-caliber pistols—when they weren't cloaking tommy guns.

To say the Progressives had lost the battle on this one would be an understatement. Prohibition had come out of the late nineteenth-century Progressive movement as a final shot across the bow to stop the loosening of morals. It was a woman's movement headed by Carry Nation, with a hatchet, steel bifocals, and a crow-black dress. She was six feet tall and promised American women that she would stop the awful scourge causing their husbands to drink, to fornicate, and to squander the family's income. Her methodology was one of destruction. This is how she described a normal attack on a saloon:

> *I ran behind the bar and smashed the mirror and all the bottles under it, picked up the cash register, threw it down, then broke the faucets of the refrigerator, opened the door and cut the rubber tubes that conducted the beer. Of course it began to fly all over the house. I threw over the slot machine, breaking it up and I got from it a sharp piece of iron with which I opened the bungs of the beer kegs, and opened the faucets of the barrels, and then the beer flew in every direction and I was completely saturated. A policeman came in and very good naturedly arrested me.*[3]

The elbowing of the saloon into small towns across America alarmed Nation. Whereas there had been 100,000 saloons in 1870, by 1900 there were 300,000. San Francisco alone had 3,000 such establishments. Bars offered not only drink but also a respite from the grueling march of American capitalism. The working man could forget his grind, and the white-collar worker could drown his stress. Unsurprisingly, the organization that pushed the Volstead Act on a country of drinkers was called the Anti-Saloon League. Congress, split between the drys and the wets, battled for thirty years. Drinking also became a racial issue, as the Southern drys claimed that liquor contributed to the Negro's lust for white women and getting rid of booze would keep him under control.

Prohibition was quickly linked to the woman's movement and the quest for the vote. Progressivism was a large train in the early twentieth century, and the back-scratching among the causes, from women's rights to working conditions to Prohibition, allowed for a linkage that should never have occurred. Those who campaigned to stop drinking in America shared the same fervor as settlement house pioneers like Jane Addams and Lillian Wald, with their empathy for the huddled masses.

Once enacted into law, Prohibition quickly became synonymous with speakeasies and drinking to excess. There was no shame. Everyone did it. No one really slowed his or her drinking, though statistically Prohibition did cut down on national consumption. But popular culture grabbed onto the speakeasy, and people knew the password to whisper into a slot in a dark Chicago alley to gain entrance to another world.

In F. Scott Fitzgerald's *The Great Gatsby*, a character accuses Gatsby of buying up drugstores to disseminate bootleg whiskey. The government had gone after industrial alcohol by adding methanol to make it poisonous. Denatured alcohol, as it was called, would kill ten thousand Americans before all was said and done. But medicinal alcohol was still legal, and so drugstores became a bootlegger's haven and even offered price lists for customers. Charles Walgreen claimed to have built his Chicago-based drugstore chain on his malted milkshakes. He went from 20 stores to 525 in the 1920s, and it wasn't because of his soda fountains.[4]

Prohibition did for drinking in the 1920s what rock and roll did for music in the 1950s. Everyone wanted booze, and critic Edmund Wilson noted that in 1927 there were ninety-seven different terms for being drunk, including "squiffy," "zozzled," "corned," "scorched," "embalmed," "buried," "blasted," "smashed," and "lit."[5] Drinking became a frenzied sport. Nothing less than the cocktail party was invented during Prohibition, with men and women socializing while drinking together. As novelist Willa Cather wrote in the 1920s, "Nobody stays home anymore."[6]

New York had 32,000 drinking spots by the end of the 1920s, and Chicago had close to that. Dancing and powder rooms made the speakeasy attractive to women, who appeared in movies dancing on tables and guzzling martinis. As songwriter Alec Wilder said, "A pretty girl in a speakeasy was the most beautiful girl in the world."[7] White and black people began drinking together, and cross acculturalization was the result, with the Harlem Cave and the Cozy Corner becoming famous spots where well-known people drank and danced in an era when the races did not mix at all.

F. Scott Fitzgerald led the charge, and gin was the drink of choice. This ubiquitous alcohol became famous as "bathtub gin," and Prohibition never lost a certain youth component. To be young in America was to drink to excess. Zelda Fitzgerald pioneered the flapper style, but America did the rest, and "partying" was born. But to do it, people needed a steady flow of alcohol, and the government was out of the business and had forced the big manufacturers to shut down. Enter Al Capone.

His lasting defense was that he was simply providing a service: "Public Service is my motto."[8] Capone was not wrong. Imagine if the government banned cigarettes. Someone would step in to meet the demand represented by people addicted to nicotine. Al Capone codified the business of providing alcohol for the second largest city in the United States. But because the government did not sanction it, the normal recourse for resolving disputes was not open to Capone and his associates. They resorted instead to murder, torture, and the annihilation of whole gangs.

So, by 1929, with a world's fair on the way in Chicago, the business of providing alcohol for a thirsty people deprived of their favorite vice had created a thriving underworld that generated millions upon millions of dollars. To keep the business rolling, everyone had to be in on it, and so democracy, or at least the rule of law, had ceased to function, giving way to extortion and murder. Anyone who testified against someone else ended up dead. Anyone who thought about testifying ended up dead. Those seven corpses taken from the garage on Valentine's Day and now lying in the morgue could tell no story. But the Big Fellah, Snorky, Big Al—he might be able to shed some light on what happened.

One thing was for sure: Chicago was totally out of control.

The Big Man

HE WAS AS BIG AS BABE RUTH AND AS ADDICTED TO MEDIA AS DONALD Trump. He was concerned about the freshness of his milk and responsible for dairies' dating their milk for spoilage. He was as popular as a president, and crowds gathered whenever he appeared in court. He wore a bullet-proof vest, had bars installed on the windows of his Cicero home, and never opened the drapes. He had personally beat two men to death with a baseball bat and shot another man three times in the head for assaulting a man who worked for him. He was a family man who liked to cook and spend time with his wife of twenty years and his seven-year-old son, Sonny. He appeared constantly in newspapers and newsreels and was known worldwide, much like Ernest Hemingway. He would change dress, media, movies, speech, politics, drinking, and income tax law. He was chosen as *Time*'s Man of the Year for 1930 and appeared on the magazine's cover.

And now, after the St. Valentine's Day Massacre, he was sitting in a checkered sport coat with white flannels and a matching white fedora in a Dade County office building in Florida. It was hot, and his cheeks shone with sweat. As the stenographer settled herself, he stared at Brook-lyn prosecutor Louis Goldstein, Dade County prosecutor Robert Taylor, and county sheriff M. P. Lanham. Perhaps he marveled at how far he had come. Just seven years before he was outside a Chicago speakeasy in the snow, trying to lure people in for girls and drinks. Maybe he thought about stealing fruit in Brooklyn so he could eat. Or joining the Five Points Gang as a kid with a sixth-grade education. Or how he left Brooklyn to work in Chicago for a 50 percent cut of Johnny Torrio's bootlegging proceeds. And when Torrio was shot in 1925 and miraculously survived, the boss got out of the business, returned to Brooklyn, and gave everything to Capone.

The "Capone outfit" consolidated over the ensuing years.[1] Between 1922 and 1926, 250 gangsters were killed in Chicago. The Windy City's homicide rate was 24 percent higher than anywhere else in the country. Cars mysteriously appeared in quiet neighborhoods; police opened the trunks and found decomposing corpses, shot fifteen or twenty times, with skulls bashed in, eyes burned out, features melted away by acid. Al Capone could have changed tracks and used his organizational skills in any corporation in America. He understood systems and systematically took over bootlegging, gambling, and prostitution. Everyone got protection, and everyone had to pay for it. Any threat met with overwhelming force. Torture with a blowtorch and a knife by an enforcer who hung a man on a meat hook in a basement became standard. Capone originated the CEO far removed from business operations who filters his income through tax shelters. He pioneered the use of offshore accounts and tax havens in his use of checks made out to phony businesses that made their way back into his account. At the time paying income tax for most Americans was a voluntary act—there was no IRS.

In 1924 Nathan Leopold and Richard Loeb, two wealthy young men in Chicago, murdered a young boy to prove that they could commit the perfect crime. Chicago was horrified, and so was Al Capone. He later offered to help solve the kidnapping of Charles Lindbergh's baby and frowned on any kind of violence not related to the mob. The word "benevolent" would be used when he opened soup kitchens during the Great Depression. Now this multifaceted man was about to be asked if he had murdered seven men in Chicago.

The voice of Robert Taylor echoed in the high-ceilinged office with the slow-turning fan.

"Do you remember when you first met Parker Henderson?"

"About two years ago."

"That was when he was running the Ponce de Leon Hotel?"

"Yes."

"Who was staying there with you that winter?"

"I don't remember."

"Under what name did you register?"

"My own name."

"You didn't register under the name A. Costa?"

"No."

"You left money with Henderson, $1,000 to $5,000 at a time?"

"I don't remember."

"You didn't receive any money by Western Union from Chicago?"

"I don't remember. I'll try to find out."

"Then you keep a record of your money transactions?"

"Absolutely."

"How much did you give Parker Henderson to buy your home?"

"Fifty thousand dollars."

"Was that in cash?"

"Yes."

"Besides gambling, you're a bootlegger, aren't you?"

"No, I was never a bootlegger."

"Do you know Jake Guzik?"

"Yes."

"What does he do?"[2]

At this point Al Capone shifted his weight and pushed up his hat. Florida was hot, and the room seemed a bit warmer. This was not going as usual. Interviewers generally asked him if he had killed so and so, and he always said he was a peaceful businessman. But these guys seemed more interested in his money. The government's right to tax American income had only been on the books since 1913 with the passage of the Sixteenth Amendment. Most Americans still were not aware of it.

"He fights," he answered.

"And do you know anybody who sent you money under the name of A. Costa?"

"No."

"But you did receive money from Chicago?"

"That is correct. All of it comes from Chicago, from my gambling business."

"Are you going to buy Cat Cay?"

"I don't' know. I don't think I will get it."

"How much do they want for it?"

"Half a million."

"Did you get any money from Charlie Fishetti while you were staying at the Ponce de Leon?"

Capone stared at the prosecutor, finally fed up with the strange questioning: "What has money got to do with it?"[3]

After the interview ended, Al might have picked up one of the Florida papers. The huge black headlines still screamed about the massacre. Of course, he knew all about it; he just didn't think it would create such a fury. An article from Chicago's *Herald Examiner* announced:

> *Chicago gangsters graduated yesterday from murder to massacre.*
> *They killed seven men in a group. There were just a few seconds of machine gun and shotgun fire. Then six of them lay dead and a seventh was dying.*
> *It was like the precise work of an execution squad of the Mexican army, like the assassination of Czar Nicholas and his family.*[4]

The accompanying photo broke taboos against graphic violence, with the mechanic John May lying next to a portion of his brain. The poor boy from Brooklyn who made $100 million a year in cold, hard cash had set the world on edge. The massacre wasn't a declaration of war, but it was close.

And yet, years later, Al Capone's niece would write a book titled *Uncle Al Capone*, the cover showing Al relaxing in his front yard, a couple of cigars in his pocket. Deidre Marie Capone describes a kind man who liked popcorn and barbecues and was proud that he could provide for his family. She paints an extremely American portrait, complete with a vacation home in Wisconsin. On being asked about Uncle Al and the people his outfit had killed, her aunt responded,

> *Remember what we've always taught you. Family is everything. There were people out there trying to kill Al for their own gain— because he was the biggest competition there was. And they were willing to go so far as to threaten his family. When you were just a little*

*girl, some of them were willing to threaten you. That's where Al drew
the line. He didn't tolerate backstabbing, and he didn't tolerate people
who wanted to hurt us. . . . No one in our family was ever involved in
any cold-blooded killing. . . . If somebody is trying to hurt you, aren't
you permitted to protect yourself?*[5]

Aunt Maffie then told Deidre that she never knew a gangster who helped
people as much as Uncle Al. "He would have given his life to save your
life or mine. So don't be so hard on him. . . . OK? Capiche?"[6]

Such was the view of Uncle Al held by a little girl who had listened
to the radio with him, sat in his lap, and listened to his big laugh. In
February 1929, in Chicago and Washington, DC, the view was much
different. Vice President Charles Dawes, trying to finance a world's fair
in 1933 by asking corporate CEOs to kick in millions, felt like he had
just been exposed as a con man. His brother Rufus was beside himself
as president of the fair. The US vice president wanted the crime solved
quickly, and Chicago was trying to piece it all together. There was a
good chance the police really had been the perpetrators, and maybe
Capone had nothing to do with it at all. Maybe Bugsy Moran's men
had double-crossed some cops, who took matters into their own hands.
The story was that Moran's men had stolen a truck of liquor from some
crooked policemen, and this was payback.

Then Walter Winchell reported two weeks after the Valentine's Day
attack that "Scarface Capone may have retired, but his phone bill from
Miami to Chicago was four and half grand."[7] Cook County's state attorney felt the heat and ordered police to close the 10,000 speakeasies in the
city. Some action is better than no action. Then the Cook County coroner
convened a blue-ribbon coroner's jury, and, for publicity as well as a starting point, its members all marched down to the garage on North Clark
Street and reenacted the massacre. The jurymen stared at the chipped
brick wall, walked over the blood stains on the greasy floor, and looked at
the chair splintered by bullets. Police officers and reporters crammed into
the oil-scented garage and took pictures while stand-ins lined up with
their hands in the air, like the doomed Moran gang. In the end nothing
came of the reenactment but a lot of press.

Of course, the publicity was all bad. Images of the actual event showed dead men with split-open heads. The reenactment photos made it seem the massacre had occurred again, and the world relived it over and over in the papers. A letter to the editor in the *Chicago Tribune* summed up the problem for the city: "What a wonderful advertisement to be broadcast all over the world, to boost Chicago for the 1933 World's Fair."[8] Another, more practical writer reminded Chicagoans that the city's bootleggers provided far better beer than their New York counterparts and mostly killed each other, not ordinary citizens. "So let's give Soltis, Moran and Capone their due."[9] This beer drinker was willing to put up with a few flying bullets for a quality brew.

Some suggested throwing in the towel and having the Illinois legislature cease enforcing the liquor laws. The noble experiment obviously wasn't working. Then Capone got a subpoena ordering him to appear before a federal grand jury. He said he was too sick to travel. Three weeks after Valentine's Day, on March 4, 1929, Herbert Hoover became the nation's thirty-first president and talked about restoring law and order in the country. J. Edgar Hoover was taking over the Justice Department, and the first order of business was to fire all political appointees and install men loyal to him and not susceptible to bribes. Hoover sensed an opening to strengthen his Bureau of Investigation and sent men down to Miami to see if Al Capone was really sick.

Meanwhile, a group of prominent Chicago officials, including Frank Loesch, president of the Chicago Crime Commission, went to Washington, DC, to see the president. They were having a fair and getting really panicky. They pleaded with him to get personally involved with restoring order in Chicago. President Hoover would later record the meeting in his memoirs: "They gave me chapter and verse for their statement that Chicago was in the hands of the gangsters and that the police and magistrates were completely under their control, that the governor of the state was futile, that the federal government was the only force by which the city's ability to govern itself could be restored."[10]

It was an amazing moment. City officials admitted that a major American metropolis had lost democratic rule and was now under the thumb of one man who had more money than Chicago itself and ruled by murder and intimidation with citizens' sanction because he supplied a drug that they demanded. In 1929 a law gone bad had subverted Chicago's rule of law, and organized crime had replaced the normal machinery of government. Mayor Bill Thompson won election with Capone's help: his henchmen had used intimidation and murder and thrown pineapple bombs at opposing polling stations. The real mayor of Chicago was lolling in Miami, sipping a tall one, while Bill Thompson was busy taking bribes, drinking, spending time with prostitutes, and getting press. Everyone had been bought off or otherwise silenced, and the press had made sure Capone the celebrity could rule by despotic enforcement. The men pleading with President Hoover were not being dramatic; they had lost control of their city.

Technically Hoover could do little. But he knew also that Capone's activities were undermining American democracy, if not American culture. Chicago could not govern itself, much less invite the world to come to its fair. Hoover gave a quiet order to all law enforcement agencies to get Al Capone, and this began the ritual that would occur every morning on the White House lawn.

Hoover liked to toss around a medicine ball with members of his cabinet, a type of exercise where a little effort was thought to go a long way. Riding a bicycle fell into this category. Americans really didn't work out, but they did things that seemed fun and might give them some exercise as well. Hooverball was played on a court sixty-six feet long and thirty feet wide with an eight-foot net. A medicine ball weighed about six pounds, and teams consisted of two to four players who hefted it back and forth. As in volleyball, points were scored when the other team failed to catch the ball or get it over the net. You could not run with the ball, and "good sportsmanship was required."[11]

Hoover used this time to go over pressing issues of the day and regularly asked, while pounding back the medicine ball in his duck trousers and button-down shirt, "Did you get Capone yet?"[12] Not only had they not done so, but, even worse, they couldn't even get him to come to Chicago for grand jury testimony.

Soon Herbert Hoover would be distracted from Chicago and Al Capone. The stock market was beginning to make funny noises.

CHAPTER NINE

The Big Fellah Comes Home

THEN AL CAPONE WENT BACK TO CHICAGO. HE SNEAKED INTO THE courthouse wearing his pearl-grey spats and black oxfords with his trademark wide-brimmed fedora. US Attorney General George Johnson heard a commotion outside his office. The man who loved publicity could not help himself. Flashbulb smoke curled up into the room. The reporters wanted to know how he had slipped in, and Al said he had left his brother and a few others in Indiana and driven in alone.

Pop, pop, pop.

The flashbulbs anoint the celebrity. The streets are awash in people rushing to get a glimpse of the gangster. Who cares about that crazy fair they are having in four years? Al Capone is in town. There's Al with his lawyers, Ben Epstein and William Waugh. Pop, pop, pop. Al Capone looks great. He is tan and has lost some weight; he looks very much the successful, confident businessman. His hair is still jet black, and his eyes rove easily, but a glint speaks of something darker, more sinister. Police are called to control the crowd of 1,500 people in the building and outside. This is before television or the Internet; yet Chicagoans flock to see the celebrity in their midst, and even though Al is not a movie star, lately he has been thinking about selling his story to the "pictyahs." Autographs for the working men and the suits, and the rest can tell their wives and kids they saw the Big Fellah; they saw Al Capone.

"I ought to go into vaudeville," Capone muses, beaming, loving it. "Look at the crowd I get."[1]

Look at it. Modern mass communication is just beginning to infect America. Ernest Hemingway is experimenting with media promotion, as is Errol Flynn and a lone flyer named Charles Lindbergh. The latter will explode onto the scene, become America's first superstar, and experience the dark side of American fame. Right now celebrity is the new drug, and for a poor wop from Brooklyn, it is nothing short of amazing. Money and dames and bullets mean nothing compared to it. Capone is turning his right cheek to the reporters.

"Just my good side, boys."[2]

Pop, pop, pop.

The smoke is thick in the room when George Johnson bursts in and realizes his witness has turned the building upside down.

"Get out of here! Get out of here! This isn't a photograph gallery for hoodlums!"

Capone laughs. "So long, boys!"[3]

Johnson slams the doors and keeps Capone waiting all day. It is all he can do to the gangster with fame, money, and influence on his side. Capone beats it to his lawyer's office in the Marquette Building for a corned-beef sandwich and a glass of milk. It is late in the afternoon when he is finally brought before the grand jury to answer questions for an hour and a half. An assistant district attorney announces that Capone has received immunity for his testimony. He says little beyond "I don't know" or "I don't remember."

George Johnson tells him to come back in six days, and Capone is annoyed. He can't go back to Florida. The papers wonder if the gangster is being set up for the Valentine Day's murders, but Attorney General Johnson can charge him with nothing but contempt for not coming to Chicago sooner. So Capone cools his heels while Chicago thaws, with the great flat ice bobbing in Lake Michigan and the coal soot falling on melting snow. So far 1929 hasn't been too bad, but there is a feeling in the air almost like the calm before the storm. People hope the Chicago Cubs can come back from a two-decade losing streak since their World Series win. Rogers Hornsby has signed on and might be the man to turn the team around.

There had been building in the city, with the Chicago Stadium and Civic Opera House getting ready to open. And that fair to be held in less than four years was getting closer. Press releases from the office of Rufus Dawes were making the rounds, and Robert Isham Randolph, president of the Chicago Association of Commerce, had once again declared that the city would be safe and scrubbed of crime by the time the fair opened. Tell that to the big man giving interviews and lounging in the Lexington Hotel. Then Chicagoans opened the newspaper on March 27, 1929, and read, "US Arrests Capone."

It was a big, big bust. Al Capone, the most notorious gangster of the twentieth century—or any century, for that matter—was being held on contempt charges. A whopping $1,000 fine and possible year in jail were the best US District Attorney Johnson could do. Capone posted a $500 bond, returned to his luxurious accommodations, and then left for Florida. But here comes the real insult to the city that could not hold its most notorious prisoner.

Cut to Hammond, Indiana. A couple of cops are driving along Sheffield Avenue when two black sedans blow past. They circle around and find two dead men in a Cadillac. They have been beaten with bats, then shot, then shot again and beaten some more for good measure. Their skulls are mush, and their ears are bloody stubs. Another car nearby contains a third man in the same condition. The victims are John Scalise, Joseph Guinta, and Albert Anselmi. A scene in the 1987 movie *The Untouchables* speculates about how they met their end: having betrayed Capone, they show up to a meeting only to be beaten to death with a baseball bat by the big man himself. "Enthusiasms . . . enthusiasms . . ." Everyone remembers the scene.

At first people believe the Moran gang did it to avenge the St. Valentine's Day Massacre. But the better story is that Al Capone has found traitors in his organization and uses a gang meeting as a teachable moment. While the other gangsters look on, Capone beats the traitors until they are dead. Everyone wants to believe this scene because it is so Chicago, so Capone, so Hollywood. In truth, Al Capone would have been hard pressed to beat three men to death with a baseball bat. Better to have an enforcer do it and dispose of the bodies in that godforsaken shithole of a state, Indiana.

Besides, no one really knows where Al Capone is. He has attended a meeting but without a baseball bat. Gangsters from all over the country have converged on Atlantic City to rein in a blood bath that all agree is bad for business. Even the gangsters are shocked by the St. Valentine's Day Massacre and want to put an end to killing that is doing no one any good and costing them money. After the meeting ends, Big Al, Frankie Rio, and other bodyguards leave Atlantic City and start driving for New York, where they plan to catch a train back to Chicago. The weather is miserable, with rain blowing sideways and a low grey sky. Capone is wearing his trademark dark overcoat, with a .38-caliber snub-nosed revolver in the right pocket. In 1929 technology tended to break down, and Capone's car stops running just south of Camden, New Jersey. They decide to hop a commuter train to Philadelphia, where they buy tickets for a train scheduled to leave for Chicago around 9:05 p.m.

The men decide to kill some time by catching a movie about gangsters: *Voice of the City*, a detective story starring Willard Mack. The Stanley Theatre is on Nineteenth Street, and two detectives are driving by in an undercover car. John Creeden and James Malone work for the Philadelphia Police Department and see the men in oversized fedoras with loud ties and long overcoats; they look like mobsters from Hollywood, but what's more, they look like Al Capone and his muscle. The cops pull over and hoof it back to the theater, but Capone and company are already inside, settling in with their popcorn.

The detectives don't want a shootout, and so they wait. The movie runs about an hour and half, and then people start streaming out. Detectives Creeden and Malone are nervous but don't call for backup. Who knows why? At 8:30 p.m. Capone and his men emerge, and Malone flashes his badge. Creeden grabs Rio and pins him against the wall. Al puts his hand in his right pocket, Malone grabs it, and they lock eyes.

"Easy there, Al," he says.[4]

And they slowly pull the .38 out together. The other two bodyguards melt away. Capone is booked on weapons possessions; he still wears his fedora in his mugshot. He lights up a cigarette and then stands before a magistrate, who orders him held on $35,000 bond. After midnight, he gets his lawyer and a visit from Lemuel B. Schofield, director of public safety. Schofield interviews Capone and gets some publicity for himself.

What comes out is Capone's state of mind on his career: "I went into the rackets four and a half years ago. . . . [D]uring the last two years I've been trying to get out. But once in the racket you're always in it, it seems. . . . I have a wife and an eleven-year-old boy I idolize and a beautiful home in Florida. If I could go there and forget it all I would be the happiest man in the world."[5] Capone sleeps on a bench with Rio. Ten big Philadelphia cops guard their prison cell. The next morning, as they await trial, a man asks how much the ring on Capone's finger is worth.

"About fifty thousand," Capone says with a shrug, about what the average American would see in his lifetime.[6]

Capone pleads guilty and is sentenced to one year in prison. He pulls the diamond from his hand and gives it to his lawyer.

"It's the breaks, kids," he says to Rio as he is led away.[7]

The biggest gangster in America was now in prison for one year for carrying a gun into a movie theater. People speculated that Al Capone wanted to go to jail for his own protection. Capone's sister Mafalda said years later that the idea was absurd; Al Capone would never have himself incarcerated intentionally. The Philadelphia police fired Capone's gun into a barrel to see if its bullets matched those found at the scene of the St. Valentine's Day Massacre. They didn't. Chicago was embarrassed. The cops in Philly had iced Capone for a year, while the Windy City couldn't hold him for twenty-four hours.

The truth was that Al Capone ran Chicago. He owned cops, judges, and prosecutors, and, of course, he owned William Thompson, the corrupt mayor elected through the efforts of Capone's bomb-throwing operatives. Worse, he knew how to make a witness disappear or end up in the Chicago River or turn up dead on a side street in Hammond, Indiana. To testify against the outfit was to invite death, and everyone knew it. Huey Long would take over Louisiana in the middle of the Depression and turn it into a police state, but Al Capone had taken over Chicago by force in the dark undertow of Prohibition that swept away all semblance of law and order.

But for now Capone would spend the next year in Philadelphia. Dawes brothers Rufus and Charles breathed a collective sigh. They could at least try to get a handle on what was coming. Capone was in jail, but the gang wars were still rolling. And now the other shoe was dropping. Only one thing could derail *A Century of Progress* permanently: sudden economic collapse. Impossible.

CHAPTER TEN

The Perfect Storm

THE ROARING TWENTIES WERE THE FIRST MODERN DECADE IN URBAN America. For the first time the new middle class had access to credit and goods that would have been a fantasy to their parents back in the speculative years of the nineteenth century. A perfect storm of a modern economy, an accessible credit market, mass production on a scale not known before, and a roulette wheel called the American stock market all converged on a people who, having been pent up during the years of World War I, now just wanted to have fun for as long as they could.

The jingoistic "We're in the Money" played from gramophones and new radios as electricity eliminated the drudgery of middle-class existence.[1] There were toasters, fans, washing machines, movies, radios, lights, cameras, new cars, air travel, clothes, furniture, processed food, easy mortgages, and easy credit. Beyond all that there was that shining beacon on the island of Manhattan: the stock market. And everyone was making money. Or so it seemed.

Culturally America had broken out. Prohibition made everyone into an outlaw, and women became the new rebels of the modern era. They smoked and drank and had sex and danced on tables and worked and made money and didn't want to get married, and if they got married, they got divorced, and if they had kids, they left them, and they drove cars and did the Charleston and resembled their mothers not at all.

Prosperity was not right around the corner, as Herbert Hoover would proclaim when the other shoe finally dropped; it was here. America put forth the idea that poverty could be wiped out in the modern era; you just had to jump in and purchase some stocks and buy a house and take out a loan because American businessmen had changed the world and consumerism had been born, and a fair was coming that would celebrate it. Middle-class people made less than $5,000 a year, but it didn't matter; people could buy "on time" now and didn't have to wait. They could have their cake and eat it too.[2]

Besides, people were becoming rich. The greatest bull market in the history of the nation was under way. You bought a stock, and it went up. Increases over a year of 300 percent were not uncommon. Of course, those stocks were manipulated, much as they are today, by players who suckered everyone in and then sold. The middle class was the biggest pool of suckers the players had ever seen, and they would buy anything. Anaconda Copper was an example of the hoodwinking perpetrated on the public.[3]

In 1928 the stock was a dog, with copper prices on the floor and not moving. Investors pumped the stock up with big buys and put out press releases touting the rise in copper prices. The stock shot up from 48 to 128 in three months, but of course the investors only stayed in long enough to make a profit; when they pulled the plug, the stock crashed, taking the middle class's money with it. Al Capone's sale of Prohibition beer was nothing compared to the Ponzi scheme of Wall Street in the late 1920s. In fact, Capone knew it before anyone else. "These stock guys are crooked," he said from his cell.[4]

There are no firm estimates of how many Americans had invested in stocks by 1929, but it was probably more than 2.5 million people. Everyone, it seemed, was in the market or wanted to get in. The movies talked about the market; the radio talked about the market; celebrities talked about the market. Groucho Marx quipped, "The little judgement I had told me to sell, but like all the other suckers I was greedy. I was loathe to relinquish any stock that was sure to double in a few months."[5]

The problem was that the economy rested on quicksand. The stock market, while ubiquitous, was a small part of the economy and did not represent the health of the nation's financial underpinning. Florida had never come back from a hurricane that had devastated the state in 1926. Farmers had struggled all through the 1920s, and, of course, the Achille's heel of every major recession is the purchase of homes by a middle class that can ill afford them. Mortgage debt had doubled during the 1920s, and families had moved up by selling their homes for a profit in order to move into bigger houses with bigger mortgages.[6] As long as everything kept moving, it all worked.

In 1929 the housing market hiccupped, and Americans started to run out of money. Maybe they had bought too many cars or too many houses or too many toasters or too much stock. The easy money dried up, and things started to roll backward. The stock market shrugged off the economic realities by taking off for the sky. People had to keep up somehow, so they bought on margin. Just one more buy, one more stock, then I sell—the mantra of the margin buyer convinced that lucky sevens will finally come up.

And then, on October 24, 1929, while Big Al snoozed in his cozy cell between meals brought by his wife and son, the market lost 11 percent of its value. A massive hiccup. Big Al was probably enjoying some brandy and a cigar when the market bounced back the next day and everyone breathed a collective sigh of relief. Then the market fell again on Monday, and brokers crowded the floor with sell orders. By now Big Al may have been out in the prison yard for his constitutional. The newspapers quoted business leaders telling the public to buy, buy, buy because the market was sound; it would not go lower, and these deals were amazing. Then the tidal wave hit, with sell orders inundating traders on Tuesday. Everyone lost faith at the same time, and the newspapers said the jig was up; the floor had fallen, and it was every man for himself. On Black Tuesday, October 29, the market lost 13 percent.[7] Even investment by business titans could not stop the flood of selling. Two weeks later the market had lost half its value.

We can relate to this somewhat in the wake of the 2008 Great Recession, when housing prices crashed to the floor. In 1929, $30 billion vanished in less than two weeks.[8] This was middle-class money. This was entrepreneurial money. This was business money. Most may not have jumped from their skyscraper windows, but that doesn't mean they didn't feel like doing so. People who lost their money raced to the local bank to withdraw their savings. In fact, everyone hightailed it to the bank, and the phrase "a run on the banks" was born.[9] Banks ran out of money and closed.

A third of the nation's banks failed at a time when depositors' money was not federally insured. There was no safety net. There was no recourse if a bank went under and took a person's life savings with it. That person was simply wiped out. And worse, there was no backup. Homes were foreclosed, and families lived in alleys or under bridges or disbanded. Many sold their children to other families in desperation. There was no unemployment insurance, no food stamp program, no Medicaid, welfare, Social Security, or workman's compensation. There were only starvation and church-run soup kitchens.

The crash ended the Roaring Twenties and ushered in the Great Depression. The reality was almost unbelievable. A reporter for the *New Republic* described a scene in New York City in 1931: "There is a line of men three or sometimes four abreast and a block long and wedged so tightly no passerby can break through. The reason for this is those at the head of line will eat tonight."[10] Men who had decent jobs one day were selling apples the next. Fifty-four men arrested in Times Square considered themselves lucky because they would be fed.

President Herbert Hoover believed in laissez-faire and that the American people just had to wait for the economy to right itself. He did not put stock in government intervention or stimulus programs. He served as the poster boy in 2008 for what not to do when the economy crashes. Americans began to starve. A 1932 *New York Times* article read, "Found starving under a rude canvas shelter in a patch of woods on Flatboard Ridge, where they had lived for five days on wild berries and apples, a woman and her sixteen-year-old daughter were fed and clothed today by the police and placed in the city almshouse."[11]

In Chicago men stood on every street corner. The city itself was bankrupt. Bread lines stretched for blocks. Al Capone joked from prison, "Tell them, I deny absolutely that I am responsible."[12] In the irony of all ironies, Al Capone would come to the rescue of the downtrodden by opening soup kitchens all over Chicago. This did not jive with his reputation as public enemy number one, but times were hard. Hoovervilles sprang up around the country.[13] Families lived in boxes, crates, old cars, basements, barns—anywhere they could find shelter.

Winter came, and life went on. Charles Lindbergh had married Anne Morrow and settled in New Jersey. Commander Richard Byrd had pioneered the first flight to the South Pole. Al Capone relaxed in jail while the outfit kept up the supply of booze to speakeasies and murdered anyone who got in the way. And two brothers, Charles and Rufus Dawes, figured they needed $20 million to fund a world's fair in Chicago in 1933, calling it *A Century of Progress*. The laughter would have been deafening, were it not for the crying.

CHAPTER ELEVEN

Financing a Fair

RUFUS DAWES WAS NOT HIS BROTHER. HE DIDN'T SMOKE HIS PIPE upside down or write songs that would become hits thirty years later. He wasn't the nation's vice president and had never created an economic reparations model for the Germans to repay their debt from World War I. But his brother had always been like that. Even when they were kids, everyone had gravitated toward Charles while Rufus worked quietly in the background. Charles was a renaissance man who could have easily ended up a musician if he hadn't gotten a law degree and discovered that he had a knack not only for writing songs but also for making money—something Rufus needed badly in 1929, when he had no idea how he was going to raise one red cent for a world's fair when the bottom had just fallen out of the economy and Al Capone was still the reigning king of Chicago.

Dawes sat in his office and read about William Wrigley Jr. and William Abbot, both of whom predicted the fair would be a disaster. There was absolutely no public money for the enterprise, and Chicago was bankrupt. And had anyone forgotten about the crime problem? The fair, they announced, "would be the biggest fiasco ever occurring in Chicago."[1]

In reading about the first Chicago fair in 1893, one comes away with a real sense of the titanic struggle that Daniel Burnham Sr., John Root, and Frederick Law Olmstead waged in creating the White City, and that drama lies at the heart of the Columbian Exposition. The devil in the White City might have been Dr. H. H. Holmes, but it was also creating

55

a vision of art through architecture under very short deadlines with mercurial personalities and giving form to an event that would ring out the traditions of the nineteenth century and ring in those of the twentieth. At times the protagonists seem like a bunch of crotchety artists who must have their way or their oversized egos might just inflate and block out all progress.

The drama of the 1933 fair seems to have lacked this element; instead, it involved two very real antagonists who were not abstract concepts to be realized along Chicago's lakefront. These villains were terrestrial and bore no relation to architects intent on creating something never before seen in the city. One, of course, was Al Capone, and the second was the Great Depression. These two forces posed an equal threat, and only by eliminating one and working creatively around the other would the 1933 fair take place. But what of the great technical aspects of creating a fair? Bring on the Dawes brothers.

Charles and Rufus were, like most brothers, very different men. They came from Marietta, Ohio, members of a distinguished family that included great-great-grandfather William Dawes, who rode with Paul Revere on the night of April 18, 1775. Charles Dawes was the creative one and Rufus the cautious conservative. But Rufus did little without consulting his brother, and before he became president of the 1933 Chicago World's Fair, he did so again. He told the committee of the world's fair that "after due deliberation and consultation with his brother, Vice President Charles G. Dawes . . . he had decided to accept."[2] The two had worked together in business for thirty years and established the dividing line early. Charles would handle the financial end of things, while Rufus dealt with the nuts and bolts. Each man was perfectly suited to his task.

George Woodruff of the National Bank of the Republic, who would serve as treasurer of the Chicago World's Fair, noted that previous fairs had not made money. He warned that the 1933 fair must generate income and, to do so, must be run on a strict business model—which brings us to the lack of the high drama so pleasurable to readers but devastating to the smooth building and running of a fair. In this way the Dawes brothers were the perfect choice. The fair brochure states, "The Dawes plan is bold like Charley and conservative like Rufus."[3] An article in *Time* magazine reported that "Rufus never crossed or argued with his older brother but simply let him explode and then went ahead and did what needed to be done."[4]

The brothers were similar men in some respects. Both lived in the upscale neighborhood on Lake Michigan in Evanston. They had visited the Columbian Exposition as young men in their twenties and seen the Ferris wheel on the Midway. They had been fascinated with the buildings of the White City, and both followed their father's edict in all their business and personal relations: "The only goal in life is the development of character."[5] Their father had been a Union general in the Civil War and served in the House of Representatives; when he became ill in 1889, Rufus had taken charge of the family lumber business.

Charles asserted himself in politics, losing a run for the US Senate in 1900. He soon realized that his calling lay in the financial realm and became president of the Central Trust Company of Illinois, soon referred to as the Dawes Bank. He then organized the Minute Men of the Constitution to fight crime and corruption in the state.[6] This organization was certainly a precursor to what would later be known as the Secret Six. After becoming vice president under Calvin Coolidge, he saw the shift in America from small-town values to an embrace of business models based on a bureaucratic division of labor. Corporate culture was supplanting the nuclear, relationship-based economic model of the small town with a different model perfected by Henry Ford with his assembly lines. Everyone did his part, but not necessarily as part of the whole.

These techniques would become the driving force behind the fair. The Dawes brothers and their general manager, Major Lenox R. Lohr, would apply modern business methods to the chaotic enterprise. Sally Rand might become the biggest draw of the fair, and Al Capone might pose an existential threat to the city, and the Great Depression might just destroy the whole thing, but the fast-developing corporation called America could compartmentalize and solve these problems one by one. Each would be dealt with in due time.

All this explains the low drama, but where was the money to come from? Chicago was bankrupt, and the US government was in fallback mode. So who had an extra $20 million to throw a world's fair? The only man with that kind of money was mopping floors in a Philadelphia prison. So what about Herbert Hoover? What was he doing? Exactly nothing. He had decided, like Thomas Jefferson, that Americans were best left to their own devices. *A Century of Progress* was on its own.

It is probably fair to say at this point that the 1933 World's Fair *was* the Great Depression. The fair came together under the black cloud of the worst economic calamity to beset the nation, and funds were raised in keeping with the old aphorism "necessity is the mother of invention." In 1928 it had been firmly established that the fair would celebrate not only the centennial of the city but also, and more important, the amazing progress of the last one hundred years. At a meeting of the Union Club on December 23, 1928, Dawes changed the theme of the fair and proposed financing it with private funds—a radical move, as the federal government, the state, and the city had financed the last fair. But Dawes knew that even if the money were there, it would come with conditions, and to succeed the fair must go its own way. The name would be changed from Chicago's Second World's Fair Centennial Celebration to *A Century of Progress*, with the focus on science and technology.

Now the organizers had to get the word out to the public. They sent out 1,200 invitations to civic and commercial organizations, urging them to appoint delegates to meet with the world's fair committee to become part of the planning. "Then a mass meeting was held in the Auditorium Theatre on March 19th 1928 to which all Chicagoans were invited to come and show their civic loyalty by lending a hand to the Centennial."[7] Dawes and the others wanted to dip a toe in the water before they jumped in and proposed the membership drive to that end. People could buy a "Membership at Large" for $5.[8] Rufus came up with this brilliant idea, which would do two things: test the public sentiment and develop early financing. The memberships would be offered to the public through the Chicago press and civic organizations. Each would include a certificate entitling the holder to ten admission tickets to the exposition.

If the membership drive didn't produce satisfactory results, then they knew they were looking at a "local" fair and would adjust accordingly. The finance committee decided that the proceeds from the membership drive would be held until the fair opened. This gave them a hedge against the possibility that the fair didn't open and the money had to be returned. The sale of 118,773 memberships raised $637,754 from citizens giving $5 for an event four years in the future. A second drive offered founder and sustaining memberships for $1,000 and $500, with the only return promised being that investors could deduct the cost from their income taxes.

This effort raised $271,400, which, along with the other money, was deposited in the National Bank of the Republic under the terms of a trust indenture. Basically, the organization committee had to borrow money from itself to begin construction—again, a hedge against the possibility the fair did not open and every cent had to be returned to the subscribers. But the committee had seed money, and the subscription drive had raised awareness as well as funds and guaranteed attendance in the opening weeks of the fair. Many of the certificates issued to those who bought the $5 subscriptions were found years later in safes and at estates sales, showing the pride their owners felt in being part of history.

But in May 1929, Rufus sat in his office in the Burnham Building and covered his eyes. They had run through their bank credit, and the situation was desperate. Two committees had studied the problem and come to the same conclusion: they saw no way to finance the enterprise's major expenses. This was before the crash, and the fair looked like it might not happen. The fair organizers had to come up with $20 million and had nowhere to get it. Rufus had said he would raise the money from private business, but the phone wasn't ringing. So he turned to his brother, the vice president of the United States.

The phone rang, and Rufus picked up the receiver.

"Rufus, don't worry. Julius Rosenwald is in."

It was his brother, who always signed his letters to Rufus the same way: "your affectionate brother." Rufus did the same. Even when they fought, they remained cordial. Charles Dawes was a big-picture man, and Rufus did the heavy lifting. He had to take Charles's vision and make it a reality. He had done this with the Dawes Plan after World War I. Rufus served on the reparations committee for a dollar and found the reparation schedule didn't really work. The plan was never adopted, but Charles still became famous for it.

Now, sitting in his drafty office in Chicago, he waited to hear the verdict. Tail between his legs, he had called his brother and confessed that he didn't know where or how to get the money for the fair. He had begun to believe that Wrigley and Abbot were right. Maybe they had lost their minds. Maybe it was best to fold up the whole project.

"Rosenwald is in," Charles repeated.

Rufus didn't breathe. Then he did.

"How much?"

Charles paused. The long-distance line buzzed.

"He said fill in the amount. He gave me a blank check."

Rufus felt his bony knees.

"You're kidding."

"No."

Rufus paused again.

"How much are you going to fill it in for?"

"A million."

"Nineteen to go," he murmured.

He hung up and realized that nothing had changed. His big brother had come to his rescue again; he felt the same relief as when they were boys and Charles had backed him against a neighborhood bully. He knew Charles would somehow get the other $19 million. He had the Midas touch. Little did he know that his brother already had commitments from business leaders. The fair would be a Charles Dawes operation, and that meant a cash basis.

Then George Woodruff proposed the gold note idea. Gold notes would be sold and guaranteed by 40 percent of the gate receipts and further secured by pledges of individual guarantors: "$10,000,000 in bonds were to be issued in various denominations, bearing coupons paying 6% interest and maturing in October 15, 1935."[9] It was brilliant. The notes were issued on October 28, 1929, one day before Black Tuesday and the start of the Great Depression. Charles Dawes would have to get the guarantees during the bleakest times the nation had ever known.

It was the fair's second stress test. If the bonds could not be secured up front, they would be worthless. Charles Dawes, in the weeks after the US stock market lost half its value, secured $12.176 million in signed guarantees. It was a testament to him, but also to the American capitalists who saw that the only way out was forward. Already Dawes was selling the fair as an economic engine to get the country moving again, and in that vein he personally shepherded the first block of bonds to market. As Lenox Lohr later wrote, "Subscriptions of $6,610,000 were received from grantors and $912,000 from others. . . . [T]o dispose of securities in so nebulous and uncertain an enterprise as a World's Fair, still four years off, during days when personal fortunes were toppling and when a chaotic future was ahead called for salesmanship and faith of a high order."[10]

People who bought these bonds had no guarantee that they would pay off at the promised 6 percent, but they turned out to be one of the few reliable investments in 1929. The subscriptions provided that calls could be made for a given amount, to be paid on thirty days' notice. As construction proceeded, calls were made and cash raised ($612,000 on the first call), which put the fair on a cash basis. The calls would bring in a total of $5,999,200 and fund the initial construction.

Charles Dawes accepted chairmanship of the finance committee. Millions more would be needed, and the Great Depression forced him and others on the committee to come up with creative ways to keep construction going. The gold notes turned into currency, with contractors accepting them on the promise of being paid years down the line. Even department stores took the notes for laying wood floors. Cash was so scarce during the early years of the Great Depression that businesses ventured into new areas with new currency.

For now, there was money to get started, and the rest would come from the corporations that funded exhibits and buildings. Finance committee chair Dawes had dictatorial power as the commander of the purse strings. Sometimes the Depression helped in keeping the fair's construction costs down. A low bid came in for a large concrete job, and the contractor was called in to explain how he could undercut everyone else. The exposition could not afford work stoppage because someone had tried to win business, then gone bankrupt. Lenox Lohr later recalled, "The contractor explained that he had a warehouse full of cement which was rapidly deteriorating and while it could be used on the sand foundations at the Exposition it could not be used in high construction. Mountains of sand and gravel had been standing untouched in his yard due to the cessation of building construction. His machinery was rusting and would be ruined if not used. His foreman and principal workers were already being carried on his payrolls. . . . [H]e almost convinced the Exposition authorities it would be a privilege to do the job for nothing."[11]

The fair became a study in cutting corners and improvising when it became apparent the Great Depression was there to stay. Charles Dawes immediately vetoed spending $2 million on publicity, correctly saying, "One gang murder on the front page destroys all preceding propaganda of the self-praising kind. The best propaganda for Chicago is the Century of Progress. The fair had to open on time and do it with the funds they had. If they ran out of money or the exhibits were not completed on time, then so be it."[12]

Efficiency was preeminent, and Charles proved very efficient when he told Rufus he would get the money. He had swung it in 1929 during the start of the Great Depression by pitching the fair as a new beginning and finding companies and individuals not wiped out in the crash. That in itself was no easy feat. Then he rammed a resolution through Congress endorsing the fair and presenting his brother's vision of *A Century of Progress*, a fair of science and technology. The resolution passed before Charles left office, with the stipulation that the government did not have to contribute one cent to the fair.

Rufus later traveled to the White House with his wife and Lenox Lohr and lunched with President Hoover and Charles. Then Hoover issued a proclamation inviting foreign nations to participate in the Chicago World's Fair. The next morning the president asked his men the same question over Hooverball: "Did you get Capone yet?"[13]

CHAPTER TWELVE

The Untouchables

OSCAR FRALEY NEEDED A STORY. LIKE A LOT OF WRITERS, HE WAS always on the hunt for an idea, or a concept, or a person he could market. After their early literary aspirations, for most writers selling becomes pre-eminent. You have to eat, and you have to pay the rent, and Fraley needed to do both when he bumped into a drunk named Elliot Ness, who was interested in selling his story about Al Capone for $300. Fraley listened to what he had to say and then crafted his own story. That is another thing good writers do: they embellish, they exaggerate, and they create a story where there is none.

If you ask Americans over a certain age who was responsible for apprehending Al Capone, they will answer, without hesitation, "Elliot Ness." But they would be wrong. Because of Oscar Fraley and later Kevin Costner, the idea of the lone crusader has taken hold in American lore. It boils down to a man who could not be bought who hired other men who couldn't be bought; their virtue ultimately enabled them to take down Al Capone. You can almost see Fraley tapping away in his Chicago apartment, getting his story just right.

What a jackpot. The book, *The Untouchables*, sold well and then became a television series. Its final incarnation was a movie. Elliot Ness as played by Kevin Costner came alive. We saw the man appearing as the single warrior, pure as the driven snow, working in the grimy, coal-smeared landscape of Capone's corrupt Chicago. Only Ness, with his beautiful wife and baby and his homespun small-town values, could stop the antichrist Capone. In the movie, he did. In real life . . . not a chance.

The man who gave Fraley his story was a shadow of the fictional Elliot Ness. In reality, by the time Ness was twenty-seven, he was a stalled-out Prohibition agent looking to make his mark. But he had not even made a dent in the Capone organization. Chicago was still pumping beer and wine into the speakeasies, and Big Al was making a cool $100 million a year. The flatbed trucks with the tarps ran all night long, and despite occasional busts, nothing had really changed.

Ness had a problem. He was prone to depression and to drink. Like a lot of men, his ambitions had outstripped his reality. Years later he said he "felt like chucking the whole business."[1] How close was Kevin Costner's portrayal to the man? Ness was tall and lean and broader in the chest than the actor. His face was oval, with a dimpled chin, but his eyes were dark and brooding. The depression that dogged him remained even years later, when he ran for the mayoralty of Cleveland.

Ness did write his own story at one point. It ran about twenty pages and amounted to a confession that he had really been along for the ride. However, Ness was like the character in the movie in that he did follow the rules. Even as a boy he had helped his mother and obeyed his teachers and worked in the family bakery when required. His hair was always neat, and so were his clothes. He was a Dudley Do-Right type, and the other South Side boys were wary of him. He might just rat them out. He liked to read, and, of course, he read detective novels.

When he went to college at the University of Chicago, he received the gentlemen's C and took a bachelor's in business. He began his career investigating people who wanted to open credit accounts at retail stores. He couldn't stand this first job, but his brother-in-law came to his rescue and changed Ness's life forever. Alexander Jamie was the chief investigator for the Bureau of Prohibition in Chicago. He pulled strings and got his wife's brother a gig as a Prohibition agent at about $75 a week.

In 1927 and 1928 he was looking to arrest anyone. There was no personal vendetta like the one the movie sets up between Robert De Niro's Capone and Costner's Ness. The men did not know each other. Like any new agent, Ness just wanted to catch someone. So he and his fellow agents rumbled around in a Cadillac looking for bootleggers, stills, or speakeasies. They had small fish to fry in the Martino gang, which they hoped to infiltrate, but Ness screamed rookie and cop.

So they raided Joseph Martino's stills and settled for busting the gangsters they could find. The mobsters merely set up new operations, and now Ness had no chance of getting inside the mob to find out which corrupt judges and cops were taking payoffs. That, at least, would have been a starting point. But then Ness did get closer to Capone. In his story Ness explained that he was assigned to George Johnson to assist revenue agents concentrating on the Capone brothers' income, especially Al's. It was his job to bust businesses that might be paying Capone.

Here Fraley took license with the story and created a legend. He constructs a scene in which Ness complains to Johnson that all the agents are corrupt. Fraley had just stumbled on the hook of the story. Good writers lurch back and forth until they discover what they are really writing about. In this scene Ness says,

> *Suppose the Prohibition bureau picked a small select squad. . . . Let's say ten or a dozen men. Every man could be investigated thoroughly and they could be brought in from other cities, if necessary, to insure that they had no hookup with the Chicago mobsters. No rotten apples. Get it? Now if this squad were given a free hand and backing, when they did make arrests—I'll guarantee it could dry up this town. And when that happens, and the big money stops rolling into the Capone mob, pretty soon they don't have twenty-five million a year to be handing out for protection. Then everybody starts to go to work on them, like they were supposed to do in the first place and you've got them licked.*[2]

It was pure Fraley because there is no evidence that George Johnson ever had this conversation or authorized this flying squad for Ness. Johnson was already beginning to pivot to trying to convict Capone for income tax evasion. Ness continued to bust speakeasies and liquor transports, but Fraley's account, which forms the core of *The Untouchables*, is all fiction. In truth, other men, like Frank Wilson, were working behind the scenes to get Capone.

Wilson was a wan, sallow man with the jaw of a boxer. His father had been a policeman in Buffalo, and since he was a boy, he had wanted to be like his father and enforce the law. But he was blind as a bat and couldn't see the target on the long end of a rifle, so he became the cop equivalent of a revenue investigator. He would get his man and didn't mind reading ledgers for hours on end, looking for the smoking gun that would show income where there supposedly was none. And then sometimes he hit the streets for interviews and became a cop in name, if not with a gun.

Elmer Irey, his supervisor, later testified that Wilson "will sit quietly looking at books eighteen hours a day, seven days a week, forever, if he wants to find something in those books."[3] He would sit in a small, cramped office, no more than a closet, chain-smoking cheap cigars in the Old Post Office Building in Chicago. He worked on a steel-topped desk, poking through anything that could shed light on how Al Capone made his money. His agents began hanging around the Lexington Hotel to see what they could discover. Wilson concluded that Capone was smarter than he'd thought. "He did all his business through front men," he later said.[4]

Frank Wilson settled for arresting Capone's brother for income tax invasion while Al sat in jail in Philadelphia. Along with others in Washington, DC, Frank Wilson had given up hope of busting Al Capone on Prohibition violations. The Prohibition agents like Ness could not get past the first layer, and if they did, judges were waiting to let Capone off. Besides, most of the Prohibition agents were on the take. Bribes were part of the job, and the money flowed. Ness did not take bribes; he had about $500 in the bank and didn't need them. His brother-in-law didn't take bribes either, but here is where it gets interesting: Jamie didn't have to take bribes because a group of businessmen led by Robert Isham Randolph, president of the Chicago Association of Commerce, was already paying him.

They called themselves the Secret Six and had $1 million to spend to stop Al Capone.[5] They were six millionaires whose identities wouldn't be revealed until fifty years later. The real Untouchables had a mandate to get rid of Capone because Chicago was about to break ground for the 1933 World's Fair.

Chapter Thirteen

Birth of the Nymph

She was from Damascus, Syria, and somehow ended up at the Columbian Exposition. Mother and Father strolled through the Midway in 1893 with little Johnny or little Susie, and then Father was gone. He had entered a tent that looked like something out of the *Arabian Nights*, and there she was: Little Egypt. Father sat down in the darkness and watched the belly dance. By 1893 standards, she wore nothing except a translucent skirt and a large bikini top. But Father saw only her smooth, brown, undulating belly. He had been born before the Civil War, and the World's Fair of 1893 had just transported him to a different time, a different place. Sodom and Gomorrah beckoned while Mother and the kids toured the amusements.

The young woman from Damascus, Fahreda Mahzur, would be sixty-two when the next fair began in 1933. She would be shocked by the insipient nudity of Sally Rand and others who offered their bodies any way they could. But she had pioneered public entertainment in that late nineteenth-century show; thousands had crowded the Midway to see Little Egypt after riding on the Ferris wheel and packing the beer gardens. Oriental women offered their own belly dance, wearing even less clothing than Fahreda. Middle-class Americans who had traveled to see the wonders of the world had never seen that much skin and were more familiar with the ubiquitous Gibson girl held up by advertisers as the feminine ideal of the time. Americans with newfound leisure and money wanted a taste of the exotic. Of course, this didn't mean that some didn't object.

Bertha Palmer, president of the Board of Lady Managers, objected to Little Egypt's act, and the fair director general released a statement: "Restrain all future exhibits within the limits of stage propriety as recognized in the country."[1] No one did a thing, and the belly dance began to morph into the "cooch" dance of the burlesque shows. Small midwestern towns now adopted the hoochie coochie at their own dusty fairs. F. Scott Fitzgerald in the early mid-1920s would pen a story for the *Saturday Evening Post*, "A Night at the Fair," in which young teenagers are enthralled by "a real *hoochie coochie* show."[2]

The dancers were part and parcel of the amusement section of the fair now. Any traveling fair would carry, sandwiched between the freaks of nature and the games, a hoochie coochie burlesque that was essentially "an exhibition of wordless, female eroticism and exoticism."[3] The "cooch" was a precursor to the striptease that appeared thirty years later: "Burlesque dancers usually removed their brassieres and remained topless while on stage. Many women posed wearing only a G string. None of the dancers made much of an effort to create an illusion of art. The women now just wanted to take their clothes off."[4]

Since the Columbian Exposition an urban culture had asserted itself, and this played into the success of the Midways at both fairs (and later of Sally Rand). Amusement parks were the first video games for young people. New games and daring exhibits in the first quarter of the twentieth century brought young people together at these fairs, and, as on the Internet, the options and choices were many. Radio and movies were distracting little Johnny and Susie from playing sports or outdoor games. As happened with the rise of the computer, which put going outside to play in constant tension with surfing the web, tastes changed, and when these kids became adults, the hoochie coochie didn't quite do it for them anymore.

Even Charles Dawes understood these drives of the modern fairgoer. He reminded Rufus that while the Sky Ride and the Hall of Science were interesting, "what is going to draw your crowds is not museums, or scientific charts or similar museum exhibits. . . . [P]eople come to see a show, the great surviving memory of the Chicago World's Fair being the Midway."[5] Lenox Lohr, who would be responsible for organizing and actually building the exposition, had toured fairs in Europe and noted that "while the fair's theme must have its appeal through these higher concepts of education, science and culture . . . people visit an exposition with a carnival spirit, hoping to be amused and diverted from humdrum routine experience by dreams of fantasy."[6] Charles Dawes also knew that the fair amusements of the Midway would do the heavy lifting by providing a steady stream of revenue. He had no idea then what Sally Rand would do for his bottom line during the 1933 World's Fair.

But sex sells, and Chicago knew this more than any other city. As Cheryl Ganz writes in *The 1933 Chicago World's Fair*, "Since the turn of the twentieth century, public display of women's bodies had been on the increase, from women bicycling in bloomers to 'modern' flappers dancing sensual dances and frequenting nightclubs. In some ways the public had been desensitized to risqué behavior. At the same time, it craved even more. And Chicago was no stranger to nightclubs and girlie shows."[7]

The red-light district of Chicago was on South State Street in the Loop and would only be a short distance from the fair. The burlesque theaters featured "programs of comic skits, films, strip acts, singing, and dancing."[8] Surprisingly, both men and women went to these shows and paid from "ten to twenty-five cents at the seamier sites and $1.75 at a classier venue." Women often made up one-third of the audience, but both sexes wanted to escape the grinding reality of the Great Depression into some sort of fantasy. The Chicago police looked the other way and allowed the striptease to make its appearance.

At bottom the burlesque was a way for women to make money. And this was what Sally Rand had in mind as she stood in the back of The Paramount. She had no way of knowing it, but the times had changed, and the fact that she had no costume and only two ostrich-feather fans worked in her favor. "The shift in attitudes toward drinking, smoking, wearing makeup and experiencing premarital sex culminated in heightened emphasis on eroticism."[9]

Some would say Sally's decision to go out and dance nude behind two seven-foot fans had roots far back in her own psychological makeup— that she had no alternative at that point and literally nothing to lose. Her last show, *Sweethearts on Parade*, had closed, and she and a dozen other chorus girls in the same predicament were looking for a spot at The Paramount. She saw two other dancers from *Sweethearts*, and they had all lined up on the stage and done a walk across earlier in the day.

Big Ed Callahan, the owner, shook his head.

"Girls. Business here in the Loop is taking a nose dive. We have to come up with something to get the customers in. . . . [W]e've all got to eat this year. If you want the job, come in with your costume at ten o'clock tonight. That's all."[10]

The two dancers before her had asked Sally what she was going to wear, and Sally confessed she didn't know. The secondhand store where she found the long silk chemise couldn't help her because the time was now, and she was in a cab. The cabbie stared at her fans. "Honey, why don't you just fly over there? You got wings."[11]

When Sally arrived, The Paramount was deserted. She went into a dressing room and saw five girls getting ready. As Holly Knox writes in *Sally Rand: From Film to Fans*, "A woman putting on fake eyelashes patted the dressing table next to her. 'This one is yours honey and I hope you're ready cause curtain is in ten.'"

"My wardrobe isn't ready. I'm new here. It's my first night."

The brunette shrugged.

"Callahan said you're first. That's the rule here, honey; the newest girl goes on first. Isadora over there has been here over a week. She goes last."

Another girl dressed as a harem dancer planted the seed and suggested she go on nude: "You'll never get the gown done in time. I saw someone dance with only the fans once."

Sally sat down and began to apply makeup and wondered if things could get any worse.

"I hope they have a phonograph here."

The woman shrugged.

"Sorry, no phonograph. All we have is Hector. He's Callahan's nephew. He plays the piano."[12]

Sally groaned. Holly Knox, who worked with Sally Rand in later years, claimed to have interviewed the star and built her scenes from Sally's recollections. The small, self-published book is one of the few on Sally Rand, and while choppy and obviously a first attempt at writing a

biography, it does have the ring of someone who took notes while inter-
viewing her subject. This is Knox's version of the tryout in The Paramount
on that cold Depression-era night.

> *The lights were bright on the tiny stage of the Paramount club and the
> piano player was not sober, but the essence of Sally's future was estab-
> lished that night. She manipulated the huge ostrich fans slowly and
> gracefully to the strains of "Claire de Lune." She artfully showed only
> teasing glimpses of her body, caressing the fans as she pirouetted on the
> small stage. A unity evolved with the fans and the woman. At times
> the fans assumed a lifelike amorosity. Her dance was eight breath-
> taking minutes long. At the end of it, when she threw up her fans
> like the Winged Victory statue, even the dancers who were watching
> backstage applauded loudly.*[13]

Sally was hired. But what did Eddie Callahan see that night? Probably something akin to what John Van Guilder, a businessman from
Knoxville, Tennessee, saw when he opened the newspaper in the worst
year of the Depression—1933—and read the rags-to-riches story of Sally
Rand. Fascinated, and needing release from the grim economic news,
he went to Chicago and bought a ticket on the Midway to Sally Rand's
show. The lights dimmed as he settled into the theater, and then something happened. The world of failed banks and soup lines faded away.
By now Sally was using a large plastic bubble to hide behind, and as the
music flowed out from the darkness, Van Guilder saw a nymph from
another world. A single blue spotlight illuminated her painted white
body, and Van Guilder later recalled, "With all the grace of a woodland
nymph, she toyed and danced around and played with and tossed into
the air her transparent soap bubble. Somehow, one felt as though secretly
watching some little woodland creature at play in the moonlight."[14]

Van Guilder was so taken with Sally Rand's dance that he arranged
to meet her backstage and offered to buy the bubble from her. She
could not part with it but gave the businessman from Tennessee an
autographed picture and a kiss. Van Guilder sent her roses with a
note expressing his belief that she had made the world a better place.

Certainly for John Van Guilder she had. No doubt Eddie Callahan saw the same thing in his theater that night—a vision that would transport people from the grim realities of the early Depression years and give them a glimmer of hope that at least, for a little while, they could see something beautiful, if not magical. Sally Rand had nailed the theme of the 1933 Chicago World's Fair for all time.

Chapter Fourteen

Death in the Underground

WHILE AL CAPONE MOPPED FLOORS OUTSIDE THE WARDEN'S OFFICE IN Philadelphia, Jake Lingle, a reporter for the *Chicago Tribune*, ducked into a pedestrian crossing that ran under Michigan Avenue. Chicago had been built on a swamp, and in the nineteenth century the entire city was raised up. Beneath Michigan Avenue and Wacker Drive was Lower Michigan and Lower Wacker. John Belushi's famous "Cheeburger Cheeburger" skit parodied the Billy Goat Tavern on the lower level.

The area beneath Michigan Avenue was eternally damp and dark. It usually smelled like urine, and on hot days it was hard to breathe, with the fetid scent of human waste wafting up. But you could skip the crowds, park your car in the lower-level garages, and get where you wanted to go. All the trains came into Chicago on the original level of the city. It was a great improvement, as people were no longer being decapitated or cut in half by monsters puffing steam and wood smoke.

Maybe Jake Lingle had just read an article on Capone in jail. Some really believed Capone managed to have himself arrested so he could relax with a sure alibi for a year. Supposedly he read a biography of Napoleon and then pontificated about the man and his life: "The trouble with that guy was he got the swelled head. He overplayed his hand and they made a bum out of him. He should have had the sense after that Elba jolt to kiss himself out of the game."[1] It is hard to believe Al Capone said any of this, but maybe he did read while he was in prison. In the same article Capone said that all the reports of him having it easy in prison had been exaggerated.

Lingle specialized in covering gangsters. Some said he got too close and crossed the line. Lingle lived high and invested heavily in the market. He had much more money in his bank account than the average *Tribune* reporter in 1930. He bet heavily on the horses, which he was headed to do when he went into the subterranean cool air, which actually felt good on a hot, sticky June day. He was going to grab the 1:30 p.m. Illinois Central train to the Washington Park Race Track in Homewood, Illinois.

He walked quickly, his ever-present cigar clenched between his teeth, and didn't hear the man walk up behind him. The man was about six feet tall, and his vision was level with the back of Lingle's head. The man pulled a .38 from his pocket and fired. Lingle fell forward, the cigar still clenched in his teeth. The man walked to the stairway leading back up to Michigan Avenue and melted into the crowd. It was just another murder in a city of murders, but this one crossed the line for Colonel Robert R. McCormack, who owned the *Chicago Tribune*. McCormack saw it as an assault on the freedom of the press and reacted the same way he had in World War I: "I remembered that one should always reply to a sudden attack with an immediate counter offensive. It seemed then that the choice was war or surrender, battle or the inevitable servitude of coward-ice. I did not know the man who was killed, I had no idea of his private affairs . . . but I had seen the gangland rise from the murder of humble immigrants until it reached the employee of a newspaper."[2]

Colonel McCormack took the elevator down from the twenty-fourth floor of the Tribune Building on Michigan Avenue and oversaw the story and the investigation into Lingle's death. He immediately offered $25,000 for any news related to the assassin. In doing so, he unwittingly took the first step in what would become a movement by wealthy citizens to take back control of Chicago and get rid of Al Capone. The next morning a banner across the front page read, "Gunman Slays Alfred Lingle in I.C. Subway."[3] "Alfred Lingle, better known to his world of newspaper work as Jake Lingle, and for the last eighteen years a reporter of the Tribune, was shot to death yesterday in the Illinois Central subway at the east end of the Michigan Boulevard at Randolph Street. The Tribune offers $25,000 as reward for the information which will lead to the conviction of the slayer or slayers."[4] The article then connected Lingle's slaying with the 1926 murder of Don Mellett, a Canton, Ohio, editor shot down by gangsters. "These two are the only outstanding cases in which newspapermen paid with their lives for working against organized criminals."[5]

The article was followed the next day with an editorial titled "The Challenge." It elaborated on the cold-blooded murder, and then it essentially declared war against the gangsters who had taken over Chicago: "The meaning of this murder is plain. It was committed in reprisal and was an attempt to intimidate. Mr. Lingle was a police reporter and exceptionally well informed. His personal friendships included the highest police officers and the contacts of his work had made him familiar with most of the big and little fellows of gangland. What made him valuable to his newspaper marked him as dangerous to the killers. . . . [T]he Tribune accepts this challenge. It is war."[6]

The paper was McCormack's mouthpiece, and the war he talked about was his personal one against Al Capone. For the first time a private citizen was considering avenues other than the police. The *Tribune* launched its own investigation into Lingle headed by the colonel. At first glance Lingle's career seemed typical. He began as a $12 a week copyboy and moved up to legman, a reporter who gathered facts for other reporters. At this stage he was writing nothing, but he was a fast learner and hung around the private detective agencies to glean information about criminals. World War I put him into naval intelligence, where he honed his investigative skills. After the war Lingle came into his own and became familiar with Big Jim Colosimo and Johnny Torrio. At the same time, he got to know cops who could make a young reporter's career. He became friends with police chief Bill Russell and another up-and-coming gangster, Al Capone.

When Jake Lingle died, he was making $65 a week. He told friends of a mysterious inheritance, and when the crash came he said he had lost a fortune, but his original investment was still there. He rode in a limousine, and at the racetracks he bet $1,000 on a single race. The reporter's life didn't add up in McCormack's investigation, and he knew he would have to dig further. But he didn't trust the police or anyone else in Chicago law enforcement. Here we see the road that would eventually lead to the Secret Six. For the first time, a separate, private force, more along the lines of a vigilante group or posse, was created.

McCormack hired two men to find the killers of Jake Lingle: Charles Rathburn as prosecutor and Pat Roche as chief investigator. McCormack ran the private endeavor by state's attorney John Swanson, who accepted it as another way to get Capone. Ultimately the investigation would reveal that Lingle had been in bed with the gangsters and was killed for a debt. But McCormack had galvanized the public into action. The Newspaper Publishers of Chicago on June 11 adopted a resolution that not only summed up McCormack's view but also laid bare the truth of Chicago and what the city needed to do to survive, much less hold a world's fair in three years.

The intolerable outrages of the last year against civic decency and public security in Chicago have culminated dramatically in the cowardly murder of Alfred J. Lingle, a newspaper reporter. The undersigned Chicago daily newspapers interpret that murder as an especially significant challenge to the millions of decent citizens who have suffered the vicious activities, in defiance of law and order, of some paltry hundreds of criminal vagrants known as gangsters. Considering the causes and connotations of the unbelievable total of one hundred gang murders in little more than a year and acting in accord and unison we pledge our resources to the cleanup of gang, police, official and any other public viciousness where it may appear in order that corruption and the resulting gang activities may be brought to an end and thereby restoring to the citizens of Chicago civic decency and security of life and property.[7]

All the major newspapers signed on to the resolution, which was printed widely and threw down the gauntlet to Al Capone and the gangsters. It could have been the preamble for the Secret Six, who were entirely independent of McCormack. But here was the model of the wealthy man who had the power and the moral imperative to take action against a scourge that had produced a lawless city in the heart of the United States. Through graft, murder, corruption, bribes, threats, and the enormous leverage brought by money and the power that comes with it, democracy had ceased to function in Chicago and been replaced by what resembled a third world strongman dictatorship. Anyone who crossed the gangsters, or, more specifically, Al Capone, ended up dead. This was common knowledge in the city and made a mockery of all law enforcement, and it led eventually to prisoner Al Capone, still in Philadelphia.

No one then knew that three groups were independently converging on Al Capone: the revenue department of the US government headed by Frank Wilson, the Secret Six headed by Robert Isham Randolph, and McCormack's band of investigators. While Elliot Ness was still hacking up barrels of beer and wiretapping phones, these three groups moved silently in the background. The Secret Six would become the most potent instrument of all. As with McCormack's band of investigators, a murder would catalyze its creation.

Chapter Fifteen

Breaking Ground

THE BOY ON NORTHERLY ISLAND SHIVERED AGAINST THE COLD, BUT HE wanted to see the plane pass overhead again. In September 1930 it wasn't normal to see low-flying planes over the city. Most people didn't have two nickels to rub together, with a president in the White House who believed all would right itself in time, while people turned off the heat in their homes, or their heat was turned off for nonpayment, and they padded around in sweaters and coats. Vacations had been canceled long ago, and abandoned homes dotted streets with half-finished buildings, creating wind tunnels when the breeze came off the lake. Many men never told their wives that they had lost their jobs; they put on their suits, then stood in soup-kitchen lines or sold apples. Sometimes riots broke out, and police had discovered that firemen were their best friends when they turned on the high-pressure water hoses. That stopped people, especially in winter.

So the boy was fishing, and if he brought something home to eat, so much the better. But that plane was coming back. This time the big, silver bird was really low—so low he could see men in the windows, all in suits and fedoras. The boy counted eight of them, and they stared at the boy and pointed at the island that was a godawful wasteland separated by a couple of lagoons from the Chicago lakefront. The boy dropped his line and watched the plane come down low three more times, with the big Pratt & Whitney engines echoing off the buildings of downtown Chicago, and then the plane lifted into the air and carried the suited men away. He had no way of knowing that eight architects had just passed overhead like gods who would alter heaven and earth and create a paradise where the boy was standing. But it wasn't a paradise yet. Major Lenox R. Lohr knew this better than anyone.

Lenox Lohr was the man. He was the man who would build what those eight architects stuffed into the silver tube imagined. He was the man who would take this useless piece of land and create *A Century of Progress*, which would open its doors in less than two years. The Dawes brothers had told him he was the man, and if Charles and Rufus said it was so, then no power on earth would cross them. Even the president steered clear.

While the 1893 fair employed dilettantish architects, the fair of 1933 would be run with military precision. Lohr was big on Taylorism and edited *Military Engineer*, a journal that expounded on the system's increased use of "specialized middle managers, thereby transforming industrial organization through scientific, labor-saving strategies."[1] In other words, the corporate model of middle managers navigating work flow in parallel departments, which would anchor American business until the great purge initiated in the 1990s and finished by the Internet, was new and revolutionary, and at a time when everyone had to make do without the aid of computers, this allowed information to flow to the proper people. In a nutshell, Lohr was the Michael Jordan of organization.

Born in 1891 in Washington, DC, Lohr took a degree in mechanical engineering at Cornell and then joined the rest of the doughboys heading over to France. He served with the Army Corps of Engineers and became a major. Lohr then taught at West Point and became a renaissance man, reorganizing the magazine of the Society of American Military Engineers and returning its circulation to a level at which it wouldn't fold. His editorials revealed a man who believed in changing the world through effective organization and teaching. He wrote that "history teaches not so much from success as from failure, for when failures are eliminated success comes automatically."[2] Lohr tipped his hand early regarding the approach he would take to the 1933 World's Fair: "He determined that with careful organization and planning, the fair would be both economically sound and educationally effective."[3]

When the Dawes brothers pitched the fair to Lohr, they defined it as a grand engineering project. Rufus added, with no irony at all, "An engineer is supposed to be able to do anything."[4] They wanted Lenox Lohr to serve as no less than the enterprise's general manger, the man who would take their vision and actually get down into the mud, sand, and water from Lake Michigan, figuratively and literally, and build it. Lohr quit the army and came to Chicago. He immediately studied early fairs: the 1893 Columbian Exposition, the 1904 St. Louis fair, and San Francisco's 1915 fair. Lohr would bring modern organization techniques and military efficiency to building the fair in Chicago on one condition: that he report only to Rufus Dawes. He had already seen the brothers' different management and leadership styles, and Lohr did not want to slip down into some crevasse of sibling rivalry, no matter how friendly. In turn, Rufus would leave Lohr alone, and those who worked for him would owe allegiance only to Lohr.

So now it was time to begin. But where? As early as 1927 the Hurley Report (which would never be acted on) had set up the boundaries of the fair on the lakefront between 12th and 57th Streets. From then on the world's fair would be connected to the Chicago lakefront. But the exposition's main buildings, its heart, would be on Northerly Island. As Lohr wrote years later, "It was fully appreciated that the Exposition's right to enclose the lagoons, even as a matter of protecting life and property on its grounds, might be disputed. Fortunately, this theoretical question was never forced to a practical issue."[5]

The western boundary of the fair ran to the Illinois Central right away, and for a time Grant Park was considered, but since the Field Museum and the Shedd Aquarium did not become part of the exposition, the presence of the buildings would have been problematic. Also, a hotel had already launched a suit to keep the view unobstructed. The northern boundary was determined with officials from the planetarium, the aquarium, and the Field Museum. Footage was reserved to keep people from encroaching, and the fairgrounds eventually included the planetarium when astronomers thought it might be good to introduce people to the heavens. The fair was being opened by a star, after all.

An original plan to build extra islands for the fair was deemed impossible given the economic climate. The fair was a baby of the Great Depression and would be tailored to the times. The Dawes brothers settled on extending the existing island to make room for fair buildings, and Charles Dawes floated a bond issue to pay for it in 1929. This left the actual construction of the extension, and that was Lohr's job.

Northerly Island did not impress Lohr. He wrote years later, "The three mile by six hundred feet strip on which the exposition was to be built was an area of waste land, relieved only by clumps of weeds and an occasional straggly poplar, with a narrow strip of planting along Leif Erickson Drive. It was entirely 'man made.' The fill above the lake bottom averaged from twenty to thirty feet in depth and varied from a miscellaneous assortment of junk and rubbish to good sand."[6] During construction they came upon rusty bed springs, tin cans, radiators, phonographs, coffee pots, and even a submerged scow. Lohr matter-of-factly described the project as "an ordinary construction job."[7] This was typical Lohr, who would break the extraordinary down to essentials. Maybe this kept him from getting overwhelmed. But the twelve-acre island extension was created with sand brought from Michigan and Indiana shores ten to thirty miles away. Suction dredges and self-unloading barges dumped the sand into running water anywhere from twelve to thirty feet deep. The fill was created behind a "bulkhead twenty feet wide consisting of fifty-four hundred piles varying in length from forty-five to fifty-five feet and filled with sixty thousand tons of small riprap stones and capped with seven thousand tons of one to five-ton cover stones."[8]

All in a day's work. Sand from Lake Michigan was then pumped in behind the bulkhead. Lohr knew that beneath the lake was a forty-five-foot layer of "soft silt like clay and sand,"[9] and then there was the hard pan or solid rock. Lohr would build his edifices on this and saw no real problems, but the first groups of surveyors didn't share his enthusiasm. Chicago in 1933 was a modern city, but parts of it were surprisingly undeveloped.

And the frontline troops, the advance guard of Lohr's army for the world's fair, were the surveyors. The rawness of the land was daunting. The fact that city was just behind them and humanity abounded in the Loop had no relevance as they stared at the wasteland of sand and scrub. Lohr would write, "There was but a single road through this strip of land. Stepping off it evidences of civilization abruptly ceased and feet sank into sand or mud or water. Among the riprap along the shore, wharf rats scurried to cover. There were no electric lines except along the Drive, and there was neither drinking water or sewage facilities."[10]

Even contemplating construction would require construction first—construction for construction, if you will. Heavy loaded trucks would have to make their way to the lakefront and to the island. Steel brought in by railroad would then have to be transported through Chicago's downtown. Lights needed to be installed, but first electricity had to be brought in. The traffic on Leif Erickson Drive would have to be diverted, as the long line of trucks would cause bottlenecks. They would have to build a road for the transport of material for the fair.

Then, once the trucks had arrived, the heavy loads would require pavement, which they had not planned for. An abandoned railroad spur would prove the solution to many of the construction problems. The line was used to build Soldier Field, and Lohr saw immediately that bringing in the massive materials by rail all the way to the fairgrounds was the answer. Electricity was brought in temporarily from the transformer at Soldier Field, with raw water pumped in from the lake in the short term for any construction requirements.

And then there were the shanties. All over the country people were living in boxcars or under bridges, in fields and alleys, and even though the icy winds and hard driving snow of the Northerly Island area and lakefront were brutal, people lived in tin shacks along the scrub brush and sand. They were left alone as the surveyors did their work and even after the first construction began, but once the area was enclosed, they were evicted.

The first construction contract was signed on September 15, 1930, to build a roadway into the grounds. Soon afterward, the earthmovers and steam shovels began to excavate. It was the beginning of construction of the 1933 World's Fair—*A Century of Progress*. The road was symbolic. All the talk and planning of the last twenty years were finally coming to fruition. Chicagoans waited for the gleaming buildings but could see only a road. As Lohr would later write, "The interested public had been indulging in roseate dreams of a blossoming panorama of buildings gardens and fountains. . . . [H]owever the vast amount of effort and money which went under the ground and into utilities . . . the average visitor was completely oblivious."[11]

By December 1930, the three-mile stretch of road was complete. Lohr had beat the winter, and the stage was now set. As he said later, "The Fair was in a position to take over the site."[12]

The Secret Six

WHILE AL CAPONE SAT IN JAIL, FRANK NITTI, ALONG WITH AL'S brother Ralph and Jake Guzik, ran the outfit. "Ralph knew the booze business and the gambling operations. Guzik was the bagman. Nitti provided the muscle."[1] Revenue agent Frank Wilson, with his bifocals, was still poring over files, and that effort resulted in an indictment against Frank for tax evasion. The police were raiding speakeasies and axing barrels of Capone beer. Elliot Ness was busy tapping phone lines and listening to gangsters speak.

Ralph Capone had operated out of a speakeasy in Cicero. Ness and his men set up their boxy vacuum tubes and heavy headphones in a basement apartment three blocks away. Ness got in his car and started driving around the speakeasy until Ralph became suspicious. He and the other gangsters began to follow and allowed one of Ness's men to climb up a telephone pole and tap the wires. Ness wrote later, "My secretary made a call to the Montmartre Café and engaged the man in light conversation. My telephone man was simultaneously raking the box. Suddenly he gave me a sign that he had found it; the bridge was made and telephone tap on the Cicero headquarters of the mob established."[2]

The transcripts of some of those calls have survived and sound like a bad movie. The takeaway was that Capone's organization still operated at the grass roots like a bunch of crooks reacting to events.

"Is Mike there?"

"No, but Dutch is."

"Let me talk to Dutch [Ralph Capone]."

"Is Blackie still there?"

"No. I sent him away twenty minutes ago. Are you still coming over?"

"Yes, but not for some time. I've got to get a fellow out of the can."

"I can go get his bond, you know, Pete."

"Oh, I can fix it all right. Say, Dutch, I want to collect a bill in East St. Louis. Have you got anyone there?"

"I might have. How much is it?"

"Thirty-eight hundred dollars—it's not a legitimate bill, you know. The guy is a businessman; he sells what we do."

"Well, I get eight hundred if I get it."

"Yes, if you get the guy here, we will make him pay."

"All right, when you get here, we will make him pay."[3]

The businessman in question would undoubtedly pay or die. This was the reality of gangster rule. Many unsolved murders involved people who had sold illegal alcohol and not paid. People who didn't pay for protection or extortion found themselves dead. Nonpayment led to the death of Philip Meagher and triggered the formation of the Secret Six. The St. Valentine's Day Massacre, while instrumental, was not the only event that pushed six millionaires to form a shadowy vigilante force that would move in the background.

On February 5, 1930, a black sedan rolled up to the curb in front of a hospital under construction at the University of Chicago. Two men in long, dark overcoats with spats and wide-brimmed fedoras stepped out. They kept their hands in their pockets. It was cold and overcast, and snow wisped in the air. They crunched across the frozen mud, weaving between workmen in overalls, and then stopped by the front entrance to the skeleton frame.

"Is Meagher here?"

A worker stood up and looked at the men, then shrugged.

"Sure, that's him over there."[4]

The two men walked over to the foreman, who was staring at some blueprints. Meagher turned as the men pulled two silver-plated .38s from their pockets and shot him six times. Then they turned and made their way back over the curves and undulations of the excavated ground. In a decade of murders, this one was different.

Colonel Robert Isham Randolph had been elected president of the Chicago Association of Commerce the previous December. The dead man's boss went to see him. He told Randolph, "My partner and I believe this shooting is the beginning of war. The first signal that the gangs are muscling in on us and mean to have a piece of the pie. If they're given half a chance, they won't let up until every contract in Chicago is tossing a divvy into the pot."[5]

Colonel Randolph was the son of Isham Randolph, an engineer who had worked for the Chicago Sanitary District. His father had found a way to reverse the flow of the Chicago River and was enshrined in Chicago history. Randolph fought in the Mexican War and World War I and believed in the countercharge. He called for a meeting of the executive committee and invited state's attorney Swanson, who told the group what "expert investigators who worked in absolute secrecy" could accomplish.[6] Randolph took Swanson's words to heart and lunched the next day with six carefully chosen men. They were some of the richest in Chicago and the most influential. At first the meeting didn't seem to be going Randolph's way.

"I don't see any great harm done. Let 'em kill each other off. Just so they don't touch decent citizens."

Randolph persisted until the richest man at the table stood.

"I can't stay here forever. I'm going, Colonel. I'll leave this on the table, put me down for ten percent of any amount you raise."[7]

The other men turned immediately and pledged support. The colonel had an instant $1 million at his disposal. A reporter sniffing around for clues to the men's identities would dub them the Secret Six.

Randolph lost no time in connecting with agencies already in the fight against Capone. His credo for the Secret Six was simply that the ends justify the means. He later said he would "try anything which will put the gangster behind bars."[8] Randolph believed law and order had broken down, and so the Secret Six would not be restrained by laws the gangsters routinely ignored. Randolph went further and gave a justification and method for men operating under his veil of secrecy. He listed four points:

1. *Continued questions by relays of inquisitors who keep the victim awake and permit him no rest may be regarded as mental torture, but I cannot believe an innocent could not support such an ordeal or be made to confess anything but the truth.*
2. *What constitutional guarantees, code of ethics or principals of justice would be violated if by any method a confession could be wrung from the kidnappers and murders of the Lindbergh baby.*
3. *No honest man needs to defend his liberties nowadays, constitutional rights are invoked only as evasions and loopholes to escape the law.*
4. *A refusal to testify shows guilt.*[9]

The fact that across town Lenox Lohr was living in a corrugated shack and overseeing an exposition billed as *A Century of Progress* epitomizes irony. Randolph had conveniently suspended all rights in order to get rid of the gangsters and saw Chicago at that moment as no different from the lawless towns of the Wild West. While Frank Wilson, Elliot Ness, and Colonel McCormack were using extraordinary means to get Capone and solve Chicago's gangster problem, no one was breaking the law. The Secret Six would not be bound by the law, however, and resembled more the lynch mobs of the South, where citizens took matters into their own hands.

Chicago was out of control, law and order had broken down, and the world's fair was looming. But it is alarming to hear the justification in Randolph's edicts, if not philosophy, where he invokes the murder of the Lindbergh baby, the heinous crime of the 1920s, implying that people could be monsters and did not deserve the rights guaranteed them by the US Constitution. He went further and justified torture (a debate that persists today) by explaining why police often brutalize suspects: "We do not hire the best brains in the country to do our police work, but none of them is so stupid as to mark or maim a prisoner so that evidence of his mistreatment may be produced to defend a guilty man."[10]

Such suspension of justice has always found a place in the American landscape of checks and balances between the rights of the accused and the objectives of the criminal justice system. Many movies and books have portrayed vigilantes who take matters into their own hands because the system is powerless against criminals who game it. Certainly Al Capone had found that in the 1920s booze and money were king and the police, judges, and citizens were easily bought off, intimidated, or murdered to blunt the laws that would have stopped him.

Randolph's group of six were truly unknown and fought back against Capone with the very weapons he was using: money and coercion. Randolph did not see using the techniques of the gangster to get rid of the gangster as problematic. Chicago had been lost, and he would use any methods, including murder, to regain control of the city. So it is not surprising that he offered more advice on torture by noting that a fist or a rubber hose tend to create a bruise or welt, while "in the hands of a strong man a telephone book can knock a victim silly and not leave a mark."[11] It is interesting to note his use of the word "victim."

But before torture must come investigation. Randolph quickly reached out to existing organizations that had taken on crime in Chicago. He began with the Employers' Association, formed to curb racketeering in labor unions. It had been effective largely through the efforts of Walter Walker, a former assistant state's attorney with a knack for investigative work. The Secret Six immediately employed his small force of investigators.

Randolph used the Prohibition unit of the Chicago federal district with the cooperation of the US Secret Service and the US district attorney in Chicago. Wilson, Ness, and others became aware of the Secret Six as a source of funds when they needed money quickly and quietly. That Randolph and McCormack worked together through the Chicago Crime Commission is a given. The tentacles of Randolph and company spread out behind the web being spun by the government and others who had been circling, trying to find a way to get rid of Al Capone before the fair opened.

And now it was time for Al Capone to come home to Chicago from Philadelphia. He had done his time, and a lot of people were waiting for him.

CHAPTER SEVENTEEN

The Modernists

THEY SAT IN FRONT OF THE FIREPLACE AT THE TOP OF THE BURNHAM Building. The flames licked the logs while the men argued. They were among the most eminent architects in the country, if not the world, and couldn't decide whether the world's fair should reflect modernism or classicism. In fact, they couldn't agree on a definition of modernism. The eight architects hadn't yet decided on the design of the 1933 World's Fair.

The problem was they had no real idea or consensus about what the fair should look like. The neoclassical White City of 1893 was already shadowing their efforts. How could anyone outdo Daniel Burnham Sr. and John Root and their magnificent collage of white Grecian buildings that spoke of Rome and the great republic that had arisen in the New World? Some believed nothing could eclipse the White City, so they should just accept that and take a shot at the 1933 World's Fair.

So while the heavy clouds of winter slid past the windows and the commission hashed out its vision, there was only one thing to do before they attacked the grand design of the fair: take a plane ride over the site. This was a novelty in 1929, and the eight men crammed into the private plane. What they saw from the air didn't help. They peered down from their windows and saw a ragged, foot-shaped piece of land different from any on which they had contemplated sticking a building or series of buildings—a small city, in fact. The lakefront was "long and narrow about three miles from end to end and it varied in width from about 100 yards to half a mile. It was all 'made' land which a few years before had been fathoms under the surface of Lake Michigan. An island of about eighty acres, Northerly Island lay abreast from the mainland from 12th Street south; an addition, yet to be built, would carry it as far as 23rd Street. Between the mainland and the island was a lagoon."[1]

The architects had their work cut out for them. When they returned they may have wondered how they had come to this sad place, so dismal in the winter months. The brooding city had a sinister quality, engendering concerns about safety. In truth, the men leading the architects were not from Chicago. While Burnham and Root had been Chicago architects leading the charge against New York snootiness in 1893, this time around the board of trustees hadn't even bothered to bolster Chicago pride. They hired two leading New York architects and called it a day.

Chicago suffered from an inferiority complex. The midwestern plains, frontier history, and gangland murders fired up the twin cylinders of insecurity that gripped the Second City and produced the decision to hire Paul Philippe Cret and Raymond Hood to design Chicago's second world's fair. That Chicago went to New York hat in hand after the blazing success of the Columbian Exposition is a little puzzling. Cret and Hood would hire the architectural commission that ultimately designed the fair, a decision instrumental in the swerve away from traditional architecture. The Burnham and Root of 1933 were Cret and Hood, two men who had only rarely even visited Chicago.

Lenox Lohr wrote years later in *Fair Management* that he had in mind something very different from the exposition of 1893: "The classical architecture which had satisfied the tastes of their generations and influenced architectural designs of succeeding periods, was not indicated for The Century of Progress. This should be radically novel."[2] *Radically novel* was a funny adjective for Paul Cret and Raymond Hood, two widely respected practitioners of the beau arts tradition. Cret had built his career designing classical buildings.

Born in Lyon, France, and educated at the École des Beaux-Arts, then in Paris at the atelier of Jean Louis Pascal, Cret began teaching at the University of Pennsylvania in 1903. While he was on a trip to France, World War I broke out, and Cret enlisted in the French army, receiving the Croix de Guerre and becoming an officer in the Legion of Honor. He began designing in 1907; his first major commission in Washington, DC, the

Pan American Union Building, would later headquarter the Organization of American States. This breakthrough in classical design led to many war memorials. In the 1920s Cret stayed in the beaux arts tradition, but modernism began to creep in when he designed the Cincinnati Union Terminal and later added the streamlined fluting on the Chicago, Burlington, and Quincy Railroad's *Pioneer Zephyr*, which debuted at the fair in 1934.

Cret played artist to Hood's technician. Born in Pawtucket, Rhode Island, Hood had attended Brown University before enrolling at the Massachusetts Institute of Technology. He then worked for the firm Cram, Goodhue and Ferguson before taking a degree at the École des Beaux-Arts in 1911. His connection to Chicago began with a competition to design the Tribune Building. He and architect John Mead Howells won, and the building became a mainstay of Michigan Avenue. Though the structure was beautiful, Hood saw himself as no more than a man designing elaborate shelters. He would write, "There has been entirely too much talk about the collaboration of architect, painter and sculptor. . . . [B]uildings are constructed for certain purposes, and the buildings of today are more practical from the standpoint of the man who is in them than the older buildings. . . . [B]eauty is utility, developed in a manner which the eye is accustomed to by habit."[3]

There you have it: Burnham and Hood's practicality versus Root and Cret's creative genius. But it is not that simple. The cross-pollination between each set of partners was strong. And Root's design of the Tribune Building, Rockefeller Center, and the RCA Building belied his self-impression as a purely technical architect. Raymond Hood becomes more complex when we consider his intersection with literature. Ayn Rand's novel *The Fountainhead* centers on Peter Keating, a realist with none of the brilliance of hero Howard Roark, based loosely on Frank Lloyd Wright. Keating is the architect who merges Old World styles with the new skyscrapers of New York after winning a contest to design a building in Chicago. Fiction and reality blend further when Keating is hired to head a committee to design a "modernistic" world's fair from which Roark is excluded, as was Frank Lloyd Wright.

Ayn Rand probably did model her character on Hood, as novelists pull from reality for their fiction, and the modernism of the world's fair in her novel certainly matches that of the Chicago Fair of 1933. But Cret and Hood first had to select the members of the architectural commission, whose formation President Rufus Dawes announced on March 2, 1928. Lohr wrote of the commission's mission years later, "Drawn from the far corners of the country and chosen with the conscious desire to find men who had eminence as designers, capability as demonstrated in existing buildings of their creation, and ability to cooperate, they gave a full measure of loyal and unselfish service."[4]

So who were these supermen and where to find them? Hood and Cret produced a first list of approximately fifty candidates; President Dawes's assistant, Allen D. Albert, came up with a second; and the board of trustees generated a third. Thirty candidates appeared on all three lists, and three qualifying criteria were established:[5] the architect's eminence as a designer, the merit of his designs as tested by buildings that had stood long enough to be judged, and, most important, his ability to cooperate with others.[6]

Based on these criteria, Arthur Brown Jr., Harvey Wiley Corbett, and Louis Ayres joined the commission. As Lisa Schrenk noted in *Building a Century of Progress*, "This initial committee revealed a strong East Coast bias. Brown, a designer in San Francisco, constituted the lone member from outside the New York area."[7] The members of the commission then picked three local architects: Edward Bennett, John Holabird, and Hubert Burnham. All three men had ties to the 1893 exposition, which was a real bonus in confronting the problems of erecting a fair on a lakefront and an island.

So everyone had to play together. The first meeting, held on May 23, 1928, generated a statement for the board of trustees: "The architecture of the buildings and grounds in 1933 will illustrate in definite form the development of the art of architecture since the great fair of 1893, not only in America but in the world at large. New elements of construction, products of modern invention and science will be the factors of architectural composition."[8]

After that, it was every man for himself.

The commission had already split along traditionalist and modernist lines, with about half the members on each side. As with a supreme court evenly divided, it would fall to Hood and Cret to break the tie and make the final decision. "The commission mirrored the great debate in American architecture over the proper direction of progressive building design in the United States."[9] Hood was concerned early on and wrote to Cret, "The committee might find itself equally divided between conservatives and those designers favoring the tested value of revival forms, and 'modernists,' those more interested in current design trends."[10]

He saw only arguments ahead and named the traditionalists as "Bennet, Brown and Ayres and the modernists as Holabird, Corbett, Cret and Himself."[11] Then providence took a hand when Ayres refused to join the commission; Hood and Cret promptly replaced him with Ralph T. Walker, an avowed modernist, and then further strengthened their hand with consultants Norman Bel Geddes and George Ferris, who leaned toward the moderns.

This did not mean entirely surrendering to function over form. Cret saw modernism as progressive above all else. He didn't believe utilitarianism should rule the day in the design of modern buildings. Cret believed that in designing buildings architects placed a very low priority on functionalism. He didn't believe in "nudist architecture," where function takes precedence and produces bland structures dedicated to serving the occupants.[12] He strongly believed architecture was a "fine art," not just a minor branch of engineering.[13] Civilizations are measured by their effort to rise above the primary stage of usefulness. Cret challenged the architects to design buildings for the fair that would "work successfully as a machine and at the same time be beautiful to look at."[14]

Subsequent meetings produced debates about modernism, with each member having his own definition: "John Holabird initially felt that modern architecture formed another step in the evolutionary development of architecture styles. Others saw it more as a set of design principles based on the issues of purpose and function set apart from style."[15] Cret would write in 1931, "Modernism is something much deeper than this or that formula or ornamentation. Ornamentation is fashion and it is only surface deep." In Cret's view, a building could only be modern if it emerged in the modern age. The commission could agree on one thing—that a skyscraper was distinctly modern, having come about in the modern age in America—and decided that a "tall vertical tower" should be part of the fair.[16]

Hood later wrote in a foreword to R. W. Sexton's *American Apartment Houses, Hotels and Apartments*, "Modern architecture consists of studying our problems from the ground up, solving each point in the most logical manner, in the light of our present day knowledge. . . . [E]ffort need not be centered on striving to create a new style or on trying to develop an architecture that is distinctively American."[17]

The commission members debated in the studio atop the Burnham Building before the massive fireplace above which Daniel Burnham Sr.'s charge was carved into the stone: "Make no little plans. They have no magic to stir men's blood and probably themselves will not be realized. Make big plans. Aim high in hope and work remembering that a noble logical diagram once recorded will never die but long after we are gone will be a living thing asserting itself with ever growing insistency. Remember that our grandsons are going to do things that would stagger us. Let your watchword be order and your beacon beauty."[18]

Shouldn't the architect with the biggest reputation in the country, and certainly Chicago, have been with them up in the clouds? Maybe no one said as much, but surely the thought occurred to Cret and Root. Ayn Rand, who built her novel around a fallen man who would come to the altar of the master of all architects, would surely have asked the question, probably in the indignant tone of all Chicagoans: Where the hell was Frank Lloyd Wright?

Chapter Eighteen

Lady Godiva

Lady Godiva was an Anglo-Saxon woman who rode naked through the streets of Coventry in the eleventh century to protest her husband's taxation of his tenants. The legend has come down through time in the image of a nude woman on a horse, long hair covering her loins, with the townspeople ordered to shutter their homes. Only one man, Tom, violated the order; the name "Peeping Tom" would forever be ascribed to voyeurs. But Sally Rand's income now depended on the Peeping Toms of the world.

While the modernists flew overhead and Lenox Lohr dumped sand into the lake to extend Northerly Island, Al Capone packed up to leave his cell, and Sally Rand had created a career at The Paramount with her seven-foot ostrich-feather fans. It was no small feat. Rand had no education and no real training beyond circus work and a few roles in some B movies for Cecil B. DeMille. The market crash in 1929 had knocked her off her feet, as it had everyone else, and sleeping in the alley was not far from her mind as she readied herself to dance.

Readying herself meant taking off all her clothes and picking up her feathers. The first night that she danced bare-breasted in front of an audience, she wore fishnet stockings. For the first year, she stuck to this "uniform," but then she started to go completely nude. The audience loved it when she raised her feathers at the end and gave them what they wanted. The Paramount did better business than any other club in the South Loop, and not because it served better booze; it was because of the cute blond with the ostrich feathers.

But the fair was looming, and Sally Rand had her eye on it. The club was fine, but she had seen herself as a movie star, not a striptease artist. Dancing in Chicago during the Great Depression beat starving, but, like every person who has tasted quicksilver fame, Sally wanted it back. As her friend Holly Knox would later write, "She was more than a little bitter with Hollywood because she had expected great things for herself there. Her family had moved out to be with her in her success and she was the one who had to leave them there because of lack of work."[1]

Sally might have been chagrined to see Kay Francis on the screen, drawling sibilant *r*'s that came out like *w*'s. The truth was that she envisioned a Hollywood comeback for herself, and headlining in a vaudeville burlesque show just didn't feed her need for fame. Ironically, we wouldn't know the name Sally Rand had she not left Hollywood and been in Chicago at the time that the city was gearing up for the 1933 World's Fair. So much of history is serendipitous, and Sally Rand's dancing less than a mile from where men would drive pilings into the earth to erect the 625-foot towers of the Sky Ride was fortuitous.

But Sally's job at The Paramount and her life were in danger. The very problems the world's fair hoped to solve reached into Sally's world one dark night. During the first summer after she had begun performing at The Paramount, she saw Big Ed talking to two men in long coats and bowlers. One of them poked Big Ed in the chest, and Sally could see her boss turning red. The men left, and he came over to the bar where Sally was sitting.

"Not only are we getting the shaft from the Government, they give gooks like that the right to push people around." Ed turned to the bartender. "Give me a Scotch . . . the good stuff."

Sally looked at her boss

"They want you to change booze dealers?"

In Chicago everyone knew where the booze came from. The gangsters supplied the beer and whiskey and inevitably wanted the clubs to buy from them exclusively. Most people didn't see the cost of their booze firsthand. Ed stared down at his drink and nodded slowly.

"They're coming back tonight with the regional boss. Said something about wanting to catch your act, Sal. That must be why I'm rating a visit from the number two boy."

Sally patted his hand.

"It'll be alright. They just don't have the right to do that!"[2]

That night Sally was stiff on stage, and the audience seemed unresponsive. Only one table in the center applauded loudly. It was as if people knew representatives of the police state were there and thought it best to be silent. One has images of Soviet Russia, where a pernicious force enters and people just strive not to be noticed. So it was with the gangsters in Chicago in the 1920s and 1930s. They represented death, and people instinctively moved away. After the show, Sally answered a knock on her dressing room door. Another dancer, Isadora, stood there with a dozen red roses. She was chewing gum and gushing: "This guy says he'll see you in front after the show."[3] Sally took the roses and knew who they were from.

"Boy, this guy must be some big shot. He gave me ten bucks to tell you he'll be waiting."

Ten dollars was a lot of money in 1931. At the time a meal at Berghoffs, the German restaurant around the corner, could be had for fifty cents. Sally Rand knew what was being asked of her. The assumption was that she took off her clothes on a stage, so she would also do it in private. A lot of men saw her as a prostitute, and more than a few of the burlesque girls had a steady income from "tricks." But Sally was a "Hollywood starlet," a self-image she carried her entire life.

Sally picked a card out of the roses and saw the initials "V. G." Vito Genovese, a notorious gangster from New Jersey, who would head up the Genovese crime family. He might have come to Chicago at this time and gone to The Paramount, though it seems doubtful. Holly Knox's rendition of events, which came from Sally Rand herself, suggests that some gangster was likely extorting money from Eddie Callahan. Vito Genovese did rise to power as an enforcer during Prohibition and may have stopped off in Chicago, but that would have put him in conflict with Al Capone.

Still, Genovese had strong ties with Lucky Luciano, whom Capone had worked for in Manhattan, so there might have been a crossover. Like Capone, he started his criminal life at fifteen stealing fruit from vendors and running errands for mobsters. Like Capone, he dropped out of school in the middle grades and saw a life of crime as his only way to make money. In the 1920s he worked for Joe Masseria, boss of a powerful gang in Manhattan. Vito's value was his propensity for violence and murder. He would blow the back of a rival's head off with a shotgun in 1930 in the Bronx. If Vito Genovese was sitting in The Paramount on that night, then Sally Rand was about to encounter evil incarnate.

She went out into the club, and there he sat, surrounded by gangsters. Holly Knox wrote later of the encounter:

She held her hand out in greeting. Vito Genovese stood up and took her hand and held it a moment too long. The other men remained seated.
"Your dance is exciting, Miss Rand . . . or should I call you Sally?"
She looked squarely into his dark eyes.
"All my friends call me Sally. Pick what category you fit in and take your choice."
Vito laughed. "Sit down with us and we'll decide that." He called the waiter. "Drinks here, please."
Sally looked up.
"My usual ginger ale."
"So Sally. Afraid to touch Ed's stuff?"
"Certainly not! I never drink when I'm working and only when I celebrate something."
Vito moved closer to her.
"Then why don't we celebrate your quitting this joint and coming to work for me at the shore?"
"I never make spur of the moment decisions."
Vito's voice became cold.
"I'll give you till tomorrow night to make up your mind. You're too good for this dump."
"Mr. Genovese . . . Ed Callahan is a good friend of mine. We have an agreement. When my contract is completed, I'll leave."
"I think he'll agree, baby." The icy voice went on. "He'll agree to anything."
Sally got up.

"If you'll excuse me, Mr. Genovese, I must get ready for the next show."

She turned her back and left.[4]

Holly Knox's rendition of events shows a proud Sally Rand leaving the gangster behind. She passes her glum boss, who by now knows the gangsters will not leave him alone. A week later white roses appeared in Sally Rand's dressing room with a card: "Red for Life and White for Death."[5] For the past week Eddie had escorted Sally home. Now she faced a clear choice.

Did Sally Rand get this death threat? In all probability, yes. Gangsters supplied the clubs with Prohibition booze; Eddie had his source, and others wanted to muscle in.

Unfortunately for Eddie Callahan, the consequence of not taking Vito Genovese seriously and agreeing to buy a small quantity of the higher-priced booze would be visited upon him a year later. Sally called after she quit the club and found out Eddie had been shot to death. But we are getting ahead of our story.

The world's fair was looming, and Sally Rand was already trying to come up with a way to take part in the biggest thing to happen in Chicago for forty years. It would save her from Vito Genovese and land her in the history books. And she would owe it all to Lady Godiva.

Chapter Nineteen

Horatio Alger Returns

It's hard to believe Dale Carnegie would cite Al Capone in his 1937 best seller *How to Win Friends and Influence People*.[1] Carnegie was fascinated with the Horatio Alger dynamic in America, where he believed anyone could rise to fabulous wealth. Alger's rags-to-riches stories pitched this dynamic to a people emerging from the rural nineteenth century into the modern urban twentieth century that would transform the country. Carnegie's book captured the very essence of that American challenge and held out the power of positive thinking as the magic key to unlock the riches of the young republic. He offered Al Capone as proof.

All celebrities are wrapped in the tinsel of our own reflected selves. We want to believe in the myth that someone like Capone, who came to America with his parents and lived in abject poverty, could rise up and make $100 million a year. The press devoured the pitch and made it fit Capone by stressing the qualities he shared in common with every American: He loved family, baseball, telling stories, his house, his neighbors, and music. He was entrepreneurial, philanthropic, generous, wise, and funny. He had a vacation home. He was living the American dream.

Amazingly, before the juggernaut of mass communication, he was an international celebrity. Whatever Al Capone did produced great newspaper copy and increased circulation. Before there were paparazzi, gumshoe reporters staked out his home, his hotel, his office. One reporter waited outside his residence in Miami, not knowing if Capone was there or not. When Al drove by, he invited the reporter in, only to have him ask if he had killed Jake Lingle. Al took it in stride and offered the man something to eat and drink, then sent him on his way.

Capone understood the press and gave an interview to the *Chicago Tribune* the day before he was to be released from prison. Readers would learn that he had lost twenty-five pounds inside and was heading back to Chicago. "Where else would I go? I live in Chicago, my business is there, my mother and my family are there."[2] A family man first and last. He told the *Tribune* he would straighten out his tax problem with the government and then head for his vacation home in Florida. Just a man who wanted to get on with his life.

But releasing an incarcerated celebrity could be problematic. The warden had Capone taken to another prison thirty miles away. As Jonathan Eig wrote in *Get Capone*, "The following morning, before dawn, reporters, photographers, and a handful of the curious began lining up outside the castlelike walls of Eastern State. By sunrise the crowd began to swell. By noon thousands of people crowded the streets and sidewalks around the massive prison. The weather was cool and damp. Newsreel shooters perched their bulky cameras on the roofs of their cars."[3]

It was all for naught. Capone was already on the *Broadway Limited*. The *Tribune* ran a banner headline at once ominous and boastful: "Capone Speeds for Chicago."[4] Was this a good thing? Reporters showed up in front of his home on South Prairie and begged for clues. Two turkeys had been ordered for the big man. Reporters offered Sonny candy in return for information about his father. The press clearly centered on the man, not the morality of his lifestyle or how he made a living.

Capone was not dumb. We have this image of a gangster in a flashy suit and a fedora who spoke in slang, but he actually pressed his case in the press. Prohibition, he maintained, had created a need, and he was simply giving people what they wanted. An interview in the *Chicago American* reveals his philosophical approach to the distribution of beer and alcohol:

> *I'm not telling anybody how to run the country, but . . . if people did not want beer and wouldn't drink it, a fellow would be crazy for going around and trying to sell it. I've seen gambling houses, in my*

*travels you understand, and I never saw anyone point a gun at a man
and make him go in. I never heard of anyone being forced to go to a
place to have some fun. . . . I don't blame the police and I don't blame
the state's attorney and I don't blame the government. They have the
pressure on them and they got to move, see?*[5]

As Capone's legend grew, so did the perception that Chicago was
out of control. Movie stars wanted to meet him. Mayors posed with him.
Capone had branded himself before branding existed, and his brand
was larger than life. He did amazing things. South Dakota invited him
to come stay in Rapid City if he found Chicago hostile. His name was
written in on election ballots in Monticello, Iowa; he received fifty votes.

Al Capone was international. The world knew of Chicago's gang
culture of tommy guns and speakeasies. Chu Ciang-ling, director of the
Richfield Oil Company, grumbled, "We have our bandits . . . but the
Chicago bandits and gangsters, especially Al Capone, seem to hog most
of the publicity." Major General Milton, stationed in Burma, a hero of
the Spanish-American War, remarked, "Scarface is as well known in the
Orient as he is here. People the world over believe they would be shot
down by machine guns five minutes after their arrival in Chicago."[6]

Clearly Chicago still had a serious public relations problem. To that
end, the men hoping to get rid of Al Capone began pursuing a dual
strategy. They continued to harass his operation with raids but shifted
to getting a conviction entirely on the issue of back taxes. It is amazing, given the amount of bloodshed in Chicago, that not one case could
be made to prove Al Capone was behind illegal bootlegging and the
attendant murders. Nailing him for tax evasion was a bit like arresting a
man for parking violations after he had just hacked up his wife. But the
government was inexperienced in pursing crime on a national level, and
tax fraud presented a novel way to apprehend a man wreaking havoc in
a major American city.

Many people thought it absurd that the government would go after a
murderer for not paying taxes on his income. But it was no joke to Lawrence Mattingly, an expert in tax cases. He and his client, Al Capone, sat
in the office of the Bureau of Internal Revenue with C. W. Herrick, the

agent in charge. Herrick started out by explaining that they wanted to get to the bottom of the issue of Capone's tax liability. As Eig writes in *Get Capone*, the conversation was a bit one-sided:

"What records have you of your income, Mr. Capone? Do you keep any records?"

"No. I never did."

"Any checking account?"

"No, sir."

"Do you own property in your name?"

"No, sir."

"How long, Mr. Capone, have you enjoyed a large income?"

"I never had much of an income, a large income."

"Have you ever filed tax returns?"

"No."

"For the years mentioned, 1926–1929, did you buy or sell real estate which was placed in the name of others?"

"I would rather let my lawyer answer that."

"Did you purchase any securities during the years under consideration?"

"No, I never had anything like that."

"Did you have any brokerage account in your name?"

"No."[7]

Al Capone was careful up to a point, and that point would prove his undoing. He admitted that he conducted most of his transactions with cash carried on his person. This implied that Capone had income and that there was a number out there. At the end of the meeting Mattingly offered to provide an estimate of his client's revenues in hopes of negotiating a settlement. Mattingly would take six months to submit that document.

Meanwhile, the Secret Six under Robert Isham Randolph were still on the hunt for Jake Lingle's and Philip Meagher's killers. Randolph would have been incredulous to hear the gentlemanly discussion in Chicago around a citizen's earnings and the best way to handle a pending tax liability. It was as if Capone were just another member of the middle class trying to take care of an oversight in paying his taxes. In reality, the bodies were still piling up, and Randolph went after the Chicago police, declaring, "Gang rule, gang violence of every kind, must be stopped, and if it is not stopped at once by the authorities, then it will be stopped by the citizens of Chicago themselves."[8]

Randolph's criticism stung, and, to show him they were doing their jobs, twenty-five detectives attending the prizefights at the Chicago Coliseum emerged with seven gangsters. Of course, brothels and speakeasies were in full swing. "Hymie Levine still made the rounds for Capone to speakeasies collecting the beer money. He always talked to the police who were drinking there while he waited for the money."[9]

The police department told the Chicago Association of Commerce and Randolph that they were keeping beer under control in the Loop by sampling. The near beer was given to a detective, who had a shot and then took back a glass of the low-alcohol beer for testing. Randolph knew it was all for show and had the Secret Six sponsor a banquet for Chicago's law enforcement in the grand ballroom of the LaSalle Hotel to push his new agenda.

Thirty officers represented the Chicago police. District Attorney George Johnson represented the federal forces, and state's attorney John Swanson came on behalf of the county. More than one thousand Chicago businessmen attended. And sprinkled among the crowd were the quiet agents of change, the Secret Six. The police were already sick of hearing about Randolph's secret organization. When a *Toronto Star* reporter asked about it, the police commissioner retorted, "The Secret Six is a myth; it's newspaper bologna."[10]

When the same reporter asked Randolph about the Secret Six, he merely smiled, prompting the reporter to later write, "Colonel Randolph's smile is exactly the kind that Bugs Moran and Scarface Al see in their nightmares. Across their path is a foreboding shadow, cast by a secret organization in the interest of law and order. And behind that secret organization is the cryptic deranging smile of Colonel Robert Isham Randolph."[11] The Secret Six weren't going away.

CHAPTER TWENTY

The Design

IN A WAY, JULIAN CARLTON *WAS* FRANK LLOYD WRIGHT. THE MAN SERvant from Barbados set fire to Wright's home and studio in Wisconsin while the architect was away in Chicago. As the fire burned, Carlton hacked Wright's lover, her two children, and four others to death with a machete. He then drank hydrochloric acid and waited to die. He didn't, but he was almost lynched on the spot. He perished from starvation in a Dodgeville jail seven weeks later. He had wreaked havoc on Frank Lloyd Wright, but Wright was well acquainted with havoc, having inflicted quite a bit of it himself.

In 1991, the American Institute of Architects voted Wright "the greatest American architect of all time."[1] He had designed 1,000 structures and completed 532, written more than twenty books, and pioneered the Prairie School movement in architecture. He never graduated from high school or college. He married three times, jumping from one wife to another, leaving behind children, enraged husbands and former wives, and disastrous finances. His mother had declared while pregnant that her son would grow up to build beautiful buildings.

Wright had the good fortune to land in Chicago after the great fire, when the city was rebuilding. His impressions included crowded streets and grimy buildings lacking any originality. He found work as a draftsman with the architectural firm of Joseph Lyman Silsbee. But Wright felt underpaid at $8 a week and quit for a position at Beers, Clay & Dutton; then he quit again to become a designer at Adler & Sullivan. As luck would have it, he came under the wing of Louis Sullivan. He had violent altercations with the other architects at the firm, married, had six children, and was constantly broke. It was said that Frank Lloyd Wright had champagne tastes on a beer budget.

But his reputation grew, and he established his own practice in the Schiller Building. There he developed the Prairie School and built many homes. Then he left his wife for his neighbor's. He left for Europe and later returned to Wisconsin, where Julian Carlton went on his rampage. After the bodies had been buried, Wright married again, but this second wife became addicted to morphine, and the marriage fell apart after a year. Wright moved into his rebuilt home in Wisconsin. It burned to the ground after crossed wires from a telephone system sparked a fire.

Wright rebuilt his home again and then was arrested in Tonka Bay, Minnesota, charged with violating the Mann Act (taking a prostitute across state lines to have sex). The charges were dropped, and Wright married again. Around 1929, a commission was set up to build the Chicago World's Fair, and Frank Lloyd Wright was left out. Paul Philippe Cret and Raymond Hood, along with Rufus Dawes, had good reason. After the flying over Northerly Island, they now had to come up with a plan in which each architect would present his concept and the best of the designs would be combined into a final. Frank Lloyd Wright did not play well with others. The mad genius was probably the greatest living architect of all time. But did anybody want that kind of ego in a collaborative venture like the 1933 Chicago World's Fair? In short, no one wanted a Julian Carlton raising hell.

Cret and Hood had brought together eight architects who needed to act as one. They were laying out a small city, and each would contribute a design, the best parts of which would go into the final plan. But architects were egotists who saw their buildings as expressions of themselves. Hood was one of the few who separated himself from his designs; Frank Lloyd Wright, while extreme, manifested traits all architects shared to some degree.

As Lenox Lohr wrote of the early meetings, "With heads in clouds there were dreams of jeweled skyscrapers, pits a mile deep, moving sidewalks, and chains of picturesque islands strung like pearls along Lake Michigan's shore."[2] Lohr went on to say that the architects had a different set of parameters to consider than the men who designed the exposition of 1893: "Since the great fairs of the past there had been radical changes in physical conditions and ways of thinking. Differences in climate, location, transportation facilities, method of financing, management and media. . . . [A]bove all, people were more traveled, more sophisticated and less easily thrilled."[3]

Paramount for the architects was moving large groups of people through the exposition. Mechanical sidewalks were brought up early as a way to reduce fatigue for visitors walking through the fair. This was not a novel idea, as Lisa Schrenk points out in *Building a Century of Progress*: "Mechanical people movers had appeared at earlier expositions. A cart that traveled on two widely spaced tracks at the Paris exposition in 1899 offered fairgoers an aerial view of the exhibits inside the building."[4] Planners for the 1893 fair in Chicago had also included movable sidewalks but junked the idea when concessioners complained they would hurt push-car revenues.

The committee members brought their plans to a meeting on January 21, 1929. Despite professing their belief in modernist architecture, the plans "revealed that most had not yet moved beyond the lessons of their formal training." Even the architects regarded the studies as "rather traditional developments of the best world's fair training of the early years."[5] Clearly a lot of liberal thinking had paid lip service to modern design, but when it came to actually designing the fair, the architects fell back on classical massing, masonry, and beaux arts planning.

The truth was that no one was quite sure what an innovative, modern fair would look like. As Lohr would write, "All of the early sketches had stressed vertical architecture and all were symmetrical, following in the respect of former expositions."[6] Before the designs were submitted, a list of agreed-on elements was established; this was part of the beau arts tradition and might have contributed to the "stifled" aspect of the designs: "Multistoried buildings, vertical and horizontal transportation systems, no automobile parking . . . provisions for making pageants viewable, water incorporated not only within the grounds but throughout the buildings, artificial light for illumination inside and outside, a major axis running parallel to the lakeshore and a minor cross axis at Twenty-Third Street,

and an attempt to use a more economical type of fireproof construction."[7]
"The parti [list] for the exposition design consisted of a dominant building celebrating scientific developments in the middle of the site, a water
portal at the north end of the fairgrounds, an airport extending into Lake
Michigan and moving sidewalks connecting the exhibition buildings. The
commissioners also agreed the pavilion should be three or four stories
high, totaling five million square feet."[8]

No one had a design everyone could agree on yet. Worse, no one
had come up with a design that would incorporate technology, science,
economics (this was before the crash), and modernism. The designs were
boring and reductive, if not derivative of the 1893 fair. Maybe someone
should have invited Frank Lloyd Wright and reckoned with the madman.
Originality was proving elusive, and the studio atop the Burnham Building had produced nothing to snap the architects out of their collective
classical stupor.

Then, in the fall of 1929, the antihero of Ayn Rand's novel, Raymond
Hood, came back from Europe and presented his exposition plan. The
other members were startled. Hood had ignored the parti. Moreover, his
plan called for an asymmetrical layout. Lohr saw it this way: "All of the
early sketches had stressed vertical architecture, and all were symmetrical,
following in this respect former expositions. It was a dramatic moment
when . . . Raymond Hood presented a plan radically different from any
that had been previously submitted. It was unsymmetrical. The balance
of tower with tower and pillar with pillar was absent."[9]

The other members (except Cret) were outraged. Hood had got rid
of the airport and the moving sidewalks. "His design included a diverse
group of elements informally situated along either side of a long rect-
angular basin, highlighted by a massive setback tower located off center.
. . . [O]n the north end of the grounds, a large ramp crisscrossed the water
leading to a terrace that overlooked the grounds to the south. A series of
X shaped pylons flanked a long cascading fountain leading from the top
of the terrace to the large basin."[10]

Hood told the other members that he'd had an epiphany in Europe:
he'd realized the symmetrical plans were "monotonous"[11] and the informal layout would give them flexibility. Cret agreed. Both men were cog-

nizant of the impact that the recent market crash would have on the fair. The design would have to be flexible, adjustable as funds became available or vanished. Harvey Wiley Corbett argued that the committee shouldn't even consider Hood's plan, as he had ignored the parti. The other members disagreed after Cret and Hood pointed out the benefits of the new design. A vote was taken, and Hood's plan won by five hands. *A Century of Progress* had just lived up to its name and broken with the past.

CHAPTER TWENTY-ONE

The Secret Six Get to Work

IN 1930 A LITERARY CHARACTER NAME WINNIE THE POOH WAS licensed. A comic strip appeared in newspapers about a weird little mouse named Mickey. A patent was granted for something called a field effect transistor, and a company called 3M began to sell an invention by Richard Gurley Drew called Scotch Tape. President Herbert Hoover maintained that the economy would recover, even though $16 billion had disappeared in the stock market over the course of a single week. And Colonel Robert Isham Randolph hired an operating director for the Secret Six.

Alexander Jamie, who had gotten his brother-in-law Elliot Ness a job, was the chief special agent of the Prohibition bureau in Chicago. Randolph had to ask President Hoover to give Jamie a leave of absence. In May he had made a spectacular bust at an airfield in Cicero as he awaited a shipment of booze from Canada. In the darkness Jamie could barely see his hand in front of him. He and the other agents waited in black cars with the lights off. Parked on the far side of the landing field in Cicero, they could hear the planes circling without lights above. Jamie heard a plane touch down with $1 million worth of Old Smuggler and Johnny Walker Scotch from Windsor, Ontario. He could hear the trucks idling across the field with Capone's henchmen waiting to make the pickup. When they moved, he would move.

The plane had barely stopped when the booze was pushed out of the fuselage through a sliding door. Another plane was circling above and waiting to land. Jamie heard the trucks start and gave his men the signal.

They would cut the plane off and surprise Capone's men. Jamie sped across the landing field and then darted across the path of the one of the trucks. He pulled out his gun, ran up to the first truck, and put his pistol to the driver's head.

"You're under arrest!"[1]

The bust resulted in a federal grand jury returning one hundred indictments against Ralph Capone and two hundred others. Jamie was one of the best agents in the field and incorruptible. This was not lost on Colonel Randolph, who was sure he had found his man. The first thing Jamie did was put together an organizational chart of the Capone outfit. He discovered that Capone modeled his organization on big business. As Dennis Hoffman wrote in *Scarface Al and the Crime Crusaders*, "Capone as dictator had as two aides a powerful labor racketeer in Chicago and an ex-convict. . . . [Next came] gang lieutenants, each in charge of a particular branch of the enterprise. . . . Next in line came the 'fixer' who dealt with policemen and other public officials . . . and a 'traffic manager' attended to deliveries of beer and liquor."[2] The rest of Capone's organization was departmentalized for the process of producing beer and bottling and shipping.

The Secret Six were essentially businessmen and operated the way businessmen do when facing a tough competitor. They studied Capone's organization from the top down, the market, and the best way to take away his ability to make money. They found that in Cook County there were "20,000 beer joints, places that varied in size from large soft-drink parlors, saloons, and night clubs to beer flats."[3] In the Loop investigators found 160 speakeasies that served whiskey and gin, but Capone made his real money on the sale of beer. "It sold at the standard rate of one dollar a bottle or twenty-five cents a glass."[4]

Bootleggers supplied the 20,000 spots, and the majority were Capone's. Other gangs paid Capone for the privilege of selling beer in Chicago. The Secret Six determined that Capone controlled all means of production from manufacture to distribution and owned many breweries. New manufacturing facilities could be started up at will if other breweries were raided. Randolph's investigators estimated that every week, the 20,000 spots sold 5 barrels of beer each for a total of about 100,000 barrels. Chicagoans—man, woman, and child—drank six pints of beer a week.

A lot of the beer was bottled in Capone plants and labeled Canadian Ale. The Secret Six determined that "it cost Capone $1.80 to brew a barrel of beer and that other manufacturing charges, such as cooperage, brought the total to more than $3. The standard price charged to speakeasies . . . was $55, leaving a gross profit of $52. . . . The armed guards who accompanied the trucks" cost $100 to $150 a week. Al Capone, they determined, had 2,000 people on payroll between "brewers, truckmen, armed guards, collectors, fixers, [and] gambling houses, [which] did not include the more than half of Chicago's 6,000 policeman who took bribes."[5]

Randolph proposed a special unit under Alexander Jamie to start disrupting Capone's operation where it would hurt. He wanted to thwart his ability to manufacture beer first. Enter Jamie's brother-in-law Elliot Ness. It turns out the famous scene in the movie *The Untouchables* with Ness in a building-smashing truck is true. Ness immediately began crashing into distilleries with a ten-ton truck with a steel bumper covering the entire grill. In a very short time he and his "Untouchables" had "destroyed $1 million worth of trucks, equipment, beer, and whiskey."[6] Then Randolph opened a speakeasy at 60 East 30th Street and called it the Garage Café. The Secret Six paid about $12,000 to make it look like a "real joint" and sold beer and liquor in violation of the Volstead Act. In this sense, they could go where law enforcement could not. They simply opened a bar and sold booze like every other gangster. The colonel hired Sam Constantino, a Sicilian paid informant, and Pat Horan, an undercover policeman, to tend bar. Constantino would later be convicted for running an interstate stolen-goods ring—a perfect bartender for the Secret Six.

Randolph's organization had one thing the police did not—money—and it was their secret weapon. They bought information from lower members of Capone's gang at the Garage Café for anywhere from $100 to $1,000. The speakeasy stayed open for six months before Capone got wise. Constantino came to Randolph and gave him the keys, saying, "I'm takin' it on the lam. Here's the keys and I'm goin' and goin' for good."[7] Capone had returned to Chicago to find his operation under assault, and for the first time he couldn't buy off the culprits. He couldn't even find them and faced a shadowy organization pushing the levers of power from behind a curtain.

Capone did hear rumors about the Secret Six. One night in February 1930, Randolph received a call: "I have the Big Fellow planted in a hotel near the Loop where you can talk to him without being seen. Will you go?"[8] Randolph, who had fought in World War I, said he would. He pocketed a .45-caliber pistol, told his wife where he was headed, and began to drive to the Lexington Hotel to see Al Capone.

CHAPTER TWENTY-TWO

Beginning to Build the Rainbow City

A CITY NAMED *A CENTURY OF PROGRESS* WAS STARTING TO GO UP ALONG the lakefront. Behind it was Gotham—dark, brooding, gangster ridden, with soup lines and suited men shooting each other with Thompson submachine guns. The coal-burning furnaces darkened the skies as the citizenry of Chicago beared up under the Great Depression and read the splashy headlines of the latest murder by Al Capone and company. Some thought the United States was on the verge of collapse, and communism was enjoying a jolt in popularity as people doubted whether capitalism was the answer. One reason corporations contributed so heavily to the fair was the fear that the United States would go "Bolshevik."[1] Perhaps this was a last chance to demonstrate that capitalism was the future and consumerism would be the new culture.

A Century of Progress was the first "corporate" fair; from then on, all fairs would be sponsored by the private sector. The era of the civic-minded and civic-funded fair was dead. Fairs were now a showplace for goods and services and an opportunity to generate money from the fruits of capitalism. The location of the 1933 fair was no accident. One had to leave Chicago and enter a new city on the shores of gleaming Lake Michigan. The cerulean blue of the lake contrasted with the black-and-white photoplay of mobsters, poverty, industrial squalor, and the patinated buildings that would be even more drab against the bright rainbow colors of the Rainbow City.

Fairs are a fantasy, and *A Century of Progress* would take Americans somewhere over the rainbow, where science, technology, corporations, goods, services, and a robust economy would save them. The world that had produced the Columbian Exposition was gone. It had rested on purple prose and romanticism, reflected in the neoclassical buildings of the White City. This new fair would run on organization and mechanization; products would literally be put together in front of people.

This clean, bright world was not part of the "old world" of Chicago. It was the future. The men working to get rid of Al Capone were suturing up the wound in the belly of Chicago. There could be no bleeding over from one city into another. This Rainbow City must be pristine, and that vision had to be built. It was no small task, but military engineer Lenox Lohr had trained for it. It was no accident that after World War I a military footing would be applied to large projects like the fair. Only the military mind could produce a city on a lakefront in two years.

Lenox Lohr found after the first winter that the lakeshore was eroding. The shoreline would have to be rebuilt with heavy riprap before construction could proceed. Already railroad cars of heavy equipment were being diverted to newly laid track leading to the fair. As many as 82 freight cars would arrive in a single day; 4,698 cars total would be switched onto tracks leading to the fair before opening day; 17,000 feet of track was made available for incoming shipments. A three-hundred-by-twenty-five-foot freight house was constructed at the south end of the Travel and Transport Building to house incoming shipments.

The Rainbow City would need its own water supply, electric plant, police force, roads, transportation, parking, sanitation, traffic force, firemen, fireboxes, railroad, secret service, bus line, telephone service, hospital, food service, sewer, and public health department. To build this city, heavy equipment was brought in by rail to alter the land and the sea, and trucks immediately began lining up outside the gates to bring the necessary material. The fire department would have two companies, "one a hook and ladder and the other a pumper." Three fire stations were set up on the grounds, and the fair was divided into twelve zones with fireboxes. There would be 104 alarms during the fair, and most of the fires were caused, as in any city, by "cigarettes, defective flues, electric wiring, overheated motors, gasoline vapors, ignition of motion picture films and fireworks."[2]

The men and women working for the world's fair enjoyed health benefits unheard of in 1931: "The health program began at home with the employees of the exposition and was then extended to exhibitors and concessionaires. Two types of physical examinations were required of employees and were given without cost. One was a general examination for communicable diseases, the other a special examination for those engaging in certain types of work such as food handling and care of children. All workers were required to be vaccinated against smallpox and were subject to reexamination after absence of forty-eight hours or more."[3] At the time there was no health insurance, and during the Great Depression people received no health care at all. But the Rainbow City was futuristic, and in the future people would be healthy and well looked after.

The Administration Building was completed first, and this would be Lohr's command headquarters. "After construction began for each building a temporary fence was thrown up around it with a field shack as headquarters for the contractor and the exposition staff who were involved with the project."[4] The Dawes brothers decided a series of preopenings would be good publicity and generate revenue. For ten cents Chicagoans could tour the fairgrounds and see the newly constructed Fort Dearborn, which opened on May 16, 1931. Certain portions of the Hall of Science and the dome of the Travel and Transport Building were made accessible. But for these preopenings, there had to be "guides" and watchmen to guard the construction sites. A motorized night patrol covered the grounds on the lookout for prowlers and fires. Special guards were hired for exhibits. The watchmen would also be on guard during the fair for "pickpockets, shortchange artists and confidence men."[5]

The guides, overseen by Major Robert Wigglesworth, would be the first people to greet visitors. Wigglesworth had almost military criteria for his guides: "Each must be five ten inches or taller, pass a strict physical examination, have a satisfactory IQ, a high school education, and be of good general appearance without physical defect."[6] The Institute of Juvenile Research arranged special tests.

The applicants underwent a grueling examination process. In a first test they received a list of fifty names with a blank opposite each. They were to

indicate whether these [individuals] were statesmen, actors, athletes, musicians, or leading industrialists. No one was expected to know all the names but the test was more an evaluation of the courage to admit the applicant didn't know the answer. The Exposition could not have their guides making things up when people asked them a question. The second test [was] a bit bizarre. A math test was given in absolute quiet. Then a second test was given but now a radio was turned up full blast, men ran through the room at intervals ringing bells, knocking against tables and chairs or letting out fiendish yells.[7]

The exposition was looking for candidates who could concentrate under adverse circumstances. An early stress test washed out those who were uncomfortable with being asked where the bathrooms were at the same time that a child was screaming.

A military-style chain of command reflected Lohr's and Wigglesworth's backgrounds. The grounds had been divided into four zones for four guide companies. As Lohr later wrote, "The Chief of the Guide section selected as company commanders men who had considerable military experience and were accustomed to positions of command. The headquarters staff consisted of an executive officer, adjutant, personnel officer, quartermaster and a lieutenant in charge of the night detail."[8]

A lagoon patrol of fifteen men was organized with "lifesaving qualifications and men who were experienced on outboard motors. The duties of the Lagoon patrol consisted mainly of patrolling the lagoon and functioning at events such as outboard motor races . . . and fireworks."[9] The exposition employed 1,700 guides while the buildings were being constructed to direct traffic and clear the grounds of stragglers and those seeking employment. Heading into the worst year of the Great Depression, with a quarter of the nation unemployed, the young men who had passed the stress test would be tested again.

The great blue expanse of Lake Michigan was testing Lohr's men engaged in pounding in pilings. The military engineer had to bring massive amounts of lake water into the new city along with massive amounts of electricity. It was no small feat, but Lenox Lohr was learning quickly that there was nothing small about the 1933 World's Fair. A photo shows Lohr in his suit with his foot up on a wheelbarrow. He is surrounded by mud and looking at blueprints with Daniel Burnham Jr. The Rainbow City would soon rise.

Charles Dawes, who found financing for the fair (*Source:* Library of Congress, reproduction number LC-USZ6-849)

Official 1934 World's Fair Poster—Beverly Shores, Century of Progress Architectural District, Lake Front Drive, Beverly Shores, Porter County, Indiana (*Source:* Library of Congress, reproduction number HABS IND, 64-BEVSH, 1--1)

Sally Rand (*Source:* Library of Congress, reproduction number LC-USZ62-112036)

A Century of Progress overview (*Source:* Library of Congress, reproduction number LC-USZ62-127584)

President Hoover presenting to Rufus Dawes, brother of the ambassador to England, a proclamation he has issued authorizing and inviting the public to attend the "Century of Progress" fair to be held in Chicago in 1933. The citizens of Chicago raised $5,000,000 for the fair. Dawes was president of the fair; on the right is Major L. R. Lohr, general manager. (White House, Washington, DC) (*Source:* Library of Congress, reproduction number LC-DIG-hec-35577 [digital file from original negative])

NBC and Lenox R. Lohr, president (*Source:* Library of Congress, reproduction number LC-H22-D-5389 [P&P])

Raymond Hood, architect-in-chief, Rockefeller Center, July 3, 1931 (*Source:* Library of Congress, reproduction number LC-G612-16473)

Sally Rand on a publicity tour after the world's fair (*Source:* Library of Congress, reproduction number LC-DIG-hec-24649)

CHAPTER TWENTY-THREE

Gold Diggers

IN THE NEW CAPITALISM OF THE EARLY TWENTIETH CENTURY, BUSBY Berkeley's *Gold Diggers* told the story of Sally Rand and many other attractive, young, white women looking for fame and fortune.[1] The film told it like it was: if you were pretty and sexy, then you had a shot at hooking up with one of the new millionaires minted by the overheated economy of the 1920s. At a time when only 2 percent of the population went to college, the vast majority of young women like Sally Rand heading to New York or Hollywood had only a few tangible assets. Professions for women in the 1920s ranged from teacher or nurse to starlet; the next best thing was marrying well.

Berkeley's story line took this idea to its logical conclusion, and his musical script revolved around young girls who blatantly admitted to being "gold diggers" and believed that enticing a wealthy man into marriage was as legitimate a profession as any other. As Cheryl Ganz writes in *The 1933 Chicago World's Fair*, "The film used the themes of race, class, and the commodification of sex that had been popularized in during the century's early decades. . . . Its gold-digger chorus girls portrayed modern, aggressive women, always native-born whites, whom professional misfortune might push into prostitution. Seeking security and upward mobility, these attractive characters contrived traps for wealthy men."[2]

Sally Rand took the techniques of Ziegfeld's Follies, with their "ornamental dancers,"[3] a step further. Was Sally's endgame to catch a rich husband? On the surface it would seem that she was out to recapture the fame that had eluded her in Hollywood. The shows at The Paramount were a springboard, as far as she was concerned, and the world's fair was now looming over Chicago. It was the event of the new century, and Sally Rand had to be a part of it.

Like the girls in *Gold Diggers*, Sally planned to cash in once she made it and marry well. But maybe a closer model for Rand was a dancer in Paris named Isadora Duncan. "Duncan had performed in revealing tunics that exposed her limbs, a provocative style that pioneered dance as modern art."[4] But Duncan performed during good times for socialites. Rand's audience was the middle classes hit by the hard times of the Great Depression. They needed more than a woman in a tunic; they needed sex, and sex was sure to sell at the world's fair.

But Sally, while popular at The Paramount, had no easy access to the fair. The rush of those looking for work with *A Century of Progress* had developed into a bottleneck. There were too many seekers for too few jobs, and Sally wasn't even sure what she would do and where. Her friend Holly Knox relays a conversation she had with Eddie Callahan one night, and we can only assume Sally recounted it herself.

In her recollection of that night thirty years later, we glimpse the gold digger scheming to break through. Rand had found out about the Streets of Paris concession and saw herself as the Isadora Duncan of Paris with her ostrich feathers. She was not far off. Carmen Miranda and Esther Williams would personify sex with their bare midriffs in the movies beginning in the 1930s and lasting all the way through the 1950s. Women as objects of sex had arrived, and the world's fair could catapult Sally back into Hollywood. On a local level, the fan dance was an obvious fit for the Midway, where freaks and sex and hot dogs all mingled together.

So on a particularly hot, sticky night at The Paramount, she hatched her plan. The fair was less than two years away when she sat down on a black leather stool at the end of the bar and ordered a ginger ale.

Big Ed smiled. "Sally, I'll buy a real drink. We got the good stuff today."

"I'm not ready for that right now, Ed. I need all my faculties and a sympathetic ear, please."

"What's troubling you honey?"

"It's the goddamned world's fair commissioners! These idiots won't even let me talk to them. I've tried every avenue I can think of to get into see them. I've used up every friend and connection I've got in Chicago, but they refuse to see me. Hell! Lady Godiva couldn't even get into see those bluenoses."

"Who?"

Sally eyes widened, and she pounded her fist on the bar excitedly.

"That's it, Ed! Lady Godiva!"

Big Ed looked at her.

"Sally, you haven't had some of our bad scotch, have you?"

Sally clutched his hand.

"No, Ed. I've just come up with an idea. One that will make those SOBs sit up and take notice. Will you help me? It's something that I know will work!"

"You know I will, Sal."[5]

And so the die was cast. Hackneyed dialogue aside, these lines contain some markers of veracity. Sally was from a small town and viewed urban sophisticates as a bunch of "bluenoses." This would accord with Berkeley's girls, who spoke in slang and lacked the refined, patrician accents of the upper classes. Sally was as much an outsider as the *Gold Diggers* girls as she tried to get in to see someone who would give her a chance. The commission she talked about would have been the one set up by Rufus Dawes, but Lenox Lohr had already departmentalized the fair, with a very clear, detailed application process for employment. Sally would have been washed out early on. Your vocation? Fan dancer. No need.

In a way, she was right. The traditional approach would not gain her access. She would literally have to break open the fair and make the organizers recognize her value. Eddie and Sally's scheming in the bar was essential to her success because they had to create the need for a woman who would dance naked behind feathers. Like Al Capone, Sally was self-made and would continue reinventing herself to survive and thrive. The country was still a nation of entrepreneurs who knew their best shot was to make things up as they went along. Ironically, the first corporate fair of America would change all that.

Corporations had started out as mercantile endeavors to further the common good. The biggest example was government sponsorship of the railroads: laying track across the country helped settle it. But after the Civil War the mercantile aspect of corporations in American lost out to the profit motive. Corporations' interests diverged from those of the nation, giving rise to trusts with allegiance to Wall Street, not the people. Antagonism between government and big business became a permanent dividing line in American politics. The 1933 World's Fair was purely a corporate affair, created and sponsored to sell goods. The concept of a vehicle to push consumer products was even more important during the Great Depression and further veered from the fair of 1893.

Sally Rand was a child of the early century, when individual initiative could change lives and destinies. Ironically, this gold digger would be the biggest financial draw at the fair, yielding her fame but not fortune. At the end of her life, Sally's papers would contain the sad legal decrees of multiple divorces and bankruptcies, with letters from hotels all over the country. Busby Berkeley's movie didn't show what happened to the gold diggers after they found fame and married the men of their dreams.

Chapter Twenty-Four

Meeting Al Capone

IN 1931 WARNER BROTHERS RELEASED *PUBLIC ENEMY NUMBER ONE*, A rags-to-riches gangster story starring James Cagney. Cagney played a new character in American film. The antihero had arrived, along with Humphrey Bogart and Edward G. Robinson, and mirrored Americans' conflicted feelings about their government during the Great Depression. Criminals with money were not necessarily bad. Al Capone fit this character perfectly. Cagney even dressed like Capone, with flashy suits and a beautiful Jean Harlow on his arm. Audiences watched Cagney fight his way up, showing compassion for the downtrodden along the way. Only once he had reached the top did he stray and the inexorable forces of law and order take him down.

Audiences came out of darkened theaters in 1931 not entirely sure which was the bad guy: James Cagney or the government. All through the film, they had secretly rooted for him, with his larger-than-life personality and his tough-guy swagger. He broke all the rules and even hit a woman in the face, but the world was upside-down, and no one was sure who would come out on top. Capone could have been dropped into the movie and played the part without acting at all. And if he thought the audience was rooting for him, he would have been right.

Colonel Robert Isham Randolph did not see the movie. He was driving to see a real gangster with a .45-caliber pistol on the seat beside him. It was a cold February night in 1931. He parked outside the Lexington Hotel, walked across a thin crust of snow, went in a back door, and stepped onto a freight elevator. A suited man pulled the iron grill shut and eyed him closely as they ascended. Randolph felt the weight of the pistol inside his coat and was surprised no one had searched him. Did it occur to him that he could solve Chicago's problem with one bullet? Of course, he knew he would never leave alive if he shot Al Capone.

The elevator stopped, and the silent gangster led him through a series of doors, past another man in a suit. He finally entered a suite where Al Capone was sitting behind a desk bigger than Randolph's at the Chamber of Commerce. Capone stood, and the two shook hands.

"Hell, Colonel, I'd know you anywhere—you look just like your pictures."

"Hell, Al, I'd never have recognized you—you are much bigger than you appear in your photographs."[1]

With his boyish smile and high forehead, the tall, thin Randolph might have seemed younger than his forty-six years to the heavyset Capone. He gave up his coat and handed Capone the pistol he had brought. Randolph then used the phone in another room to call his wife and tell her he was fine. When he returned, Capone served him a beer and leaned back in his chair.

"Colonel, what are you trying to do to me?"

Randolph sipped the flat beer.

"Put you out of business," he replied.

Capone stared at him.

"Why do want to do that?"

"We want to clean up Chicago, put a stop to these killings and gang rule here."

Capone shook his head.

"Colonel, I don't understand you. You knock over my breweries, bust up my booze rackets, raid my gambling houses, and tap my telephone wires, but yet you're not a reformer, not a dry. Just what are you after?"

Randolph held up the beer and smiled. Capone leaned in.

"Colonel, you're putting me out of business. Even with the beer selling at $55 a barrel, we didn't make a nickel last week. You know what will happen if you put me out of business? I have 185 men on my personal payroll, and I pay them from 300 to 400 a week. They were all ex-convicts and ex-gunmen, but now they are respectable businessmen, just as respectable as the people who buy my stuff and gamble in my places. . . . If you put me out of business, I'll turn every one of those 185 respectable ex-convicts loose on Chicago."

Randolph put down his beer.

"Well, Al, to speak frankly, we are determined to put you out of business. We are burned up about the reputation you have given Chicago."

Capone leaned back and frowned.

"Say, Colonel, I'm burned up about that, too. Chicago's bad reputation is bad for my business. It keeps the tourists out of town. I'll tell you what I'll do; if the Secret Six will lay off my beer, booze, and gambling rackets, I'll police this town for you—I'll clean it up so there won't be a stickup or a murder in Cook County. I'll give you my hand on it."

Randolph shook his head.

"Can't do it, Al."

Randolph finished another glass of beer and stood up. Capone looked up.

"Say, Colonel, what do you think about the mayoral election? Should I come out for Anton Cermak or ride along with the Republicans and 'Big Bill' Thompson?"

"I think you'd better stick with Bill."

The colonel put on his coat and hat, and Capone handed him his pistol.

"So even respectable people carry these things?"

They shook.

"No hard feelings?"

"No hard feelings," said Randolph.[2]

The preceding is a Hollywood scene but probably close to the truth. Capone did want to make a deal because he was losing money. The Secret Six had studied his operation and, like any business, were exploiting the weakness of a competitor. The minute Randolph left Capone's office, he knew how important it was to oust Bill Thompson as mayor. Frank Loesch, president of the Chicago Crime Commission, had dubbed Capone public enemy number one the year before, and the noose was slowly tightening. Elliot Ness continued attacking Capone's breweries, while Randolph became a silent partner with the US Treasury Department. Elmer Irey headed its intelligence unit, with Frank Wilson and Pat O'Rourke running the investigation in Chicago. "With Secret Six money, O'Rourke purchased gaudy clothes like the gangsters wore: a white hat with a snap brim, several purple shirts, and checked suits. To infiltrate the Capone gang, O'Rourke spent more Secret Six money to rent a room at the Lexington Hotel. After signing the register 'Michael Lepito,' O'Rourke loitered. He sat reading newspapers or losing Secret Six money to Capone's henchmen."[3]

As early as 1930, Frank Wilson reported to Irey, "I know where Al gets his money, but it'll take a little proving. I can prove where Nitti gets his and how much. The same goes for Guzik. I think we should get them first and then go for Al."[4] It was a tried-and-true strategy of getting one gangster to turn against another when confronted with lengthy prison time. Frank Nitti had erred in endorsing a check that Wilson knew was from a Cicero casino. A grand jury indicted him for tax evasion on income spread over 1925, 1926, and 1927, totaling $742,887. Nitti disappeared, but there was still Jake Guzik.

Guzik had also signed some checks and was getting money from gambling houses. Agents used handwriting analysis to determine that bookkeeper Fred Ries had been depositing and withdrawing the money and giving it to Guzik. Frank Wilson went down to St. Louis and met Ries, who said he wouldn't talk. Wilson had him thrown into a roach-infested jail cell in Danville, Illinois, for four days. Ries apparently hated bugs and eventually agreed to testify against Guzik, Nitti, and Capone.

At trial, Ries fingered Guzik for receiving more than $1 million over three years. The judge sentenced him to fifteen years, and now Randolph had a witness who could testify against Capone. The problem was that there was no Witness Protection Program. If they put Ries in jail, he wouldn't testify. If they released him, he would end up dead. The Secret Six gave $10,000 to the Treasury Department to put Ries on a steamer to South America, where he stayed for ninety days as the first witness in American history to go into protection.

The Secret Six then assisted in finding Frank Nitti. They hired a private investigator to pay a member of the outfit $1,000 for information. Nitti was hiding in a bungalow in Berwyn, Illinois, just west of the city. "Secret Six detectives rented houses on two sides of the bungalow and watched for signs of Nitti. Nitti neglected to draw the shades when he went into the kitchen for a cold bottle of beer."[5] The detectives arrested him. Nitti pleaded guilty to tax evasion on income of $153,000 and was sentenced to eighteen months in Leavenworth.

Meanwhile, agent Pat O'Rourke had been leading the gangster life on Secret Six money and even traveled with Capone's men to his estate on Palm Island. O'Rourke took note of Capone's sixty-foot yacht and the gambling house he ran on the island. The Secret Six gangster also ascertained that Capone was spending $4,000 a week on beer and high-end liquors smuggled from the Bahamas. O'Rourke backed this up with evidence of Capone's spending in department stores in Chicago. A case could be made that Al Capone made and spent money, but where was it? How did he receive it? There seemed to be no way to tie the money to the man responsible for the whole organization. Then Al Capone's lawyer stepped in.

CHAPTER TWENTY-FIVE

Water, Electric, and the Sky Ride

CHICAGO HAD A PROBLEM: EVERYONE KEPT GETTING CHOLERA FROM drinking the water in Lake Michigan. The Chicago River spewed sewage in a long, brown line all along the lakefront, where intakes took the water back in to the city. Starting in 1892, an ambitious project undertook to put water cribs four miles out from the lake, with tunnels bored two hundred feet under the lake bed. Men died from the bends and from cave-ins when lake water found its way into the tunnels. But the cribs were finally completed, and cholera vanished from the city after the Chicago River was reversed in 1900.

Lenox Lohr had a problem too as he sat in his corrugated shack. The Rainbow City required 2,843 toilets and thirty drinking fountains. Lohr calculated that each person on the fairgrounds, through use of the toilets and water fountains, would use twenty gallons daily. Adding in landscape watering and cleaning raised the figure to a whopping 2.35 million gallons a day. This did not include the 1.75 million gallons for miscellaneous uses or the exhibits' combined use of 4.3 million gallons, and the fire department needed about 5,000 gallons per minute, or 26 million gallons a day, should a fire break out. Moving sewage out of the fairgrounds would take another 18 million gallons. Leakage ran about a half million gallons a day.

Lohr needed a lot of water, and the best solution he could come up with was to tap those underground tunnels and unleash Lake Michigan. The city council passed an ordinance authorizing the fair to use the water from the cribs four miles out. Lohr described the system in his book years later: "The water pumping station was located at 11th Street and Park Row, adjacent to the Illinois Central Railroad, and about a half mile from the Fair grounds. Three motor-driven centrifugal pump units, each with a capacity of 10,000,000 gallons per day, were chosen as the size and type of pumps best suited for use."[1]

Lohr had his water, but now he needed to light the fairgrounds, and that would require massive amounts of electricity. *A Century of Progress* would use lights in a way no other fair or city ever had. More than eight miles of gaseous tubing would illuminate the buildings. In the Hall of Science alone, over "1200 feet of red neon tubing,"[2] combined with 4,760 feet of gaseous tubing, would light up the exterior. The 1933 World's Fair would be the first to use new lighting techniques employing "neon, krypton, helium, and mercury vapor tubes. . . . [S]pecial-effect lighting at the fair, undertaken jointly by General Electric and Westinghouse Electric and Manufacturing Company, included color-shadow effects, color transparencies, electrical fireworks, electrical cascades, luminescent and iridescent features, and a scintillator that projected multiple arc searchlights."[3] Needless to say, *A Century of Progress* would use a lot of power, and Lohr had to figure on maximum consumption of twelve to fifteen hours a day, seven days a week, "with a reliability of service equal to that provided for a municipal distribution system."[4] In other words, he had to power a small city.

Lohr went to the source and approached Commonwealth Edison, which supplied power to Chicago. He later wrote, "It early became evident that instead of installing a power station, it would be more practical to purchase electrical energy. . . . [C]urrent was fed at twelve thousand volts from the company's feeder station at Soldier Field and four thousand volts from the station at 31st Street."[5] *A Century of Progress* required the same amount of power as a small town in Wisconsin. Workers electrocuted themselves by cutting into 4,000-volt lines with axes and saws. A separate emergency system was installed in case of power failure on the main line.

The real test would take place on the opening night. Only then would Lohr know if he had enough power. Now that he had water and electricity, there remained one thorn that no one seemed able to extract:

What exhibit or ride would equal the 1893 exposition's Ferris wheel? Each fair needed a representative esoteric feature that would stand out in visitors' minds. The 1889 Paris fair had the Eiffel Tower, the Columbian Exposition had the Ferris wheel, and the 1933 fair was looking for something comparable. There was no money, and time was of the essence, with less than two years until the opening. Shades of Daniel Burnham Sr.'s plight in trying to find the perfect main event during the fair of 1893 haunted Lohr and the world's fair committee. Where was George Ferris when you needed him?

CHAPTER TWENTY-SIX

One Hundred Thousand

FRANK WILSON SAT IN HIS OFFICE IN THE SOUTH LOOP AND LISTENED to the traffic outside his open window. The shaded desk lamp cut the light off beneath his eyes and made the creases even darker. After trying to catch Al Capone for two years, he had come up with nothing. Capone had done more time for carrying a gun in Philadelphia than he had served for anything the government could put together. Wilson leaned back and stared at his thumbed files smudged with fountain pen ink. He simply had no way to prove income for a man who was making $100 million a year.

Chicago had buckled under the pressure of the Great Depression, and soup lines lined the streets in the South Loop. Even now Wilson could hear the steam engines and the rerouted freight trains bringing heavy machinery to the lakefront for the 1933 World's Fair. It was an even bet that it would never come off. Banks were closing every day, and unemployment was riding up to a quarter of the population. "Who the hell would go to a world's fair?" he muttered under his breath.

Wilson lit a cigarette, rubbed the back of his neck, and slipped his fingers under his glasses. His eyes felt swollen from staring at figures for so long. Washington was running out of patience. Attorney General William Mitchell was sending William J. Froelick to take over the investigation of Capone in Chicago. That had sent his boss, George Johnson, into a rage, but you couldn't blame them. No smoking gun—or any kind of gun—had turned up that would allow them to put Capone away. Thank God for the Secret Six and Elliot Ness, who were at least hitting Capone where it hurt.

Wilson put his cigarette in the ashtray and stood to put the files away. He pulled the file drawer open but accidentally bumped it with his hip, and it slammed shut. He didn't have the key, as the file drawer had been open when he arrived. Wilson breathed wearily. He couldn't just leave the files on his desk. He opened the door to a musty storeroom and pulled the cord on the overhead light. He found a dust-coated file cabinet and opened the drawer. Aged envelopes lay in the bottom. Wilson pulled one out and felt the heft of a book.

The package was wrapped like a Christmas present, with string tied around the four sides. Wilson carried it back to his desk, took out his scissors, and clipped the string. He pulled off the brown paper, and three dirty ledgers lay on his desk. Wilson opened the first and began reading. The dates jumped out at him: 1924, 1925, 1926. The ledger had been seized five years before from the Ship, formerly known as the Hawthorne Smoke Shop, one of the biggest gambling houses in Cicero. Ness probably raided the place and threw everything into a box; then someone had shoved it all into a filing cabinet.

Frank Wilson leaned back and put his wingtips up on the desk. He lit another cigarette and read through the ledgers: $500,000 had been paid out over a twenty-four-month period, with $6,537.42 going to "Town," probably payoffs to the police. "Then came four payments of $5720.22 each" to Frank, Lou, D, and JaA.[1] The figures were subtotaled at the bottom of every page. Wilson turned to the next page and stopped. Across the top of the page was written "Frank paid $17,500 for Al."[2]

It was one of those legendary moments, but by all accounts true. Treasury agent Frank Wilson was at the end of his tether after trudging the "crummy streets" of Cicero looking for clues. He did find the ledgers in the file drawer and did connect them to a Leslie Shumway as their author. After four months he located Shumway in hiding in Miami and spotted him at the Biscayne Bay Kennel Club. He tailed him home and then went back to his hotel.

The next morning, he rang Shumway's doorbell and brought him to the Federal Building in Miami. Jonathan Eig in *Get Capone* writes of the meeting:

"I'm investigating the tax liability of one Alfonse Capone," Wilson told Shumway as the men settled in.

"Oh, you're mistaken," he said finally. "I don't know Al Capone."

Wilson put a hand on Shumway's shoulder.

"I know you're in a helluva spot."[3]

The bald and bespectacled Frank Wilson could be as tough as any gangster. He painted a grim picture for Shumway. The bookkeeper could either testify or Wilson would have him arrested publicly, and Capone's men would surely kill him. Shumway told his wife he was going to visit a sick relative and went back to Chicago with Wilson.

Interestingly, Shumway said the outfit had avoided paying out money directly to Capone not because they were concealing an income trail but because he was known to bet crazily on the horses. After Shumway testified before a secret grand jury, the Secret Six provided funds to hide him in California to keep him alive for trial. The grand jury charged Al Capone on March 13, 1931, with evading taxes in 1924.[4]

Frank Wilson had also caught another break. The year before, Capone's lawyer, Lawrence Mattingly, had taken a gamble. He had met Wilson in his office, taken a letter from his coat, and thrown it on the desk.

"This is the best we can do. Mr. Capone is willing to pay tax on these figures."[5]

The letter was a short summation of the finances of one Al Capone. In summary, Capone's lawyer Mattingly wrote, "I am of the opinion that his taxable income . . . might be fairly fixed at not to exceed $26,000."[6] This was an estimation of what he owed. Mattingly then sold his client down the river by estimating that Capone had made no more than $100,000 in each of 1928 and 1929.

Frank Wilson had filed away the letter, with its amazing admission. The government had no hard proof until Wilson opened the dusty ledgers in his office. In 1929 $100,000 was real money. The star baseball player Babe Ruth only made $70,000, while the president of International Business Machines clocked in at $60,000. Top movie producers like Irving Thalberg earned a salary of $200,000. Unlike today, there were no write-offs. A 24 percent tax rate had Al Capone owing about $50,000 for the two years.

Mattingly had hoped to strike a deal but had instead put the first nail in his client's coffin. On June 5 a federal grand jury indicated Al Capone on twenty-two counts of tax evasion for 1925–1929.[7] The unpaid taxes were now $215,030. Capone posted a $50,000 bond and was released. A third grand jury indicted the gangster for offenses on evidence amassed by Elliot Ness. The noose was growing tight, but Al Capone had yet to lose a trial in Chicago, and there was no reason to think this time would be any different. The judges and juries were still bribable, and witnesses could easily end up dead.

The Secret Six's undercover man at the Lexington Hotel, Pat O'Rourke, may have saved Frank Wilson's life when he heard from other gangsters that assassins had been brought in from New York to kill Wilson, Arthur Madden, George Johnson, and Pat Roche. The agents changed hotels accompanied by police. Wilson still worked late in his office, focusing on the upcoming trial of Al Capone. The steam engines' roar in the evening air from the lakefront construction was strangely soothing. It sounded like progress.

Chapter Twenty-Seven

The Depression Fair

THE FIRST STEEL GIRDER WAS PUT INTO PLACE FOR THE ADMINISTRA-tion Building. Fair president Rufus Dawes dedicated the moment: "We pledge ourselves to the use of this land for the enjoyment, education, and entertainment of the people of the world. The exposition will fittingly portray the history of Chicago and be worthy of the city's proud position among the cities of the world."[1] The Administration Building was erected first because the fair organization could work on the grounds and quit paying rent in Loop offices. From the first, Lenox Lohr had been cognizant that times were bad and getting worse.

Fort Dearborn went up second. It was considered an anchor, an emblem, and an early tourist attraction that could be opened immediately to generate revenue. The fair committee thought the log fort's contrast with the new skyscrapers of Chicago would perfectly symbolize one hundred years of progress since the city incorporated as a village. The fort would open on May 1, 1931, and the pre-fair admissions would cover the cost of its construction.

The third structure Lohr began, sinking pilings into the shifting sands along Lake Michigan, was the Travel and Transport Building. This would house locomotives and ships under a cantilevered "floating" roof. Its placement two miles away from the nearest structure had Lohr and Daniel Burnham Jr. nervous. The question was simple: What would fill the intervening space in the fairgrounds? The answer was people, but it was a gamble that people would come at all in 1933.

The final building erected with cash from the bonds was the Hall of Science. These initial four buildings were Lohr's stake in the side of the mountain, and if there was to be a fair, then they had to be built with the cash on hand and on time. During the Great Depression, nothing was certain.

The clay model of the fair created to follow the commission's ground plan in 1930 had already been altered substantially. The original plan placed the Hall of Science in the middle of the lagoon, but costs led Paul Cret to relocate it on the shore, and the miniature clay building was moved over. The second change was abandonment of Ralph Walker's Tower of Water and Light at the south end of the lagoon. Sketched as a lofty structure with water cascading down its three surfaces, it would have been an impressive edifice, a memorable fixture of the fair rivaling the Eiffel Tower in size and beauty. But it entailed technical uncertainties, and there was no money to pay for its high cost. The Sky Ride that took its place became the dominant feature of the fair and provided the thrill of a unique structure coupled with an experience. It wasn't the Tower of Water and Light, but it was close and, most important, cheaper.

Lenox Lohr was building a fair during the worst times in the history of the United States, if not the world. A drought had added to the nation's woes, and industrial production had slowed by 25 percent in 1931. The market had stayed down after the crash, and any hope of a rebound was gone. More than one thousand banks had failed, and men with good jobs and homes were now on the streets. The fabric of the middle class was unraveling quickly. Producer and director Herman Shumlin described a New York scene for Studs Terkel's *Hard Times: An Oral History of the Great Depression*: "Two or three blocks along Times Square, you'd see these men, silent, shuffling along in line. Getting this handout of coffee and doughnuts, dealt out from great trucks, Hearst's New York Evening Journal, in large letters, painted on the sides. Shabby clothes, but you could see they had been pretty good clothes. Their faces, I'd stand and watch their faces and I'd see that flat, opaque, expressionless look which spelled for me human disaster."[2]

In Chicago 120,000 people were out of work, and there were no relief programs. Businessmen asked Chicagoans to donate a day's pay every month and for the rich to donate more. A $5 million fund was set up for food, coal, and jobs. Churches ran soup kitchens, but they were small and ineffectual. Except for one thriving soup kitchen at 935 South State, which was feeding 2,200 men three times a day at a cost of $300 a day. "Lines snaked from State Street to Roosevelt Road, almost two blocks away. No questions were asked; anyone who wanted food got it."[3] Women in aprons served men at tables of eight. Soup and coffee and doughnuts were available around the clock, and the word was Al Capone was responsible. A kitchen worker told a reporter, "Nobody else was doing it and Mr. Capone couldn't stand it seeing so many poor fellows dying of starvation. Not heart failure mind you . . . but starvation."[4] It's hard to know for sure, but all signs point to Al Capone benevolently feeding the down and out of Chicago.

So while the biggest gangster in Chicago was tending to the city's poor, the Dawes brothers, Lenox Lohr, Raymond Hood, Daniel Burnham Jr., and Paul Cret were trying to build a world's fair along the lakefront. Lohr was the man on the spot, directing construction and explaining to contractors why he had no funds to pay them. The water system—including water for the fire hydrants on the grounds—was about to be installed when he learned that $200,000, funds considered certain, had suddenly vanished. The plans called for piping circling the fairgrounds, which was standard construction practice. The bids were in hand, and the contractors had been hired. Then the date for redeeming the gold notes came and went.

Lohr later wrote about the innovations devised on the spot when the funds dried up: "The laying of the pipe had to begin, but there was no cash on hand to pay for it. . . . [A] solution was found. Over the protests of the engineering department, the loop system was scrapped and a single line ordered and put in which could be paid for with the funds on hand."[5] Then, to satisfy the requirement for water to fight fires, Lohr had ramps built close to the shore so that fire engines could back up, drop their hoses, and suck in Lake Michigan water. Lohr saved $100,000 with such shortcuts, proving once again that necessity is the mother of invention.

But even during construction of the four initial buildings, the fair ran out of cash. "By the summer of 1932 there still remained unsold

3,000,000, worth of the original issue of gold notes."[6] The Depression had wiped out private fortunes along with middle-class savings, and no one could buy anything. With the gold notes sitting in a vault and corporations sitting on materials, their labor forces already on payroll, a deal was struck: the gold notes would serve as currency to pay for the fair. This was bartering on a vast scale and highly risky for the contractors and service providers. If the fair went bust, the gold notes would be worthless, and the way the economy was heading, this was a very real possibility. But the times dictated the means, and with no new construction jobs on the horizon, the 1933 World's Fair was the only gig in town. The contractors accepted $2,581,400 in gold notes to construct the fair.

Then, in a show of faith, fair employees accepted the securities as part of their salaries, many of them as much as half. These bonds were no good until redeemed, and people had to eat, but $309,500 in gold notes was used for payroll. In a sense, the people, the city, and even the country were all in the same boat, and the world's fair was beginning to look like pushback against the unrelenting bad times. When Lohr and company ran out of gold notes, the contractors offered to work on credit. Basically the fair was being constructed on the promise of payment and nothing else: $1.8 million in work was performed with no collateral at all. If the fair wasn't successful, then countless contractors and service providers would be wiped out.

Under these circumstances, Lohr altered the clay model again, slashing $1 million off the drawing boards by eliminating "more trees and landscaping, more elaborate illumination, more decorative items such as fountains, statuary groups and incidental buildings."[7] The contractors were more than willing to extend another $1 million in credit, but, like a blackjack player who has upped his bet to his limit, Lohr knew eventually these companies would have to be paid back.

The rest of the buildings would be built with money from corporate exhibitors and subject to Lohr's "necessity policy."[8] Structures that had to go up before the gates opened would be built first. Next would come those buildings that would generate revenues above their costs. Then they would erect structures with aesthetic value, that added something pleasing to the eye to the overall fair.

When creation of a chain of islands in the lagoons was proposed, the *Chicago Tribune* caught wind of it. A farmer wrote in to offer to sell an island to the organizers: "I see in the papers that you are going to build a lot of islands. Well I have a lake on my farm, and in the middle of it there is an island about two acres in size which I would be glad to sell you cheaply."[9] No islands were built in the lagoons. Nor would there be moving sidewalks or a monorail system to assist people in moving about. Fairgoers would simply have to walk.

The buildings under construction ended up needing protection from the elements during the winter, and aluminum paint was used as a sealer for the gypsum board and plywood. Workers were advised to apply thick coats, for there might not be money for the final colors. The Rainbow City would look more like a fleet of grey battleships a year before the fair opened.

Chapter Twenty-Eight

Nymphs

THE TAXI LET SALLY RAND OUT NEXT TO THE FENCE. SHE STOOD OUT-side the construction and watched a line of freight cars making their way toward the lake. Booming and whistling, the steam shovels moved around like giant monsters. Men swung around on the skeleton buildings like acrobats, and two unfinished towers, one of them across the lagoon, reached to the sky. She could smell the lake and the dry scent of earth exposed by the shovels. It looked like they were building a city.

She walked lightly toward the galvanized fence and saw a young man in a uniform. He was staring at her. Sally waved, and he raised his hand uncertainly. One of the new guards, he looked all of thirteen. The world's fair had hired thousands already, but it had not hired her. She walked up to the fence and clutched the cold steel. The guard walked quickly toward her. He had pimples.

"Can I help you, ma'am?"

"No. Just looking, kid."

He stared at her uncertainly.

"The employment office is closed."

"Yeah, I know."

She had gone to the office in the Loop and filled out the forms. Nothing. There was no job for her at the 1933 World's Fair. She knew vaguely about the Midway and the Streets of Paris. A couple of girls had gotten hired to serve food and drinks, but no one knew who would hire a woman who danced naked except for some body paint and feathers.

There was no application for that position. But she had to be part of the fair, no two ways about it. She could not stay at The Paramount forever, with the creepy gangsters and the watered-down booze.

Sally really wanted to get back to Hollywood—to the lights. She stared at the thin necklace of light bulbs that had just winked on over the fairgrounds. Everything was wire and pipes and holes in the ground and guys hanging off girders in the air, but it felt like the future. All these railroad cars dumping off all this material for this vision that spoke to her: the world's fair didn't give a damn about the Great Depression, and neither did she.

She read the Chicago papers that derided the fair as folly. They said Chicago was nuts to put on such an event when the city was bankrupt and Al Capone was running soup kitchens because the city couldn't afford to. People said organizers should just stop, admit the fair was a mistake, and not throw good money after bad. But the world's fair was going on, and so was Sally Rand.

She didn't stop when Cecil B. DeMille told her that her career was over because of her lisp. She didn't fold up her tent when she lost jobs with the circus, vaudeville, or nightclubs, or even when she was sleeping in alleys. She was going to be a star. It was 1931, and this century was going to be big. She could feel it in her bones, even though the times were bad and getting worse. Even while the country stumbled, it felt more to her like a sleeping giant lurching. Something big was on the horizon. She had seen it in Hollywood. They were just warming up out there. Movies would take over the world the way radio had.

Sally felt her eyes water in the cold wind. Nothing was going to stop this fair. Nothing. It would show the world what America was capable of. It was the reason she had left home. It was the reason she had gone to Hollywood. She was twenty-seven, and the century was thirty-one years old. The men building this fair knew it too. They all knew it represented a vision of what American would become.

Sally noticed that the young man in the uniform had left. He probably had to get home for a nice hot meal. It was nice to have someone cook for you. Sally turned and started back to the city. The lights were on in the tall buildings, and she could hear the traffic now. She felt like she was leaving another world, something like a city over a rainbow. She watched the buses on Michigan Avenue and the overhead L train rattle over the tracks, sparks flashing blue against the encroaching darkness. She had to go on tonight, but she would be back. One way or another, Sally Rand would be back.

CHAPTER TWENTY-NINE

Springtime in Chicago

THE REFLECTIVE COMPONENT OF AMERICAN CULTURE HAD KICKED IN by the early 1930s. Al Capone was a cultural phenomenon; at the same time, he was a deadly killer. We are used to this now, but in the late 1920s and early 1930s, the celebrity engendered by the mass media was something new. At the very time that the IRS, Elliot Ness, and the Secret Six were targeting Al Capone, Hollywood was developing a cottage industry based on the character the United States was trying to extinguish.

Little Caesar, starring Edward G. Robinson as a cruel little mobster named Rico Bandello, was a Robin Hood story of stealing from the rich and giving to the poor. "The first underworld movie of the talking era, *Little Caesar* set the tone for future gangster films."[1] Bandello is not all bad; he's basically a businessman—like Al Capone. Killing is a last resort, and a man has to do what a man has to do. Bandello dresses impeccably, is streetwise, and, of course, rose from nothing. Hollywood had capitalized on the scent that Sally Rand and others had detected in the beginning of the American century. Simply put, anyone could make it if they were willing to do whatever it took.

The Secret Six was willing to do what was needed, and the tide had turned. The famous scene in the beginning of *The Untouchables*, when Kevin Costner rides in a truck that bashes into a warehouse full of Prohibition booze, is accurate. Elliot Ness had been running around doing the low-level grunt work of raiding speakeasies and gambling joints. But on the morning of March 25 he drove a truck through the doors of a brewery and found 23,000 gallons of beer in fourteen vats.

Photographers were on hand. The axes tore into the vats, and the beer poured out in a thick river of foam that filled the building and then rolled out the doors. The men look like they are standing in a sudsy river in the newspaper photos. Ness continued his beer blitz, and Al Capone's operation began to bleed badly. The Secret Six had determined that attacking Capone's means of production was the best way to cripple his empire.

But Capone now had a trial coming up, and it was spring in Chicago. The smoking, frozen lake looked less menacing to the workmen who had fought through the winter and continued work on the buildings for the world's fair. The St. Patrick's Day Parade marched down Michigan Avenue, and people stared at the green of the Chicago River, wondering if the municipality really colored it. The parks began to look more like places for visitors than frozen wastelands, and those who could thanked God they still had a home. Those in the bread lines and soup kitchens wondered if the economy might come back, like the breezes from the south.

Al Capone wanted to go down to Florida, but his lawyers had to work a deal out with the government on the tax-evasion charges. In an ominous sign for Capone, voters tossed out Bill Thompson and elected Anton J. Cermak on a promise to clean up Chicago. The city went wild with a ticker tape parade; it felt to some like a war had ended. The spring and Cermak's election suggested that there might be a glimmer of light at the end of the long, dark tunnel that had been Chicago for the last eleven years. Three thousand of Thompson's patronage employees were shown the door.

George Johnson, head of the Chicago investigative team, felt he might finally be cornering that rat Al Capone. Ness continued busting up Capone's drinking establishments and getting press, and Frank Wilson had been in his office diagraming the Capone organization's cash flow, while the Secret Six stood by with ready funds. Even if prosecutors couldn't nail down Capone's exact income, a jury would see how much he spent and make the leap that the money had to come from somewhere.

Then Al Capone turned the tables. Attorney Michael Ahern came by and told Johnson that Capone knew all about the sealed indictment for tax evasion and would contest a trial in Chicago. In that moment

Capone grabbed the initiative, and Ahern put Johnson against the ropes by forcing him to begin negotiations. It was a little like a fighter coming out early and going into his opponent's locker room while he was getting ready. Ahern told Johnson that Capone would plead guilty if they could work out a reasonable sentence.

George Johnson had no choice but to tell the gangster's lawyer that he would let his bosses in Washington know he had been offered a plea deal. The meeting ended. Johnson sighed and stared out the window open to the spring breeze. He saw a marquee over the Chicago Theatre. *Little Caesar* was playing. He paused, listening to the staccato tap of a pneumatic jackhammer slamming rivets into a building by the lake. It sounded like a machine gun.

CHAPTER THIRTY

The Sky Ride

MACIEJ KALETA DECIDED TO GO THE WORLD'S FAIR ON JULY 13, 1934. President Franklin Roosevelt had requested that the fair stay open for an extra year to keep people spending money. He saw it as a beacon of light in very dark times. Maciej had a small shoe store in East Chicago, with a wife and two children aged seven and thirteen. He even told his neighbors he was going to *A Century of Progress* to wander the grounds alone.

After he paid for his fifty-cent ticket, he headed over to the Sky Ride. Its towers were 625 feet tall and eclipsed Chicago's skyscrapers. Rocket cars shot back and forth on a cable over the lagoon. A person could take an elevator all the way to the top for an incredible view of the lake and the city in the distance. People in 1933 and 1934 had never been that high. Practically no one had ridden in an airplane, making dirigibles a major draw at the fair. A person who went down a couple flights of stairs could board one of the rocket cars. Someone who went down just one floor could enter an enclosed observation space.

Maciej took the elevator all the way to the top and roamed around, taking in the view. Then he went down one flight of stairs and looked around. The floor was empty. Maciej calmly opened a window, climbed out, and jumped. He plunged 618 feet, clipping a support cable on his way down and severing his leg. His body was deflected inward and crashed into the top of the south loading platform, where people waited to go up to the top.

Only one man said he saw Maciej fall, but he didn't know more than that. No one saw him jump. His glasses were retrieved, undamaged, near his body. A note, written in Polish and found inside his jacket, read, "My dear wife and children, I am sorry to leave you, but I am forced to go."[1]

The structure on which Maciej Kaleta ended his life was initially called the gondola project. It had been scrapped for cost and feasibility. The thought of building two giant towers on opposite sides of the lagoon and shuttling cars back and forth just seemed too fantastic in the budget-tightening era of the Great Depression—not to mention a technical nightmare. The proposed Sky Ride would take over five months to plan and eight months to construct and cost over $2 million in Depression-era dollars. The two 625-foot towers were named Amos and Andy after a minstrel radio show. This was after the Heinz Company proposed a thousand-foot pickle as the attraction that would rival the Ferris wheel of 1893. Montgomery Ward had gotten into the act with the Tower of Water and Light, then decided not to pay for it, and the Architectural Commission turned back once again to the crazy gondola project.

Enter two young architects, Nathaniel Owings and Louis Skidmore, ages thirty and thirty-six. The original design was the baby of engineer William L. Hamilton, but Owings and Skidmore began to solve its technical problems. While the Ferris wheel was the vision of one man, the Sky Ride, like the fair itself, would be the product of a consortium of people and companies. Owings acquired foundations, steel, cables, elevators, glass, concrete, paint, and light fixtures from large corporations; then he convinced other suppliers of the value of demonstrating their products in action. The Sky Ride's backers would include the Valley Structural Steel Company, Inland Steel Company, Great Lakes Dredge and Dock Company, and John A. Roebling Sons Company. The Goodyear Zeppelin Corporation would build the "streamlined rocket-shaped aluminum and glass double-decked sightseeing cars, lightweight and reminiscent of airship design. The Otis Elevator Company designed, built, and maintained the eight automatic, signal-controlled, high-speed elevators that transported fairgoers to the rocket car stations or beyond to the observation platforms high above the fairgrounds."[2]

It was up to Lenox Lohr to get the Sky Ride built. The two towers were the result of the architectural committee's team approach to the fair, with many hands in on the design and planning. Now it fell to one man to supervise the different companies involved in the construction. Lohr's description twenty years later probably best summarizes what actually went into the Sky Ride:

The towers were connected by a cable suspension span which supported the track cables on which traveled ten rocket-shaped cars at a height of 219 feet. The towers were backstayed to great counterweights located 600 feet in the rear of each tower. These counterweights were designed to maintain constant tension on the cable structure during its various moments in expansion and contraction. Each tower was equipped with four elevators, two going to the observatory floor at the 600-foot level, and two to the car platform at the 219-foot level. The observatory consisted of a two-story structure, one entirely closed, with ample glass sections to allow easy visibility over the surrounding country, and the other an open observatory enclosed with steel netting.[3]

The rocket cars traveled at five hundred feet per minute and weren't exactly rockets. Steam puffed out of the back, and lights followed the cars to emulate a comet's trail. Technically the towers, the cables, and the cars pushed the limits of safety. Transporter bridges were used more in Europe than the United States.

Double-decked rocket cars, twelve in number, ran suspended from the four-cable "track" between the two towers eighteen hundred and fifty feet apart. The car seats were arranged lengthwise, so that passengers faced outwards for a better view of the panorama below them. The cars were suspended from their aerial track by four-wheel trucks, each wheel running over a separate cable to insure absolute safety. The cableway had a breaking strength of 220,000 pounds per square inch of cross section, and only one span, that of the George Washington Bridge across the Hudson River just above New York City, exceeded it in length. The steel for the towers weighed 2,000,000 pounds, and over one hundred miles of stout strands of steel were used in cables for the aerial track and the 600-foot-long backstays.[4]

The cars moved along on their own power until "an automatic gripper engaged the traction rope which furnished the power for the car until it reached the other side."[5]

For people in 1933, this was the closest they would come to an airplane ride. "Suspended two hundred feet above the lagoon with thirty-five other adventurers, the sightseer traveled at six miles an hour on the world's longest cable track. From there the visitor beheld a breathtaking panorama of the fairgrounds surrounded by three states."[6] People might have thought the future held rocket cars and would have been disappointed that the internal combustion engine still dominated transportation eighty years later.

Even the stolid military engineer Lohr waxed poetic (for an engineer) when recalling the Sky Ride: "Soft green lights flooded the top of the two sky-piercing towers with their red-patterned platforms, six hundred and twenty-eight feet from the ground. Higher than any building in Chicago, the Sky Ride stretched its massive cables more than a third of a mile across the Lagoon connecting the mainland and Island and acted as a symbol of the relationships between the basic and the social sciences, the two buildings it connected . . . its highlights shining so far above and always cutting through the darkness to guide the visitor to his destination."[7]

In the first year six million passengers would encounter a view they had never seen before. Photos of workers up on the steel towers drinking a beer give a sense of the impossible heights men would work from. Workers on boson chairs performed maintenance on the towers and the cable late at night, sliding along the cable like dangling spiders. Little did these steel workers know that some, like Maciej Kaleta, would find in the grand height of the towers the freeing moment of their lives and a passage from this world to the next.

CHAPTER THIRTY-ONE

The Trial of Al Capone

SOMETIMES THINGS WENT WRONG FOR THE SECRET SIX. AN UNDER-cover man on the state's attorney's staff played both ends against the middle and ended up getting knifed over a diamond ring he tried to dispose of with fellow gang members. He went home to recover with three knife wounds in his abdomen. Robert Isham Randolph received word that the gangsters were returning to finish the job at his home that night. He wrote years later, "We planted four men in the flat and awaited the invaders who arrived on schedule; two at the back door and two at the front. They ordered the undercover man's wife to take them to her husband. The instant they were inside the house, our men emerged from their hiding places and the battle began."[1] When it was all over, two of the gangsters were dead, two had got away, and one of the Secret Six men was mortally wounded. The undercover agent in the bed was dead as well. Chicago was still too hot to hold a world's fair.

George Johnson was thinking about the violence in Chicago as he listened to the train tracks clacking. He reached Washington, DC, the next morning, hailed a cab outside Union Station, and headed for the Justice Department. Assistant Attorney General Youngquist was waiting for him. Both men were Swedes, and both were "drys" politically. Herbert Hoover had picked Youngquist to head the Justice Department's Prohibition and Taxation Division, and he wanted to get Capone badly. Impatient with the pace of building a case, he felt Johnson wasn't being aggressive enough.

So, on this warm morning the two men faced each other in their cheap suits behind a government-issued desk as Johnson painted a picture. It wasn't pretty. He thought they would lose and should plead out the case. One has to wonder why Johnson didn't have more confidence, but he had been in Chicago a while and seen how cases against the Capone syndicate dried up and died. Capone's lawyer had already won the strategic advantage of setting the government back on its heels.

"Go back to Chicago," Youngquist said after hearing him out. "Build the strongest case you can, and don't take any deals unless you talk to me."

George Johnson caught another train back to Chicago, and Capone's lawyers came calling again. The gangster lawyers were not tax attorneys. That branch of law was just getting rolling, and the thought that a citizen should hire a tax attorney to fight the government was something new. Capone's attorneys were criminal defense lawyers who excelled at cutting deals and keeping gangsters out of jail, or at least keeping sentences to a minimum. Michael Ahern and Thomas Nash threw eighteen months on the table as an opening bid. Johnson rejected the low-ball offer out of hand, but the damage was done. Capone's attorneys had once again set the floor for negotiations, and even if they went up, this ensured his sentence would be light.

Johnson went to see Judge Jim Wilkerson on the sixth floor of the Federal Building. Wilkerson was an independent man in a town where a lot of judges had been bought off. He was idiosyncratic and fiddled constantly with a large radio on his desk. His chambers reeked of the absentminded professor, scattered with law books and ashtrays holding unfinished cigars. Heavy-jowled and a bit unkempt, he did not seem like the kind of man who could take down Al Capone.

Jim Wilkerson was the son of John Wilkerson, a Union officer who had served with William Tecumseh Sherman's regiment on its march to the sea through Atlanta. It was a story Jim Wilkerson knew well and carried with him to DePauw University in Indiana. He taught school out on the plains of Nebraska before coming back to Chicago to practice law. Twenty years later he replaced Judge Kennesaw Mountain Landis, who became the commissioner of baseball.

On July 1, 1922, 400,000 railroad workers had had enough and walked off the job. President Warren Harding interceded and tried to settle the strike but failed miserably. Attorney General Harry Daugherty had appointed Wilkerson to the bench and called in his marker. Would he order an end to the strike? Judge Wilkerson shut down the strike and forced union leaders and strikers to go back to work.

But Judge Wilkerson had tired of bootlegging cases that fell apart when witnesses vanished. So when George Johnson sat down in front of him to take his temperature on a possible plea bargain with Al Capone, he was less than confident that Wilkerson would accept it. He quickly outlined his case and explained that his two witnesses, Fred Ries and Leslie Shumway, could end up dead or recant.

And the case involved a double jeopardy component. Johnson usually charged people with "the misdemeanor failure to pay and with a felony of defrauding the government." But now the felony charge on one of his prior cases was being challenged, and if that fell apart, he could lose his convictions on Frank Nitti, Ralph Capone, and Jake Guzik. The case against Al Capone wouldn't have a snowball's chance in hell then. Plus he had a statute of limitations to worry about on the evidence from 1924 and 1925.

Wilkerson had begun fiddling with his radio. Johnson proceeded to tell the judge that the case rested on a letter from Capone's lawyer, Lawrence Mattingly, which might be deemed inadmissible. Mattingly had said the numbers were just an estimate, and they were not an admission of guilt. Wilkerson quit fiddling and leaned back.

"Anything else?"

Johnson had used all his bullets. Yet the iconoclast who had taught school out on the western plains and overreached in ending a national strike didn't give George Johnson a clue as to whether he thought he had a case. Wilkerson started to fiddle with his radio again as Johnson walked out.

Chapter Thirty-Two

Color and Light

THE WORLD WAS A DRAB PLACE IN 1932. AMERICANS WERE UNDER SIEGE by a monochromatic monster pushing down on their financial lives. This monster was black, brown, grey, dirty white, pallid brick, rusted iron, grey-sheeted aluminum. The world we know, where objects bark back at us in vivid color, didn't exist. Men dressed in dark or grey suits, the occasional loud pinstripes, or the precursor to khaki: the flannel suit. Women did much the same. The 1930s were a drab decade after the colorful 1920s. People drove around in hulking cars in muted hues of black, blacker, and grey. Sinks were white; houses were white; buildings were nondescript.

Chicago was the smudged thumbprint on a soot-covered window-pane. Coal-fired furnaces and belching locomotives made sure little color found its way into the Windy City. In black-and-white pictures of the era, the city looks awful—a smoke-hazed group of edifices pushing up on the shoulder of Lake Michigan. If an artist sketched the Great Depression, then surely charcoal would be the primary medium. The men standing in the soup lines wore long, dark overcoats, black fedoras, and black shoes. This was due in part to the limits of manufacturing and technology. Dyes were unreliable and expensive, and, besides, who would wear colored clothing anyway? Or who would want to see orange, red, or yellow buildings? Only gangsters showed a flare for color. Al Capone favored bright blue and red ties, green shirts, pearly spats, and yellow-banded fedoras. The loud tie or shirt came to symbolize gangland couture. But the working man mostly operated in a world of dull compositions resembling the pencil drawings of court reporters.

The architectural committee in Chicago made a bet that people were ready for something else. If Oz was going to be re-created (L. Frank Baum's *The Wonderful Wizard of Oz* had been published in 1900; the movie was still six years in the future in 1933), then Joseph Urban was the man to do it. Born in Vienna in 1872, the architect loved to eat. He was a porcine man with a handlebar mustache waxed at the ends. He studied architecture at the Academy of Fine Arts and received his first commission at age nineteen, when he designed Abdeen Palace in Cairo. He quickly became known for his innovative use of color and immigrated to the United States in 1911.

By the time the architectural committee contacted him, Urban had designed more than fifty theater sets, including for Ziegfeld's Follies and the Metropolitan Opera. The man just loved color; even William Randolph Hearst took notice and hired Urban to work on his films starring his mistress Marion Davies. Orson Welles would parody Davies in *Citizen Kane*. In the movie Davies has no talent, but Kane (Hearst) spares no expense to push her into the galaxy of rising stars. However, even Urban's brilliant use of color could not realize the enigmatic mogul's desire to set his concubine up as a queen of Hollywood. She fell into obscurity, and Hearst made it his life's mission to destroy Orson Welles for his unflinching assault.

Urban's use of dramatic color and light to create cinematic realms to which audiences could escape was perfect for the futuristic world of the 1933 World's Fair. For *A Century of Progress* to succeed aesthetically and financially, visitors must feel they had escaped the oppression of the Depression-era landscape and been transported into a bright, effervescent, colorful world saved by science, technology, and goods. The only comparison would probably be the advent of color television. Suddenly the grainy black-and-white past receded into memory as NBC's bright peacock proclaimed the new primary-colored reality made possible by the cathode ray.

But attitudes about color were beginning to change in 1932. "Recent developments in plastics made it possible to offer a choice of colors for a wide range of products, including tumblers, poker chips and expensive jewelry. According to *Business Week*, the brightly colored bathroom fixtures and kitchen utensils that had recently come on the market were a sign of modern times."[1]

Even psychologists were beginning to sound off and said color could change the way people think. As Lisa Schrenk noted in *Building a Century of Progress*, "Maud Maple Miles had been studying and preaching the psychological effects of color for at least a decade. She attempted to educate industry on the ability of certain colors to improve factory production."[2] If workers saw a bright red wall or a brilliant blue, they might just drive those bolts a little faster. Even corporations got in on the act, purveying colored paints for the fair. The American Asphalt Paint Company proclaimed, "Color can induce happiness instead of sadness. It can produce alertness or drowsiness, comfort or discomfort, perfect vision or indistinctness. . . . Color amuses, fascinates or annoys, inspires or disheartens, excites or repels, exaggerates or undervalues."[3] In 1933 the company pooled $1 million to promote these ideas.

Traditionally architects were a grumpy breed of cats who didn't like color. Designers believed it was dishonest to cover up the natural surfaces of a building. One has to wonder if the architect has the ego of the writer who doesn't like his writing to be altered. The building should stand for itself, warts and all, as the design would speak volumes. But ornamentation was taking a backseat along with neoclassicism (see the court at the 1893 World's Fair, the White City), and something had to spice things up. As Leon Stanhope, president of the Illinois Society of Architects, wrote in 1928, color could be used "as a replacement for expensively applied ornament."[4]

The world's fair made color almost essential with the use of new materials like gypsum board and plywood. These could not be left "without a layer of paint,"[5] and the White City had been done already, so white was out. These materials required protection from the elements, but colored paint was unstable and faded as soon as it was applied. The architectural committee solved this problem by selecting a new paint created by the American Asphalt Paint Company, casein paint, whose bright hues, through a technical breakthrough, did not fade.

In an article published in *World's Fair Weekly*, Urban's assistant gave three major reasons for using colored paint on the 10.5 million square feet of wall surfaces: It would unify the different exhibition halls into a cohesive design. Color made otherwise boring designs more interesting. And it would create a festive atmosphere where, removed from the grimy, dull buildings of Chicago, visitors would "be conscious of only the joys of living." One could make a case that the Great Depression was on Urban's mind and that he saw it as a creature to obliterate with light and color.

But Urban had to supervise the application of color, and he wasn't well. He'd had surgery and did most of his work from New York. He visualized the entire fair as a huge stage, much like the setting of a theatrical production. Shepard Vogelgesang, who would later take over when Urban died, said that he had "visualized the Exposition Buildings as the background for moving crowds. He selected his pallet for the effect that would be produced by people moving before the masses of color."[6]

Urban was used to controlling his set or his production absolutely. He wanted no suggestions for colors from the architectural committee. He did not want to pollute his vision. However, he was technically an advisor, and the fair organizers had the final say on all construction matters. The ego of Joseph Urban was being pitted against those of the eight other architects, and men like Raymond Hood would not take kindly to someone spraying his building with red, blue, and orange like a child let loose during kindergarten.

Urban ultimately used "two shades of orange, two shades of blue, white, and a touch of red to create the buildings' arresting appearance. He then used a pallet of at least twenty-four brilliant colors to create contrast and variety among the fair's buildings."[7] The great colorist would have to contend with something else he hadn't encountered on movie or stage sets: a tight budget. All colors Urban created had to be compatible with the new casein paint formula, which would be sprayed on. But the industrial prerogative leaning over his shoulder did not deter the color maestro, who immediately smashed into new ground by painting on glass, which would be illuminated and constantly change hues. But this also forced him to relinquish control to the illumination experts chaired by E. W. Lloyd, vice president of Commonwealth Edison Company.

The actual painting, and thus the implementation of Urban's vision, fell to Lenox Lohr and his men, who had to contend with rain, snow, hail, ice, wind, lake gales, and soot from the city. The casein paint, while better, did break down. Lohr noted, "The dark green blue showed the worst fading the yellow tended to lighten and lose some of its orange character; one of the reds and one of the greens became somewhat transparent and would have been unsightly had there not been an undercoat of paint the same color."[8]

Joseph Urban had planned to drive around in a convertible and supervise the painting like a general lord of the arts. But he was too ill to travel and instead relied on photographs, fair contacts, and sketches to make his decisions about colors. The Rainbow City was a conception in his mind, much like Ziegfeld's Follies or the many movies he had design for. "By specifying particular hues, he was able to tie groups of buildings together in color themes. . . . [C]ool colors were favored for the north walls, neutral colors for the east and west walls, and warm colors for the south walls."[9]

Urban ultimately saw the colors he chose as the notes in a composition, and the resulting melody was the world's fair, taking place against a backdrop of the Depression and the gang warfare in the Gotham lurking behind his phantasmagoria of light and inspiration. It was Oz to the people coming to the 1933 World's Fair. As Paul Cret later remarked, "Conservative people gasp[ed] at the violent pigments covering a whole façade and then, when they left the fairgrounds, wonder[ed] why the streets of the city were so dreadfully gray and drab."[10]

Urban never made it to Chicago, despite his desire to ride around the city in his open car. If he had come, he could have passed Al Capone or another member of the outfit in the South Loop. He would have appreciated their loud ties, bright shirts, and colorful fedoras and the way color could be used to enliven or to destroy.

CHAPTER THIRTY-THREE

The Plea Bargain

THE ICEHOUSE WAS SMOLDERING BY THE TIME THE VILLAGE OF BAR-rington's firemen arrived. They sprayed down the timbers and started pulling the small building apart. One timber didn't look right. It resembled a bumpy and fat burnt log. As they sprayed it down, it steamed and sizzled like an overdone steak. When the cops arrived, the firemen pointed at the log, told them it was their problem, and left.

It would take three days, two gold crowns, and a false tooth to identify Mike Heitler, a small-time Jewish gangster who had been around a long time. His car was found in Itasca. His last-known whereabouts were the Legion Cigar Store and then a diner at the Chicago and Northwestern train station. He had been playing poker with some of Capone's men, and that was good enough for the police. They raided the Lexington Hotel and then a dance hall and then the Hawthorne Inn in Cicero. Capone was gone.

Everyone thought Heitler was an informant planning to testify against Capone, but it turned out he was just a hoodlum with a big gambling debt. Really, Al Capone should have killed Fred Ries and Leslie Shumway. But where were they? He couldn't find out anything. They had vanished. There was no cop he could bribe, no judge to buy off. Worse, there were no witnesses to kill. He would have to do what every other citizen in the American justice system did: rely on his lawyer.

George Johnson didn't wait any longer and rolled the dice. He announced the indictment of Al Capone on June 5: "Between 1924 and 1929, the government alleged Capone had earned at least $1,038,654.84."

Capone had failed to pay taxes of $215,080.48, for which the maximum penalty was "thirty-two years in jail and $80,000 in fines."[1] The gangster was arrested and posted $5,000 on a $50,000 bond. Then Elliot Ness came as close as he ever would to nabbing public enemy number one. The wiretaps and brewery busts had yielded enough evidence to indict Capone as "leader of a conspiracy to violate Prohibition laws."

That wouldn't stick, and if it did, the sentence was nominal. The only thing Johnson really had was failure of the most notorious gangster in the world—who had murdered, beaten, extorted, and stolen at will for more than a decade and terrorized a major American city—to pay his taxes. It was trifling, but it amounted to a multipronged D-day assault on Capone, the man, and his empire.

With no one to rub out, Capone sent his lawyer, Michael Ahern, back to see Johnson. The agent in charge was torn between trying to get a real conviction that would put Capone away for at least ten years or going for a quick plea bargain that would satisfy the president and the city that was holding a world's fair and wanted Capone dealt with now. A trial could drag on for years and last right up to and beyond the fair's opening.

Johnson's biggest problem—one that all lawyers wrestle with and usually settle under the basic maxim "A bird in the hand is worth two in the bush"—was that he just wasn't sure of his case. The vagaries of tax law, the statute of limitations, the chances of an appeal, and the nature of the charges themselves weakened his confidence. America had arisen out of the concept of no taxation without representation. Most Americans hated paying taxes, and prosecuting a murderous gangster for not filing his tax returns seemed absurd even to Johnson at times. At least Elliot Ness was busting down doors, arresting goons, and getting his name in the paper.

So George Johnson covered himself and talked with Washington. The word was that Herbert Hoover wanted Capone off the streets now. The city wanted him off the streets. Johnson would offer Capone's attorney two and a half years with no appeal, and Capone would start serving immediately. It was a light sentence and amounted to two years for tax evasion and six months for the biggest bootlegging operation in history. They were flipping cards at a shark, but it was all they had. Ahern listened in silence, then leaned forward and demanded two things. He wanted the deal in writing from Washington, and his client must face no incriminating questions before he was sentenced. Johnson agreed, and they shook.

On June 16, 1931, Al Capone entered the federal courtroom in downtown Chicago. Joseph Urban would have appreciated his yellow suit and could have pointed to the juxtaposition of color against the wainscoting of the courtroom and the black-and-white uniforms of the police. Color did brighten and stimulate, and the backroom was packed with people who were very excited to see this celebrity, this larger-than-life man who eclipsed everyone else.

The walrus-jowled judge Jim Wilkerson entered, took his seat, and glared down at Capone sitting quietly while the case number was called. It was a beautiful day, and sunshine poured in through the open windows. The pounding from the derricks and steam shovels along the lakefront floated on warm summer air. The buildings had broken the eastern skyline like skeletons reaching to the heavens. It was so rare for Chicago weather to be anything but subzero or stiflingly hot and humid.

"Alfonse Capone," proclaimed Assistant District Attorney Dwight Green, "you are charged with attempting to evade and defeat your income taxes for 1924. Do you plead guilty or not guilty?"

Capone rose from his chair.

"Guilty," he said quietly.

"In indictment 23,232, you are charged with attempting to defeat and evade your income taxes for the years 1925, 1926, 1927, 1928, and 1929, and with willful failure to file returns for the years 1928 and 1929. Do you plead guilty or not guilty?"

"Guilty," he murmured.

Then Assistant US Attorney Vide LaRue faced Capone.

"Indictment 23,256 charges you with conspiracy to violate the National Prohibition Act. How do you plead, guilty or not guilty?"

"Guilty," Capone answered.[2]

That was it. The biggest gangster in American history had pled guilty to not paying his taxes and selling some illegal beer, crimes millions of Americans had already committed. The *Chicago Herald Examiner* later wrote, "In those quiet few minutes . . . Chicago was throwing off the shackles of a man and an organization that has represented lawlessness, viciousness and a flout to its self-respect for ten years."[3]

Judge Wilkerson set the sentencing for June 30, and Capone left for the elevator. No one then knew that Al Capone would do two and a half years in prison for a lifetime of crime. It was laughable. Men who had punched their wives or stolen cars got longer sentences. The streets were crazy with people outside the courtroom. Everyone wanted to get a look at Al Capone. From Al Capone to the Beatles, mass media would change the way people viewed celebrities. They were the new gods on earth.

CHAPTER THIRTY-FOUR

The Temple of Womanhood

THE COURIER HANDED DORTHEA GOODRICH THE LETTER. SHE WAS about to walk into a ballroom at the Congress Hotel to open a meeting with the heads of Chicago's clubwomen to unveil plans for the Temple of Womanhood at the *Century of Progress* world's fair. She opened the envelope, read the letter, and felt her face burn; her eyes blurred. Lenox Lohr had just slammed the door shut on her project, informing her that "efforts in this regard are entirely without authority from A Century of Progress and must result only in embarrassment to yourself and others as no proposal for a concession of this nature will be considered by A Century of Progress."[1]

Dorthea Goodrich felt faint, but Dolly Ledgerwood Matters, a "disreputable"[2] woman, was furious. Amazingly, they were the same person. To trace the downfall of the Temple of Womanhood, we should go back to the four woman's world's fairs in 1925, 1926, 1927, and 1928. These were celebrations of working women, organized by women such as Helen M. Bennett. The fairs "emphasized women's persistent push into politics, business, and the sciences." Elizabeth Bass, chair of the 1927 women's fair, saw them as giving women the tools to push further into a world dominated by men.[3] The cross-pollination between the fairs and *A Century of Progress* began with Vice President Charles Dawes speaking at the 1927 fair and proclaiming that women's "greatest contribution to society are made in the home."[4]

Bully for Charles. His brother, Rufus, had married a very different sort of woman. Helen Dawes had six children, but, "as one of Chicago's most powerful society woman, she wielded considerable influence among the city's clubwomen. She had served as president of the woman's club of Evanston and board member of the General Federation of Women's Clubs, to which more than three million women belonged nationwide. During World War I she was Illinois vice chair on the Board of Food Conservation."[5]

Rufus, as president of the world's fair, was no progressive and saw women's role as supportive. Helen was powerful in her own right, but in a "woman's world," not a man's. Others, like Congresswoman Ruth Hanna McCormick, did not see women's role that way. She invited twenty-one women from the committees of woman's world's fairs to serve as leaders for the 1933 fair. After she lost her Senate bid in 1930 and moved to New Mexico, the women lost their supporter, and few stayed involved. So Rufus appointed his wife as chair of the social committee and called it a day.

General manager Lohr was not as backward as Rufus and Charles in his view of women. His mother and his wife were both working professionals, and the army engineer took a more utilitarian view: If someone could do the job, who gave a damn if that person was a man or a woman? To that end, he had hired Martha Steele McGrew, probably the second most powerful person during the construction phase of the fair.

McGrew was born into a middle-class family in Pulaski, Tennessee, and graduated in 1920 from George Washington University. The university's yearbook editor playfully memorialized her dedication and highly developed work ethic: "Whenever there is anything to be done, Martha is always on the job."[6] Lohr met her while he was resurrecting *Military Engineer* and hired her in 1922. She followed him to Chicago with his appointment as manager of the world's fair. She became as powerful as Helen Dawes, but on the other side of the fence, so to speak.

Lohr trusted her to "review expenditures, publicity, payroll, and employee relations."[7] She was his right-hand woman and worked day and night to keep track of the details of multifarious construction projects. Daniel Burnham Jr. corrected an employee who called her Lohr's secretary; she was his assistant, and in his absence "the rest of the staff was glad to get their orders from Miss McGrew."[8]

McGrew often made decisions when Lohr was not around, and this rankled some, especially the wife of the fair's president, Helen Dawes. As a clubwoman, she saw McGrew as a young upstart, a middle-class climber who didn't know her place. In a letter to McGrew, Helen criticized her for a lack of respect "toward the most important and influential woman of Chicago." Helen did not like that McGrew derived her power from Lohr and asserted it not through position but through action. Helen and the clubwomen thought a woman's place was in the upper echelons of the grand dames who walked faithfully in their husbands' shadows.

"If [only] you had taken the trouble when you first assumed your duties in Chicago," she continued, "to inform yourself as to what organizations in Chicago have real weight."[9] In other words, the women's clubs that she had ignored, along with Helen (and, to some degree, Rufus). Power was a sensitive issue to Helen Dawes, who felt her own husband walked in his brother's shadow and deferred too easily to Charles. Helen reprimanded, "It is hardly wise to boast to any man's wife that he moves when you pull the strings. It is particularly regrettable that you would speak so of a man in Mr. Dawes position."[10]

Apparently McGrew had said something in the press regarding her power over her male superiors. The issue would come to a head when Eleanor Roosevelt visited the fair and McGrew failed to inform Helen Dawes of the logistics involved. But this was in the future, and Helen finished up her letter by saying, "The part of our committee may be of slight importance, but it is our opinion that on account of your youth and lack of social experience, we are much better judges . . . than it is possible for you to be."[11]

This seething warfare between the society women and the new working women of the 1930s forms the backdrop to the letter Dorthea Goodrich received before she spoke in the Congress Hotel. The story of the Temple of Womanhood begins with Goodrich applying for space on the fairgrounds for an officially sponsored woman's building. "Goodrich called it the Temple of Womanhood and articulated its purpose as commemorating the progress made by women."[12] Basically it would be the hall where clubwomen and others could showcase women's accomplishments, with booths, shops, exhibits, and services for women at the fair: a women's building for women.

Lohr liked the idea immediately because Goodrich promised that her committee of clubwoman would raise the funds to construct the building, operate it, and raise additional funds with $1 admission badges, which would entitle the women who purchased them to "special privileges and office space."[13] What was there not to like about the Temple of Womanhood? For Lohr, it seemed a win-win. Goodrich lost no time and went to Daniel Burnham Jr. for a design.

She had very specific ideas for her building. It would be a domed temple to which women from around the world could come—a sort of mecca of womanhood. Burnham did his best to keep to the design dictates of the fair, where the modern fashion was in ascendency over the neoclassical. This was a bit of challenge with Goodrich's vision. At this point Lohr bowed to the powers that be and told Goodrich that "accredited representatives of the various clubs concerned need to make a request" before the fair or he could proceed.[14]

In other words, the lady's clubs headed by Helen Dawes had final say on the building's design. In particular, she needed to contact Estelle Northam of the Illinois Federation of Women's Clubs, who happened to be very good friends with Helen Dawes. She was the troll at Helen's gate and kept her informed of everything that came across her desk related to the fair. Goodrich ignored Lohr's admonishments, continued planning with Burnham, and communicated directly with Lohr. She did not contact Northam.

Her supporters went to work collecting signatures from Chicago women. Goodrich plowed full steam ahead and met with F. R. Moulton, director of concessions, who let her know a contract would be on the way and said, "We will assign you sufficient space to erect the building outlined herein."[15] The Temple of Womanhood was close to reality, and Goodrich's people sent out letters to the clubs, inviting them to the Congress Hotel for a meeting. There Lohr's courier delivered the letter telling Dorthea Goodrich that the Temple of Womanhood was dead in the water.

It would seem there was nothing good or rich about Dorthea Goodrich, a name that Dolly Ledgerwood Matters had made up. And her downfall came from an unlikely source—Martha McGrew, who had received information from another source on Goodrich's real identity. Dolly Matters was not from a social tier that the clubwomen recognized, and her past actions knocked her out altogether. Dolly Ledgerwood, probably a real-life gold digger along the lines of those portrayed in Ziegfeld's Follies, had married Fred Matters during World War I. Matters was much older, and when he died in 1916, he left a $200,000 estate. He also left a daughter.

Another woman, Jessie Ryan, had taken the child to Canada. Dolly Matters, seeing the money slipping through her fingers, sued, saying that she was the child's mother. A court disagreed and awarded the estate to Jessie Ryan and her daughter. Dolly then went to Canada, kidnapped the child, and was arrested by the police. She subsequently married a man named Frederick Ferner in 1917—but Ferner was still married, which resulted in a charge of polygamy.

So Dolly Matters did what so many people throughout history have done: she started over as a new person, Dorthea Goodrich. She joined the Illinois Federation of Women's Clubs and reestablished herself as a progressive, respectable woman. She would have been all right if Martha McGrew had not let her boss know that she had in fact lived a double life. Fearful that this scandal would damage the fair's reputation, already under assault by doubters who thought holding a fair during the Great Depression the height of lunacy, Lohr pulled the plug.

The Temple of Womanhood became an immediate casualty of Matters's duplicity, and even though she sued the world's fair, which settled with her for $1,200, no one was willing to pick up the pieces. Matters did proceed with her meeting at the Congress Hotel, but it was a setup. Mrs. A. H. Johnson of the Illinois Federation of Women's Club knew about the letter and confronted her during the meeting. When Matters refused to read it aloud, Mrs. Johnson administered the coup de grâce by reading it herself. The meeting ended, and that left only Sally Rand to represent woman at the 1933 World's Fair. Some would say she represented them very well in all their glory.

Chapter Thirty-Five

The Bad Plea Bargain

This was the golden moment. No one knew about the deal George Johnson had cut with Capone; people just knew that public enemy number one was headed for prison. Osama bin Laden might have come close to the designation of public enemy number one, and when he was finally killed, people celebrated. With Al Capone, the government celebrated. Treasury official Dwight Davis wrote to George Johnson, "Personally I do not believe there could be any more distinct accomplishment that would tend to create public confidence. . . . I personally congratulate you." Attorney General William Mitchell in Washington lauded the conviction and summed it up to reporters by saying that you can get your man "if you have honest men on the job and a real purpose."[1]

President Herbert Hoover was leaking sawdust. The Great Depression was not going away, and the American people weren't pulling themselves up by their bootstraps. In fact, the economy looked like it might just break down altogether, and at the bottom of that slippery slope was Bolshevism. Many thought capitalism had failed and communism might be the solution. The tin shanties referred to as Hoovervilles and the Bonus Army march, at which World War I veterans demanded their back pay only to be met by Douglas MacArthur and his machine guns, proved that Hoover had no clue how to solve the nation's woes. Hoover blankets, Hoover flags, and Hoovervilles dominated the news. So when Capone's arrest and conviction hit the airwaves, the president grabbed onto the news like a man finding water in the desert. He proclaimed in Springfield, Illinois, while visiting Lincoln's tomb, "There can be no man in our country who, either by his position or influence, stands above the law."[2] The man who asked his staff every day, "Have you got Capone yet?" had his answer.

Hoover shook hands with George Johnson at the governor's mansion in Springfield. Johnson later told reporters that the president had been very kind in his praise, and then he talked down his own feat in snaring Capone for tax evasion. "All I had was the imagination enough to see that the income tax law would serve to bring these big-shot hoodlums to justice."[3] Johnson didn't seem to want the limelight, so the reporters moved on. There had to be a better story than accountants ensnaring a tax cheat. There was.

Elliot Ness was giving interviews to anyone who would listen. Now *there* was a crime fighter who bashed down doors and had shoot-outs with gangsters. He was the G-man who fought it out with bad guys. He was young and called his men the Untouchables. The stories wrote themselves. No more mind-twisting numbers on income versus his tax liability. Just crusaders immune to bribes, who had courage, grit, and perseverance. The *New York Times* printed a typical Ness quote full of bravado and derring-do: "We had to weigh our problems and find a vulnerable point. . . . [W]e decided on the breweries because their product is bulky and because they have the toughest transport problems."[4]

But although convicted, Capone had yet to be sentenced, and as the glow of success began to fade, the press started to question Al Capone's deal and why should he get one at all. Somehow it leaked that the biggest gangster in history was going to jail for a piddly two and a half years. The armchair quarterbacking began almost immediately.

Frank Loesch, former president of the Chicago Crime Commission, wrote to President Hoover that the plea bargain was not making Chicagoans happy in Chicago, but that when Capone was behind bars, he would throw credit Hoover's way for getting the bad man. Hoover was looking toward the election in 1932 and hoped the economy would turn around. He wrote back to Loesch that he would very much like to take credit and that "some time when the gentleman you mention is safely tucked away and engaged in very hard labor, you can tell me all about it."[5] In other words, once Capone was behind bars, Hoover could claim victory.

On June 26 the smell of the plea bargain began to assault the olfactory senses of Attorney General Mitchell, who wrote a six-page letter to George Johnson, berating him for giving Capone time to try his case in the court of public opinion: "It was no doubt a tactical mistake to receive the guilty of plea and then allow two or three weeks to elapse before the sentence is imposed. . . . [T]he effect of that is to start the public discussing what the penalty ought to be."[6]

Even though Mitchell and Youngquist had signed off on the plea bargain, the deal had begun to stink up the halls of justice. The government began to realize it had been played and was essentially letting Capone off the hook. Mitchell charged that Johnson had had no confidence in his own case. It was true; in a letter written to announce the plea deal, Johnson had repeatedly stressed the weak and "circumstantial" context of his case against Capone and denigrated the physical evidence, the witnesses, and even the soundness of the law itself. Again, it would seem George Johnson didn't have the moxie to take on Capone.

Then Capone's lawyers asked the judge to postpone the sentencing on June 29. They then offered up dropping any sort of appeal to slow down his incarceration, and Judge Jim Wilkerson agreed. Al Capone was at liberty for the time being and free to try his case in the court of public opinion. The *New York Times* interviewed him at the Lexington Hotel, and Capone complained about the inequities of justice. "Why don't they go after all those poor bankers who took the savings of thousands of poor people and lost them in bank failures. . . . Isn't it lots worse to take the last few dollars some family had saved, perhaps to live on while the head of the family is out of a job, than to sell a little beer?"[7] Many concurred as the cyclonic Depression tore away homes, bank accounts, jobs, and lives with no end in sight.

On July 30, 1931, a line of dark police cars escorted Al Capone from the Lexington Hotel to the Federal Building. People hoping to see the gangster before he disappeared into prison lined the streets. Chicago was hot and sticky, the air still. Capone went up the back elevator and entered the warm courtroom populated with reporters, lawyers, and court personnel. The judge entered and took care of some preliminary business before looking at Al and his lawyers.

Then Judge Wilkerson astonished the courtroom by announcing that he was not bound by the plea bargain. As the final arbiter of the proper sentence, he would make a determination after getting some answers from Mr. Capone. Capone attorney Michael Ahern went nuts. Wilkerson stated that the case should never have been tried in the papers and that he was not going to just sign off. Then he lowered the boom: "It is time for somebody to impress upon this defendant that it is utterly impossible to bargain with a federal court."[8]

George Johnson backtracked, said that Attorney General Mitchell has signed off on the deal, and offered to show him a letter. Wilkerson listened silently, then shook his head and refused to hand down the sentence without hearing evidence. Ahern knew what was happening. Wilkerson had tasted the rancid meat of Capone's deal and wasn't swallowing. He was not going to give him a mere two and a half years for tax evasion. The gangster's attorney could do nothing but withdraw the plea. Johnson accepted, and Wilkerson set a trial date for October 5. Al Capone had sat quietly during all this, but observers noticed that his shirt collar was wet, and for the first time in his life, he had nothing to say.

Like Dorthea Goodrich, who thought she was home free when she entered the Congress Hotel, Al Capone had the shock of his life when he realized the deal was off. Dolly Ledgerwood Matters could relate.

CHAPTER THIRTY-SIX

Frank Lloyd Wright's Fair

FRANK LLOYD WRIGHT WAS IN ECLIPSE. LIKE ALL GREAT MEN ULTImately must, he was experiencing a cooling-down period that was very hard to accept. He had not erected a major building since the 1920s. Raymond Hood had left him out of the 1933 Chicago World's Fair, writing, "I felt that you were a strong individualist and that if an attempt was made to harness you in with other architects, the result would be more apt to be a fight than a fair." Wright responded characteristically that he could work very well with others as long as he alone designed the exposition.

But this did not stop the public outcry over the exclusion of Chicago's premier architect, even though many critics pointed out that he was well past his prime. Having the world's fair in Chicago and not inviting Frank Lloyd Wright to sit on the architectural committee was a bit like casting a movie without a leading man. Yes, Hood and Daniel Burnham Jr. were great architects, but Frank Lloyd Wright was legendary. Prominent men such as Lewis Mumford, Douglas Haskell, and Henry Churchill chimed in and derided the fair organizers for not including the great architect.

As early as October 8, 1930, in a letter to Frank Lloyd Wright, a close friend and former client, Darwin Martin, wrote that his brother William had sent him a clipping from a Chicago paper "reproaching the fair for not obtaining Wright's cooperation."[1] Other articles began appearing in the national press. "The first published by architect and critic Haskell in the *Nation* likened the exposition's design commission without Wright to an anthology of American literature without Ralph Waldo Emerson."[2] Haskell went on to denigrate the committee's "fear [that] he would seek to dominate and not cooperate." Genius need not play well with others, and Haskell believed the committee had made "too much of a minor trait."[3] To Haskell's point, Wright would later write in his biography, "Surely it was better having one architect out of employment in such parlous times than the 8 or 10 or 15 already employed at the fair. . . . [W]ere I to come they would go out."[4]

In fact, Paul Cret had suggested Wright as one of his first picks for the committee, but Hood knew a genius was a genius because he went his own way. Hood tempered his own dilettantism with a utilitarian view that architects created shelters that served the common good. Even a genius had to bow to function over form, and he knew Frank Lloyd Wright had built his personal and professional life on bowing to no one. Still, Hood was not above throwing Wright a bone.

Wright's son John, whose toy company sold Lincoln Logs, suggested that his father be allowed to design a major exhibit hall, "much as Louis Sullivan had been given the Transportation Building at the 1893 World's Columbian Exposition."[5] He wrote to committee member Harvey Wiley Corbett, "No doubt the rest of the Fair Architecture may be badly shown up by comparison with what he would do, but what of that? Wouldn't it be more appropriate to have it shown up at the Fair than after the Fair."[6]

Such is the pride of a son in his father. After making this request, John Lloyd Wright then wrote to his father that if "by any remote chance"[7] the committee asked him to design a building, he should decline the offer. Strange, but pride injured is vengeance unleashed. The architectural committee did promise Wright a building, but of course he refused. In a letter to architect Rudolph Schindler in January 1931, he wrote, "They say I am to have a corner of it when they get around to it. Probably one where I can't wiggle out very far. It would be better to refuse connection at this late day so far as the cause of an organic architecture goes."[8]

Wright was playing both ends against the middle, declining the offer but hoping the committee would press him. The *Chicago Daily News* reported in 1933, "The architect was planning to erect a steel and glass tower across from the fair entrance." *Architectural Forum* chimed in that the building would demonstrate various designs for office and apartment buildings. Wright said he had no intention of designing a building near the fairgrounds. This was true; he intended to design the entire fair.

Calling the architectural committee a bunch of "skyscraper pilots,"[9] he produced for *A Century of Progress* three designs that he called "genuine and practical as Modern Architecture."[10] It was part of Wright's grand plan to get back at Hood and others, if not to take over the designing of the Chicago World's Fair.[11] He unveiled his three designs at a meeting of the American Union of Decorative Artists and Craftsmen in New York in February 1931. He had decided the topic would be the Chicago World's Fair, and in their opening remarks, architects Woolcott and Lewis Mumford made clear they deemed it an outrage that the greatest living architect had not been asked to design the fair. Mumford called the committee's members "eclectic shams, illustrating only the latest fashion trends."[12]

Take it away, Frank. And he did. First he decimated the architects of the fair. Raymond Hood was in attendance and sat stone-faced as Wright tore into the fair committee. There was a New York element too, and Wright lashed out at Hood and Corbett, saying, "Only eclectics who had put the masks on skyscrapers were invited. . . . [T]he Fair is the latest expression of New York eclectic modernism."[13] *Time* magazine quoted him as saying, "I'm trying to bring architecture back to America as something real to America. The proposed World's Fair in Chicago is a conspicuous example of modernism sprung up overnight, of superficiality of sham and imitation. They are making a pretty cardboard picture of ancient wall masses. . . . They are specialists in spectacle. But the architecture for the fair is only bad theatre where theatre does not belong."[14]

"Perspiring with embarrassment,"[15] Hood did rebut some of the claims laid down that night by Wright and others and said that nothing more than Wright's inability to work with others had prompted the committee's decision. He may have said this after the main event at which Wright lobbed his cannon balls directly at the fair. Wright's three designs would turn out to be Hood's best argument that he had made the right decision.

Frank Lloyd Wright's first design was a 245-story skyscraper half a mile high. He called it a "genuine modern construction since it incorporated recent advances in both structure and materials."[16] The tower would be a "concrete mass with light concrete floor slabs on steel girders cantilevering out from a central core."[17] The building would then be enclosed with "light transparent glass substitutes."[18] Sixty elevators would take people up to terraces in the clouds, and if there were no clouds, planes would fly past with colored streamers. Terraces below would face Lake Michigan with parking below for 30,000 cars. There would be a park on one of the four lower terraces, and an adjacent auditorium would seat 25,000 people. Large fountains would surround the base.

His second design entailed "a massive canopy supported by a system of pylons and suspension cables. . . . [G]igantic 500-foot-wide, tented bays form the building blocks of his design."[19] The massive tent would be well over a mile long, with the pylons 275 feet tall. Hanging screens would separate individual exhibits, with the pylons able to go as high as 500 feet or as low as 150. Moving sidewalks and waterways would run through a park under the tent and take visitors to different exhibits. Water would be pumped on top of the canopy to keep it clean and create waterfalls as it ran down the sides.

About now Raymond Hood was resting easier. It was rumored that Wright drank and used cocaine, and to some it might have seemed that the great architect was under the influence. The final design would confirm their suspicions. In his third vision, Wright put the whole fair into the lake. Barges would be the basis for the entire exposition: "According to Wright, floating bridges and gardens would connect the individual barges together in a continuous varied, brilliant modern circumstance. The result would be an organic assemblage of barges extending into the lake from a central area linked to nearby parking on the mainland."[20]

Like the bolder, more audacious plots of an aging novelist, Wright's designs smacked of fantasy, if not outright insanity. Glass rods would shoot from his barges into the water, creating a lit aquarium effect all over the fair of his third design. *Time* would report that Wright "presided like a benign deity"[21] over the meeting. It is a testament to his reputation that his designs were not ridiculed. A giant skyscraper, a giant tent, and floating barges reaching far out into the lake were his answer to the 1933 World's Fair. This was Frank Lloyd Wright's Hail Mary pass and showed his disdain for the supposed impracticality of holding a world's fair during the Great Depression.

The word "ego" comes to mind in describing the fair designs. The skyscraper was totally impractical, as the volume of people attending would hit 125,000 in a single day. Sixty elevators would not suffice, and why would people go up into a giant tower to spend the day? A building big enough to hold sixty elevators was outside the scope of either the budget or existing technology. People would bottleneck at the elevators, and God forbid a fire should break out. The size and scale of the tent pushed the limits of construction, not to mention cost. Nor were floating pontoons to hold buildings practical in terms of cost or construction.

In truth, Frank Lloyd Wright was furious about his exclusion from the architectural committee of the 1933 World's Fair. He took revenge by promoting himself and his "original" designs at the fair's expense. Like a child not invited to play, he took pleasure in destroying the game. He painted the committee members as stodgy, mediocre designers and himself as a genius with a true vision of the future of modern architecture. Wright knew his ideas would never be acted on, and one has to wonder if he did it all for spite.

Frank Lloyd Wright would later defend himself, saying, "It would seem that I was present and spoke because I myself resented being out of the Commission whereas I resent only their quick turnover and pretentious scene painting as unworthy of modern architecture."[22] Raymond Hood surely had a rough night, but the aging architect had taken his best shot and lost. The world had changed, and no one could afford the impracticality of genius anymore. The Great Depression and Al Capone had moved into the ascendency, and Frank Lloyd Wright, in prizing form over function, belonged in the history books.

Chapter Thirty-Seven

Hayseeds

THE MAN WHO CHANGED JUDGE JIM WILKERSON'S MIND HAD BEEN the US president. The unverifiable word was that Herbert Hoover wanted Al Capone to go to jail and stay there. He wanted Capone to stand trial. A columnist for the *Chicago American* wrote twenty-five years later, "Two days before Capone was to come to court, Wilkerson was visited by the confidential secretary of the man in Washington," George Murray.[1] It made sense. The plea bargain was paltry, and the president was probably outraged that a gangster like Capone should get off so lightly. That was one theory. The other was that the stolid Wilkerson had communed with his radio and decided he didn't want his power usurped by a two-bit gangster.

Capone passed his time before the trial with his family and even went to a Northwestern football game on October 3, 1931, where the crowd heckled him. He left at the half, and two days later he went to a different sort of game. He wore a blue suit and didn't feel so good when he left the Lexington Hotel. He took along some cough drops and made his way to the courthouse. Once again, spectators, cameramen, and reporters jammed the streets. All were disappointed when Capone slipped past to the Dearborn Street entrance in an unmarked car.

Some reporters yelled questions, and Capone shrugged, saying he was sorry he was going to miss the third game of the World Series. Photographers blew off flashbulbs as he passed into an elevator to the sixth floor. Telegraph wires had been run to the courthouse for an ad hoc telegraph office. Local, national, and international reporters were in attendance as well. Upstairs George Johnson had witnesses against Capone lined up: "Johnny Torrio, Fred Ries, and Louis LaCava." Johnson was not taking any chances and had sent out seventy-five subpoenas.[2]

Jonathan Eig, in *Get Capone*, describes the courtroom as a "grand space, befitting the magnitude of the event at hand with ornate columns rising to the lofty ceiling, bronze sconces holding small electric lightbulbs on the walls, and a massive arch over the door. Painted above the entrance to the court were quotations from the US Constitution that had faded."[3]

An Indian summer had been hanging around, and the day was warm. Capone darkened his shirt even though the windows were open. George Johnson had on a grey suit, and Wilkerson wore no robes. He told the reporters to move back from the defense table and called the court to order. In a famous scene from *The Untouchables*, the judge swaps one jury for another and foils Capone's effort to buy his way to freedom. In reality the trial was very low drama: Wilkerson simply swapped prospective juror lists with another judge.

An informant, Eddie O'Hare, had told Frank Wilson of the Bureau of Internal Revenue that Capone had gotten to the jurors: "The big fellow is going to outsmart you. . . . They're passing out $1,000 bills. They're promising political jobs. They're using muscle, too."[4] Wilson told the judge, and Wilkerson cagily refrained from tipping his hand until the day the trial started. It was too late for Capone's men to bribe the new jury.

For the first time the fix was not in. To make matters worse, the jurors were middle- and working-class men from small towns and over the age of forty-five. They did not look at Al Capone as a celebrity. They worked hard and went to church and saw Capone as the devil. Another thing bothered Capone's attorney, Michael Ahern: these jurors had served on other juries. Men who had served before were more likely to convict.

Ahern complained to the judge, "It seems more than a coincidence that so many of these jurors are repeaters. . . . [I]t is not a fair manner of selection."[5] Wilkerson shrugged, and when Ahern asked him to throw out the pool of jurors, he simply said no. Ahern and Capone knew what this meant. Urbanites regarded bootlegging and speakeasies as necessary due to a ridiculous law. But men from small towns actually believed in the law and thought bootleggers were men of evil intent.

Ahern searched in vain for sympathetic ears. The selection of twelve jurors took less than four hours.

On Capone's side of the table, things had not gone well. Eleven jurors hailed from downstate towns in Illinois. As anyone who has lived in Chicago knows, there is Chicago and there is Illinois, and there is no resemblance between the two. Chicago was a Democratic stronghold, while the rest of the state was as red as cherry pie. The people from Illinois looked at Chicago with the same dismay as out-of-staters who saw the city as a den of gangsters, booze, and sex. To top it off, it was holding a world's fair in the middle of a depression. Insanity upon insanity.

As Eig writes, one juror from Edisonville wrote five years after the trial, "I had formed a pretty fair picture of Capone. . . . I understood that he was a terrible man who did not hesitate to murder those who stood in his way. . . . [T]o me . . . he epitomized all that was evil."[6] This was exactly what Ahern feared, and he complained to the *Chicago Tribune*, "Capone is to have no trial by his peers. It is to be by the men who reflect the opinions of the countryside."[7] A reporter from New York wrote that he detected the "fragrant whiff of green fields and growing rutabagas and parsnip in the courtroom. . . . [T]he jurors were a bunch of hayseeds, horny-handed tillers of the fruitful soil, small-town storekeepers, mechanics and clerks."[8]

To make matters worse, Judge Wilkerson had presided over Ralph Capone's trial for tax evasion, and Capone was convinced the judge had it in for him. He was right. Judge Wilkerson saw the federal court as above the fix, and to that end he had something to prove. The gangster faced a possible sentence of thirty-two years and wanted a different judge. But Ahern decided to stick with what he knew and figured if the trial was in Chicago, then a deal was always possible. Even hayseeds could be bribed.

CHAPTER THIRTY-EIGHT

The Gaseous Tube

WHILE AL CAPONE BRIBED PROSPECTIVE JURORS, LENOX LOHR REALized he had little more than a year to put on the biggest show in Chicago since the 1893 World's Fair. Could it really be the end of 1931, with 1932 just around the corner, and then the fair? Impossible. They were still trying to deal with the muck and mire of an island in the lake where timbers were driven down to hardpan thirty-two feet underground. The only way to keep the buildings from sinking was to put a mesh of steel on top of the timbers, fill it with cement, and create a floating platform. Still, the buildings sank.

But winter was coming again, and there was no time to lose. Occasionally city dwellers reported strange lights streaking across the summer sky. Suddenly green lights would shoot up into the heavens and then vanish. Or the entire lakefront would light up like the sun and then flicker out. Once a giant searchlight cut across the sky, turning from red to blue to green. No one really knew what was going on, and some reported flying saucers.

Each world's fair had furthered illumination. The Paris Exposition of 1851 brought the gas flame forward, and the Crystal Palace of London introduced the incandescent light in 1882. The Columbian Exposition outdid them all with more white lights than had ever been strung together before. The 1893 fair used more current than the entire city of Chicago in that year. So *A Century of Progress*, a science fair, had to surpass them all.

Lighting technology had made great leaps since the last exposition, and it all came down to the gaseous tube, or "neon."

Claude Neon had invented gaseous tubing in 1915, and his French firm began to sell licenses to produce the lighted tubes. "The company was selling franchise licenses for $100,000 each plus royalties, making neon lighting prohibitively expensive."[1] Most Americans had never seen it, except on the occasional sign. But after 1932 the patent had expired, opening the way for *A Century of Progress* to use Neon's light on a scale no one had attempted before.

Neon would allow the fair to do things with light that others had only dreamed of. The science of neon lighting surely presaged the splitting of the atom thirty years later. It was all made possible by the "gaseous tube." As Lenox Lohr explained in *Fair Management,*

The neon light is a glass tube of carefully figured dimensions with metal electrodes at the ends. When the air has been exhausted, a tiny amount of the so-called rare gases is admitted to the tube and sealed in. As the high voltage is applied to the ends, electrons break away from the atoms in the electrode and, traveling at terrific speed, crash into the atoms of the gas within the tube. The result of the collision is to dislodge other electrons from those atoms which knock lose still more atoms. . . . [N]ew disruptions and collisions are taking place, and as each occurs, light flares up.[2]

In reading this, we are again reminded of nuclear fission. That this controlled reaction could be harnessed to produce light and different colors with different gases made the incandescent lighting of the 1893 fair look Stone Age. The possibilities were endless, with neon gas producing an orange-red light, argon mixed with krypton and helium gas emitting a blue light, and a yellow glass tube giving off green. Joseph Urban's colors would now ignite in ways he never would have imagined.

General Electric and the Westinghouse Company took the job of illuminating the fair. Lohr had run out of money once again and offered up $350,000 in gold notes. Then Walter Ryan, director of General Electric's illuminating engineering laboratories, was made chief of illumination, with Charles Sthal of Westinghouse as his assistant. They immediately began carrying out tests in the basement of the Administration Building to find the best suitable lighting. Ryan wanted to increase the visibility of the fair by "projecting moving beams of light into the evening sky to form colorful beacons that were visible for miles."[3]

Indirect lighting, which we take for granted, was first used at the fair of 1933. In an article published in *Architectural Forum*, Ryan identified types of lighting incorporated into the event: street, path, and exterior surface lighting, building outlying and decorative lighting, water lighting, spectacular lighting, and indoor lighting.

Gaseous tube lighting stood out above the rest. The public in 1933 had never seen light emanating from the bends and curves of a tube before. As early as 1929, "the Exposition engineers were convinced that in the field of gaseous tube lighting lay possibilities for unappreciated opportunities."[4] The first use of the gaseous tubes on a grand scale occurred at the Hall of Science, which employed a mile of them. The tubes on the north and west were blue; those on the south and east were red. The tubes had the advantage of low heat and could be concealed in channels to produce indirect lighting that seemed to come from nowhere.

The Electrical Building is an amazing example of what the fair did with gaseous tubing. The initial plans called for a waterfall of 90,000 gallons per minute down the outside of the building. Hood and others immediately tallied the cost and decided to use gaseous tubing "to simulate a cascade in the great court of the Electrical Building. This section of the building was designed to represent a great dam, and for the spillway there was a tumbling waterfall of 4600 feet of tubes emitting a soft blue light that seemed to diffuse itself through the atmosphere like a fine mist."[5] Only gaseous tubing could do this.

Ryan's big idea was to draw attention to the fair and wow the visitors exhausted from walking around all day by filling the night sky with colored lights: "On the roof of the Electrical Building a huge white fan of seventeen movable, thirty-six inch, incandescent searchlights projected 21 million candlepower of light into the evening sky. The result was the largest battery of incandescent searchlights employed for special effects up to that time."[6]

The south end of the fair had twenty-four lights mounted on a two-tier step. Each light produced a 60-million-candlepower beam. Planes would drop chemical vapors into the army searchlights, which were of the same type used to light Niagara Falls, and create an artificial aurora borealis. The combined candlepower of these lights was a "staggering 1.440 billion."[7] Specially trained operators, brought in to run the lights, would switch out color filters for more dramatic effect.

The underwater lighting in the two major aquatic shows was just as dramatic: "The huge seventy-foot-tall Morning Glory Fountain in front of the Electrical Building contained 133 underwater floodlights that slowly changed color. The floodlights along with 500 jets of water guaranteed a brilliant evening show. . . . [A] large triple fountain in the lagoon drew the attention of fairgoers by including constantly changing lights."[8]

In the Rainbow City the technology of gaseous tubing intersected with the artistry of Joseph Urban. The electrons shooting and dislodging from the static atoms and sending out flares of light that broke the darkness elevated Urban's colors into new dimension. The Chicago World's Fair could only hope to do the same when it opened in 1933—ironically, the darkest year of the Great Depression.

CHAPTER THIRTY-NINE

The Trial of Al Capone

WHILE ELECTRICIANS LIT UP THE SKY ABOVE CHICAGO WITH MILLION-candlepower searchlights, prosecutor Dwight Green opened his case against Al Capone. He had a simple strategy: show these hayseeds from downstate Capone's lavish lifestyle, demonstrate that he had income, and let them decide if he was guilty of tax evasion. Green didn't have a smoking gun, but he did have a secret weapon. Now it was time to paint a picture.

So while the October light crept across the dark old floorboards of the Federal Building, Green described a lifestyle foreign to Capone's fellow citizens: a mansion in Miami, diamond rings and belt buckles, shopping sprees, a house in Cicero, residency in the Lexington Hotel. Then he turned and said Al Capone had made $1 million from 1924 to 1929 and not paid a nickel of tax. Capone's lawyer, Michael Ahern, didn't bother with an opening statement and remained seated next to Albert Fink, who specialized in tax law.

Fink was not impressive, with his bald head and airplane ears. But he had come up with a novel defense for Jake Guzik, saying that failure to pay income tax and conspiracy not to pay income tax were one and the same. This would obviate the conspiracy charge and just leave the misdemeanor. He had already informed Judge Jim Wilkerson he would use this defense again, and the judge basically shrugged and said, "Let's hear the evidence."

Prosecutor Green first established through a series of government witnesses that Al Capone had paid no tax under any alias. Capone listened and occasionally smiled. He didn't seem nervous in the least. Then came Leslie Shumway, whom the Secret Six had smuggled into the Federal Building. The accountant said he had kept the books at the Cicero gambling halls and confirmed that the books found by George Johnson were the ones he had written in.

The jurors yawned and fidgeted as Shumway confirmed the profits for Capone's gambling establishments had been around "$300,000 in 1924, $117,000 for 1925, and $170,000 in 1926."[1] A Reverend Hooper, who had raided Capone's gambling den in 1926, testified that Capone had admitted the place belonged to him. So it went like this: the ledger that Shumway kept showed income for Capone and the casino, and the reverend established that Capone owned the establishment. Attorney Ahern poked holes in the reverend's story but did little real damage. The court adjourned, and Capone and his lawyers and bodyguards posed for some pictures. When he left the building the crowds outside rushed toward him. Mounted officers pushed them back as Capone waved and chatted with some people, then jumped into a cab and disappeared.

The next day Dwight Green used his secret weapon and called George Slentz to verify the September 30, 1930, letter from Lawrence Mattingly, Capone's then lawyer. The letter admitted Capone had a tax debt and put his income for 1927, 1928, and 1929 at $26,000, $40,000, and $100,000. Capone's lawyers rushed the bench, saying the letter was inadmissible and had been presented only in an attempt to compromise with the government.

This was Dwight Green's ace in the hole. The ledgers showed income, but the thumb-smeared and faded pages didn't carry much weight with the jury. But here was a letter from Al Capone's attorney stating he had made as much as $100,000 and not paid a nickel of tax. In 1931 dollars, $100,000 was well over $1 million today. Livid, Ahern stated Capone had been trying to pay his taxes and that the letter was a show of good faith.

"Congress doesn't want to send people to jail," he said to the judge. "Congress wants people to pay their taxes . . . to come in and settle with their government before criminal or civil action."[2] Then he pointed to the cases where courts had rendered attempts to strike a deal or a plea bargain admissible. Judge Wilkerson listened and then paused, looking down at Capone's lawyer sweating in the warm courtroom.

"When a man makes such statements . . . he does so at his own peril," he pointed out. "He cannot bind the government not to prosecute him."[3]

In short, Wilkerson hated deals, he hated plea bargains, and nobody would tell him what he could admit as evidence. The jury would hear about the letter. Then Ahern changed tack and argued to the jury that the government had not allowed Capone to pay his taxes. The jurors just stared at the well-heeled lawyer in the long afternoon heat.

The government continued over the next few days to document Al Capone's spending habits, showing that money was deposited in bank accounts and wired to Miami. Again and again the prosecution put the gangster's lifestyle on display for the men of the jury. When a contractor testified about some work he did on Capone's home in Miami and charged that he was still owed $125, the slouched-down Capone sat up. The *Daily News* said, "The scar on his cheek stood out like a cord."[4] It was reported later that Capone told his attorneys that the man wasn't paid because he hadn't finished the job.

The question posed by Johnson and Green was "Where did he get all his money?" It floated around the hot courtroom like a balloon and was never answered. Capone's rich-and-famous lifestyle seemed to hover over the jurors and taunt them with their meager Depression-era existence. And then on October 10, a small incident brought home the reality of the man standing trial.

On that day the judge called for lunch, and Capone and bodyguard Phi D'Andrea started toward the door. Mike Malone, one of the Internal Revenue agents, saw a bulge in D'Andrea's jacket and knew it was a gun. He alerted Frank Wilson, and together they shoved D'Andrea into the hallway and threw him up against the wall. "D'Andrea, a pudgy man with gold-rimmed glasses, put up no struggle. He politely told Wilson and Malone he was permitted to carry the weapon because he had served as a deputy bailiff."[5] But a check revealed his license had expired; he was taken into custody and later sentenced to six months.

Again the movie *The Untouchables* exaggerated this scene as a sinister moment. But in truth, if any juror saw this, and undoubtedly some did, it did not bode well for Capone. It reminded jurors that they were trying a murderous gangster for terrorizing Chicago, and tax evasion was their only shot to get rid of him.

CHAPTER FORTY

The Disposable Fair

MAJOR LENOX LOHR WAS USED TO WORKING WITH DISPOSABLE MATE-
rials. War was all about setting up bridges and camps and then tearing
them down. The army valued efficiency, ease of use, mobility, and, above
all else, speed. Lohr wrote years later that "the problems of materials and
construction [for *A Century of Progress*] paralleled those confronting an
engineer in war time, in that they must perform for a short period at a
high degree of efficiency, yet allow speedy and economical demolition,
once their purpose has been served."[1]

There it was. The 1933 World's Fair was a one-season, one-shot affair.
It would last an extra year at President Franklin Roosevelt's request, but
Lohr and his lieutenants were all working under the assumption that the
city they were constructing would be destroyed the same year it opened.
In that way they had one foot in the quality camp and the other in the
cost-efficiency camp. The disposable fair of 1933 would later resonate in
every suburb in the United States, where homes sprung up in a matter
of days and subdivisions in a matter of months. All those plywood and
Sheetrock creations were testaments to 1933's *A Century of Progress*.

"Low cost in manufacture and fabrication and the minimum of field-
work erection were fundamental. Light weight, reflecting a saving in sup-
porting framework and foundations, was essential from the standpoint of
cost cutting."[2] The Depression was only getting worse, and money was
getting tighter. Necessity is the mother of invention, and if Lohr couldn't
build his fair on the cheap using innovative materials that would save
time and money, then they couldn't build the fair at all. Cost efficiency

was not an option, as he saw it; it was a requirement. Indeed, the destruction of the fair was on his mind even as he built it: "The necessity of demolition demanded ease and security of fastening to joints and materials that would permit easy disassembly and have a high salvage value."[3]

Spoken like the true military man. Lenox also had an ace in the hole. Since the world's fair was built on man-made land, no building codes applied. The architects and Lohr could experiment with whatever they wanted. The major went hunting immediately for new materials, and the first thing he found was plywood. Used in World War I for airplane fuselages, plywood became a viable alternative for building exteriors with the advent of waterproof glue. This lightweight, inexpensive board was perfect, as far as Lohr was concerned, and could be used just about anywhere.

Transite, "a type of precast asbestos cement wallboard,"[4] was used for the exterior of the Administration Building; "gypsum" was used for the interior. This first building set the bar for others. As Lisa Schrenk in *Building a Century of Progress* writes, "The boards were attached to a steel frame with case-hardened screws. The sides of the building were insulated with Sprayo-Flake, an experimental mixture of emulsified asphalt, sodium silicate, and shredded paper, blown in between walls with pneumatic guns, while Maize wood, a material consisting of processed corn stalks, insulated the roof."[5]

The techniques used on this first building differed radically from the artistry employed at the 1893 fair. The architectural committee and Lohr were fighting a different war than Daniel Burnham Sr., John Root, and Frederick Law Olmstead had forty years before. They had no money. The Depression was a vortex, sucking in everything in its path, and gangsters in Chicago threatened to keep people away and jeopardize the whole enterprise. Lacking both time and money, Lohr approached the entire fair as a general would, using every weapon at his disposal, and this required cutting-edge building technology.

Everything was on the table, including "precast gypsum board, five-ply Douglas fir plywood, ribbed metal siding, pressed steel plates, and prefabricated laminated insulation boards." The architects assessed each pavilion and evaluated the materials under consideration for "strength and durability, ease of securing to the framework, resistance to moisture, absorption and resistance to combustion, weight, and availability."[6] Flexibility was Lohr's guiding principle, and after the first three buildings were constructed, gypsum board became the go-to material. The Travel and Transport Building was constructed of steel panels, the Hall of Science of plywood, and the Administration Building of Transite, but the rest had exteriors of gypsum board, which could take paint and not fade.

Gypsum had come out of research in the 1920s. Known today as "drywall," it was very new in 1931. "A sandwich panel system less expensive than plywood, gypsum board consists of noncombustible gypsum plaster (ground calcium sulfate combined with water) covered in paper to make it appropriate for drywall construction. Augustine Sackett took out the first patent for gypsum board in 1894. . . . [I]n 1909 United States Gypsum took over the business." The company developed new products, including "Sheetrock," which had a finished surface. In 1931 a new advancement made Sheetrock viable for the outdoors. Half-inch Sheetrock was used "for all the exterior walls of the General Exhibits Building."[7]

Stronger and more durable adhesives also let the 1933 Chicago World's Fair use plywood more extensively than ever before. Introduction of a "German phenol resin binder in 1931 . . . made the plywood practical for exterior building construction."[8] This pressed wood took the place of Transite in the building of the Hall of Science. The wood panels were less expensive, expanded and contracted less, and required no weather stripping. Plywood was much easier to handle and had half the weight of Transite or Sheetrock. "In constructing the hall of science, workers secured standard four-by-eight panels of half-inch five-ply laminated Douglas fir to wall studs with thin battens."[9] Plywood was also used as subflooring all through the Hall of Science and covered with Masonite boards.

Lohr and his architects were changing the very nature of construction. One man could carry plywood around and attach it to a building. Men could lay panels of Sheetrock one after another and cover the side of a building in a day. New types of paint could be sprayed on, achieving massive coverage without multiple coats. The innovations cut across every facet of the building of the fair. As Lohr wrote later, "New wall coverings and methods of fastening, unheard of uses of standard materials slightly altered to a new role, raceways for electrical conduits of low cost . . . water pipes of amazing thinness, roofing and flooring materials, indirect gaseous tubes for architectural effect . . . it is certain that in the aggregate they effected a savings of hundreds of thousands of dollars."[10]

What we see as standard was innovative in the extreme in 1931. There would be no "hand shaping" on site.[11] In other words, prefabricated materials would arrive ready to go, shortening and minimizing labor and conserving materials. And when it was all over, the destruction of the fair would be as efficient. Above all else, the latest construction techniques saved time, something that Major Lohr was running out of.

So was Al Capone.

CHAPTER FORTY-ONE

Verdict

WHILE MAJOR LENOX LOHR BUILT HIS FAIR, AL CAPONE'S LAWYER paced in front of the jury in the Federal Building, throwing out reasons why his client should not be convicted. The government had failed to make its case. It had not shown that Capone earned any income. Sure, his spending habits were lavish, but was that a crime? Even when Fred Ries testified, he could only say that he had given money to Jake Guzik. He never paid Capone. Michael Ahern gesticulated; he raised his voice. The government had proved nothing . . . nothing at all!

Then George Johnson stood up in the afternoon light and approached the bench. Everyone thought the trial would continue through the week. He was not a trial lawyer and had never argued a case before a judge. But on this day he stood in front of Judge Jim Wilkerson, raised his head slightly, and said, "Your honor, the government now rests."[1]

Capone's attorneys, Ahern and Albert Fink, threw a fit. They had more witnesses to call. They wanted to prove that Capone's failure to pay income tax was an honest mistake. They wanted to show that the whole trial was a setup, ordered directly by the government in Washington, to unfairly prosecute Al Capone. They wanted to paint their client as a victim who had incorrectly assumed gambling losses would offset income, which was why he thought he didn't have to pay any taxes. It was all just a misunderstanding.

The judge didn't buy any of it. He gave the defense four hours to present its case. Ahern demanded he throw out the Mattingly letter. The judge said no. Would he reconsider the statute of limitations on the charges? No. The whole thing should be thrown out with a directed verdict. No. The next day Ahern went on a polemical tear about the duplicity of the US government in prosecuting his client.

"You are the only barrier between this defendant and the encroachment of the government," he almost shouted. "The government has sought by interference and presumption to prove this man's guilt. . . . Why do they seek conviction on this meager evidence? Because he is Alfonse Capone! Because he is the mythical Robin Hood you read so much about in all the newspapers! They have no evidence!!"[2]

The floors creaked under Aherns's hard shoes as he darted back and forth like a caged lion in front of the jury and tied his case to the big picture of Prohibition. The government had made a terrible mistake with the Volstead Act, and instead of owning up to its mistake, it was making Al Capone the "fall guy." Capone was just a man caught up in something bigger than himself. And then Ahern brought his argument back to the numbers. How much had the government really proved? He slapped his fist into his hand and went through the evidence. *Nothing. It had proved nothing.*

Ahern drank some water and paused. The Mattingly letter had no value. It was an estimate by his lawyer at the time and was never an admission of income. The United States had spent years trying to come up with some proof that Al Capone had an income, and it had failed. Fink took over and hit his core message: Capone had not paid his taxes, but he had not therefore conspired to defraud the government. Ahern took the helm again as dusky shadows fell in the courtroom. Capone didn't look bored anymore and was watching his lawyer. Ahern went back to the letter and said that, if anything, Al's lawyer had duped him. "It was all a plot, gentleman, to get this defendant to make admissions he had a tax liability!" Ahern then reframed his case as part of a vast government conspiracy. "Capone must be destroyed!"[3]

That was it. The courtroom was silent. The next day George Johnson presented the government's case. He compared Al Capone to middle-class people who went to work and paid their taxes. He then discussed the responsibility of the governed to enforce the laws and collect taxes to keep the military, the government, and the municipalities going. "Every one of those workers must pay an income tax on every dollar they earn above the sum of $1,500.00. The government has no more import-ant function . . . than to enforce [its] revenue laws."[4]

Johnson wisely left bootlegging out and stuck to the case. Capone had not paid tax on his income. He had broken the law. Then Johnson addressed Ahern's defense: "I am bewildered in this case at the manner in which the defense has attempted to weave a halo of mystery and romance around the head of this man. . . . [I]s he Robin Hood[?] . . . Was it Robin Hood in this case who bought $5,000 worth of diamond belt buckles to give to the unemployed? Was it Robin Hood in this case who bought a meat bill of $6,500? Did that go to the unemployed? It went to the house on Palm Island."[5]

Johnson next went through Capone's gambling operations and the wiring of profits "from a bank in Cicero to a Western Union office in Miami."[6] He painted Capone as sitting above the operation and reaping the profits. He then questioned the integrity of Capone as head of a large syndicate and of Capone's lawyer, Ahern. The lawyer had contorted facts to make it look like the government had it in for Capone. "This, gentle-men of the jury, is not a case of public clamor. . . . [T]he facts cry out louder as evidence of a violation of the law of the United States." He then concluded, "I am asking that you be fair and impartial to the defendant and I am asking you to be fair and impartial to the government."[7] Future generations would remember this trial, he admonished, and it was the jurors' duty to give the correct verdict to those generations.

The case was in the jury's hands.

On October 17, 1931, at 10:50 p.m., Al Capone entered the courtroom and stood next to his lawyer. The jury filed in. Even though it was Satur-day, jackhammers pounded, and the Union Pacific engines huffed toward the lakefront on the custom tracks. It seemed now trains were always heading to the world's fairgrounds, but a newly erected high fence made it hard to see anything. It was as if the long boxcars kept disappearing right into Lake Michigan.

The court was called to order, and Capone sat stone-faced next to his lawyers. Judge Wilkerson entered, and everyone stood. He sat down and looked at the jury.

"Gentlemen, have you reached a verdict?"

They had.

"You may hand your verdict to the clerk."

The clerk took the paper and read aloud.

"We, the jury, find the defendant guilty on counts one, five, nine, thirteen, and eighteen in the second indictment and not guilty on counts two, three, four, six, seven, eight, ten, eleven, twelve, fourteen, fifteen, sixteen, seventeen, nineteen, twenty, twenty-one, and twenty-two."[8]

No one, not even Capone, was quite sure what it all meant. The judge told the clerk to read the verdict again. He did. Ahern informed Capone that he could face a sentence of seventeen years, or five for each of the three felonies and one for each of the two misdemeanors, and a maximum fine of $50,000. The sentencing would take place in a week. Capone left without a word. A week later he returned to court to hear his fate.

Ahern tried to get the verdict dismissed. Judge Wilkerson barely opened his mouth and murmured, "Denied." He then asked Al Capone to rise and approach. Capone stood and walked to the bench with his hands clasped behind him like a schoolboy. Judge Wilkerson sentenced Capone to five years and fined him $10,000 for the first count. On the second count, five years and $10,000. Capone grimaced and licked his lips. On the third count, five years and $10,000. Capone squeezed his hands together. For each of the misdemeanors, he received one year and a $10,000 fine. Wilkerson "added that two of the three counts would run concurrently, and he gave Capone credit for some of the time he'd already served for contempt." The result was an aggregate sentence of eleven years in the penitentiary and fines of $50,000. A newspaper reporter said Capone trembled and turned white. Then he turned to his lawyers and shook their hands.

"Well, so long," he said. "Good-bye."[9]

A bailiff took him from the courtroom. In that moment Al Capone lost his grip on the city of Chicago. It was about 11 p.m., and there was no sound in the courtroom, save for the train whistles by the lake and the hammering of men building a fair due to open in less than two years.

CHAPTER FORTY-TWO

Racing the Clock

A LITTLE OVER A YEAR AFTER AL CAPONE WAS CONVICTED OF TAX EVA-
sion, Congress adopted a resolution to repeal the Eighteenth Amendment. The end of Prohibition would coincide with the opening of the
world's fair in May 1933, and beer would be sold. Among the concessionaires at the world's fair would be the Mueller Schlitz Garden Café, Pabst
Blue Ribbon Casino Seating, Victor Vienna Garden Café, Old Heidel-
berg Inn, and Mueller Pabst Café. The man who might have stopped the
world's fair with Prohibition-era violence was out of the picture, and the
fair had taken over his business. No fortune-teller in the Midway could
have predicted that.

Major Lenox Lohr would sell beer, but what else could he offer? The
American public liked to eat, and feeding the masses was no small feat. In
the end the fairgrounds would include ninety-eight restaurants and cafés
and fifty stands for hot dogs, hamburgers, and fried ham sandwiches.
The Doughnut Machine Corporation had ten stands; Coca-Cola, forty;
Orange Crush, sixty; root beer, twenty; candies, fifty; fruits and nuts,
fifteen; tomato juice, twenty; pineapple juice, ten; ice cream, thirty-three;
and popcorn, forty.

In January 1933 fair planners realized that two bridges to the
island would not suffice. Another would have to be built, but of course
there was no money. The bridge would have space for concessions, and
the planners hit on the idea to offer up those receipts to finance the
construction. A contractor was found who would accept the financing
terms. If the bridge wasn't paid for by June 1933, then gold notes would

cover the remainder. The bridge was built at a cost of $93,686 and paid for by the fees from the concessions.

And then there was the matter of law and order. Chicago had been battling gangsters, but who would keep the peace at the fair? *A Century of Progress* had its own police with "tropical-weight, regulation open jackets of red whipcord, full-length black trousers with yellow stripes on the sides, Sam Brown belts, regulation .38 Colt revolvers with five-inch barrels, blue swagger sticks, white pith helmets with chin straps, light blue shirts and blue ties."[1] Plainclothes men were added to this force to look out for pickpockets and petty criminals known to investigators.

Backing up the police would be the Travelers Aid Society, which already operated in railroad stations and assisted travelers with special circumstances, such as lost funds or bad news from home. A branch set up on the fairgrounds would assist 8,000 fairgoers by 1934. Many of the assists were made to lost children. During the Great Depression many children would come to the fair alone and then present themselves as lost. The policy was to give them a ride home in a police car at midnight. Children soon learned that running off to the fair and spending all your money was not a problem as long as the Travelers Aid Society was there.

The fair worked hard to solve problems peaceably, and in the end only 228 arrests were made. No gangsters were known to attend. Al Capone would have surely gone, had he been free. Public enemy number one may have been in jail, but 1933 would bring the worst year of the Great Depression, with a third of banks closing and a quarter of the population out of work. Capone's soup kitchens still functioned, and they were needed. Chicago was bankrupt. Factories closed, and Herbert Hoover had just lost the presidential election in November 1932 to a man who said citizens had nothing to fear but fear itself. In 1933 Americans feared ending up on the street or starving to death. There was no social safety net beyond help offered by churches and the occasional gangster. And there was not enough of either of those.

Incredibly, as 1933 got under way, the work of the world's fair went on. Major Lohr had long ago run out of money, and now he was running out of time. The opening day was May 27, a mere six months away, and the fairgrounds were a jumble of trucks, steam shovels, and half-built buildings.

Really, the world's fair lakefront resembled the blasted surface of the moon. Created from fill consisting of sand from Indiana, caisson clay, Loop excavations, the charred timbers and ashes of the Chicago fire, bed springs, and auto bodies, the construction site was "three miles of waste relieved by a clump of volunteer poplars on the Island. It had been untouched since the sand dredge and the dump truck had made the land."[2] And now, with the fair a scant six months away, something had to be done. Grass, trees, flowers, and vegetation of all sorts had to be planted, nourished, and hopefully established.

The World's Fair of 1893 had benefited from Frederick Law Olmstead and his brilliant landscape architects. The 1933 World's Fair started out with Ferruccio Vitale, an architect on the committee who got sick and handed the job off to Alfred Geiffert. Like the rest of the fair, the landscaping would have to stand on its own; it would have to be flexible with the asymmetrical design. There would be no overarching "grand plan,"[3] but rather a series of ad hoc plans, although Lohr had a few requirements.

One, it would have to cost very little, as there was no money. And two, the landscaping must complement the architecture and "impart the refreshing feeling of a garden."[4] Then there was the problem of how to plant and make things grow during the construction, which was steaming ahead at full bore. The fill was worthless, and they would have to import soil to have any chance at all of getting Mother Nature to cooperate with the fair.

Soil was shipped by freight train from southern Illinois, unloaded on the fairgrounds, and then trucked to the various sites. "The first order of five thousand cubic yards was delivered in the fall of 1932. . . . [A]n additional store of nine thousand cubic yards was stored at 16th street. . . . [A]n additional pile of twelve thousand yards was brought in during 1933."[5] Five hundred thousand bales of peat moss were brought in to condition the soil. Sixteen hundred trees were planted, including American elms, maples, hackberries, Wheatly elms, Lombardy poplars, various lindens, hawthorns, junipers, and arbors.

The majority of the tree planting took place during the winter and spring before the fair opened. "Twenty-five thousand shrubs were hand planted and twenty-four thousand lineal feet of hedging, mostly privet, forsythia, and two thousand vines were traced onto many walls. Seventy-five thousand square feet of flower beds were scattered around the fair with color a priority."[6] Then the grass was planted throughout to fill in. The planners knew to the day when the seeds would germinate and the first blades appear. In the spring of 1933, all the planting was finished. It was up to Mother Nature. Then it rained and rained and rained for a week. The grass seedlings were washed away, along with the fertilizer and humus-rich earth. *A Century of Progress* became a mud bath. A week before the fair opened, the planners decided to lay sod. "It started rolling in at the rate of 9000 square yards per day."[7] Men worked day and night turning the brown, broken-up earth of the fair into the smooth grounds of an English garden. *A Century of Progress* resembled a big suburban lawn by the end.

CHAPTER FORTY-THREE

Capone on Ice

THE PAPERS SHOUTED FROM THE ROOFTOPS THAT AL CAPONE WAS IN jail. The *New York Times* led the way with "Capone Convicted of Dodging Taxes," while a few people took issue with the tax-evasion conviction. "It is ludicrous that this underworld gang leader had been led to the doors of the penitentiary at last through prosecutions on income tax," wrote the *Boston Globe.*[1] Many were just relieved that he was incarcerated, and Chicagoans rejoiced. Even though Frank Nitti had taken over the operations of the outfit and men were still being mowed down with the Annihilator, Robert Isham Randolph and the Secret Six, Frank Wilson, George Johnson, and the government (and, to some degree, Elliot Ness) had succeeded in the winning of public opinion. Action had been taken. The monster had been shackled. Chicago was now safe, or at least safer. To the men working furiously on finishing the world's fair, this was enough.

Now they had to keep him in jail. Capone had made it as far as Cell Block D, the hospital wing of Cook County Jail. With any luck, he would go no further. His attorneys worked furiously, while Al feasted on tin plates of corned beef and cabbage, water, and a few bites of rice pudding—a long way from steaks at the Lexington or lobsters in Miami. Michael Ahern and company filed a stay to keep their client in Cook County while the appeals went through. If Capone was shipped off to federal prison, they would lose access to him, as well as the impression that their client's conviction was not the train wreck that it seemed.

George Johnson received telegrams saying that Capone was getting special treatment in Cook County. The telegrams went further and said he was running the outfit from jail by phone and messenger. And indeed he was. His visitors included "Jake Guzik, Frankie Rio, Red Barker, Murray Humphreys, and Johnny Torrio."[2] They were not coming to make him feel better; they were doing business. Whiskey was served, and women also were making their way in to the big man.

The *Chicago Herald* announced, "Capone Runs Underworld from Cell."[3] George Johnson visited to see if this was true and found that most of it was not. Still, Capone was winning the battle for public opinion, and the government had a vested interest in never letting him take the reins again. Johnson clamped down on Capone and restricted his visitors to his lawyers and relatives. Then the warden David C. Moneypenny was caught taking Capone's Cadillac for a drive to Springfield, and Johnson clamped down harder.

On March 1, 1932, the Lindbergh baby was kidnapped from his bedroom, and Capone offered his services to find the culprits. Charles Lindbergh was a modern international celebrity. He entertained Capone's offer, which hinged on the gangster being let out of jail to do the work. Frank Wilson killed the proposal and told Lindbergh that Capone had no knowledge of the crime that could help them. Wilson had been working on the case and came up with the idea to record the serial numbers on the money paid to the kidnappers. This would lead to Bruno Richard Hauptman and his garage, where thousands of dollars were found, traced, and identified as the ransom money.

Capone sat in Cook County as his lawyers gave him the bad news: His appeals had failed, and the US Supreme Court would not hear his case. He was going to Leavenworth, Kansas, to do time in the federal penitentiary. Elliot Ness would have one more brush with fame when he escorted Al Capone to the Dearborn Station. In his biography he said they had exchanged words, but in truth they rode in separate cars. The closest Elliot Ness ever came to Al Capone was trailing him to the train station. The rest was pure Hollywood.

The *Dixie Flyer* left Chicago on May 3, 1932, with Capone handcuffed to a car thief named Vito Moirci. Federal agents watched while he smoked cigars, chatted with reporters, and posed for photographers. At every stop crowds peered in the windows of the Pullman car. Capone smiled and waved, much like a baseball player heading off to training camp. When asked what he thought about it all, Capone replied, "I'm not sore at anybody, but I hope Chicago will be better off. . . . [T]hey'll find that sending me away won't help Chicago much."[4] Capone was right. Repeal of Prohibition, not the imprisonment of Al Capone, would end the gangster wars.

Throughout the trip Capone maintained that he had just been giving people what they wanted and blamed the president for the vendetta against him. He could have just paid his taxes, but Herbert Hoover needed to distract people from the Great Depression. Capone's assertions weren't wrong, but he also failed to take responsibility for destroying the reputation of a major American city or to acknowledge that he was his own worst enemy. Even going to jail, he could not stay away from the press, and one could argue that if he had not made himself a target through publicity, he might not have been convicted.

Leavenworth was not a pleasant place. Built and opened in 1903, it was designed to break the will of inmates. The walls of the prison were four feet thick and thirty-seven feet high and enclosed twenty-three acres. His arrival there would begin the US government's tacit campaign to break Al Capone. He had put Chicago and Washington through hell, and convicting him had cost time and money and demanded huge resources. Now the United States would make sure he never resumed his role as head of the outfit.

Capone surrendered the "$231 in his pocket" when he arrived as well as "religious medals, a rosary, a nail clipper, a fountain pen, a wallet, and a single key. He received a pair of blue denim overalls with the number 40886 stitched on a trouser leg. In his medical examination he weighed in at 255 pounds . . . 20/20 vision in his right eye and 20/40 in his left. His blood pressure was . . . 130/100. . . . [H]e was suffering from arthritis, a deviated septum," and a severely swollen prostate gland.[5]

Al Capone was thirty-three years old, with an average IQ of 95. A blood test came back positive for "nervous system syphilis."[6] He had contracted it when he was twenty-one, and now it was coming back. In 15 percent of the cases syphilis caused brain damage, leading to dementia and sometimes blindness or death. Al Capone was destined to be among the 15 percent. The prison hospital put him on bismuth therapy and a series of other chemicals that his family later claimed robbed him of his mind.

Al Capone cobbled shoes for eight hours a day in the prison factory. The newspapers reported again that he was receiving special treatment, getting to wear silk underwear, having money smuggled in, and being allowed more time to play softball and tennis. His cellmate would claim that Capone hid cash in the hollowed-out handle of his tennis racket. The government investigated and found nothing amiss. In reality, Al Capone was becoming just another number in the US penal system, and people were beginning to forget his name. Besides, a world's fair was opening in Chicago in the summer of 1933, and it was supposed to be the biggest yet.

Chapter Forty-Four

Lady Godiva Again

Lenox Lohr described the world's fair's opening like this: "A little orange-colored ray of starlight completed a forty-year journey and turned on the lights for a Century of Progress."[1] In modern terms, a bit of starlight hit a telescope, then a photoelectric cell, and switched on the lights. But let's keep it dramatic.

Forty years before, during the fair of 1893, the star Arcturus had beamed its pinpoint of light at the earth; now that beam was striking a photoelectric cell that converted the light energy into electricity that raced through Western Union lines toward Chicago, then entered a circuit closing a relay that fired up a generator, releasing the massive power into the searchlights and colored beams lighting the Rainbow City at the 1933 Chicago World's Fair.

It was May 27, and 120,000 people had showed up for the opening-day ceremonies; a respectable crowd of the Chicago upper crust cheered as the city's second world's fair in forty years opened its gates that night. A naked woman sitting astride a snow-white horse heard the cheer and watched the colored lights shoot up into the heavens. The searchlights were the most powerful the fair promoters could come up with and returned the starlight that had beamed from Arcturus when the Columbian Exposition had opened in 1893. The woman on the horse gliding across the lake toward the fair knew none of this (and wouldn't have cared even if she did).

Earlier that day, Sally had walked up to the front gate and been stopped by a thug of a guard. She had nothing on except the body paint, her blond wig, and the cape, bright against the early darkness. Still, the short man with few teeth shook his head: "No. You can't enter without no invitation." The man's eyes had passed over her, but Sally realized then that he wasn't budging. It was the opening extravaganza of the 1933 Chicago World's Fair, *A Century of Progress*, and she, Sally Rand, wasn't part of it. It was only for the mayor and his cronies and the Gold Coast jeweled bats and their husbands who went to the burlesque shows on State Street that Sally danced in. Some were from the North Shore, and there were plenty of gangsters in attendance from the look of the mugs hanging around the black Cadillacs. Anybody who was anybody was there, but not Sally Rand.

She stomped back to her army tent and ducked under the green flap, cursing Charlie Web, the beer commissioner who had said he would get her in. Charlie was nowhere to be seen, and Sally was freezing after walking across the landfill the fair had been built on.

Eddie Callahan met her in the tent, his squinty eyes shining.

"What are you doin' back, babe?"

"They won't let me in," she muttered, slumping down in front of a makeshift table and putting her legs up, not caring what Eddie saw.

He saw a lot, judging from the way his jaw dropped. Sally pulled the cape around to cover her privates. What did she care? At least he wanted to see her. Callahan recovered his composure and grunted, rubbing his jaw. Sally turned to the short promoter, cigarette smoke shooting from her mouth. "I gotta get into that fair, Eddie. This is my last chance . . . I'll do anything, but I gotta get in there and be part of this. There's nothing but the fair now. . . . This is like the movies for me. If I don't make it now, I got nothing left."

"Let me think, let me think," Eddie muttered, staring toward the muckety-muck extravaganza going on behind the high fence. It burned him the way the high society excluded him because he was Irish and ran a burlesque show at The Paramount. The Irish and the Italians were equally detested in America, with the greatest prejudice reserved for southern Italians. Callahan blinked and couldn't believe what he was seeing. A man was walking outside the tent with a white, saddled horse. The same inspiration washed over Eddie that had made him put money down on the club when everyone said he was crazy. Eddie saw the horse, like the club, as sheer providence. He pulled out the wad of cash he always kept on him just in case.

"Hold on a minute, babe," he said, walking into the darkness.

"Yeah, sure." She shrugged. "I got nowhere else to go."

Sally sat dejectedly, feeling just like she had when Cecil B. DeMille told her he couldn't use her anymore. She had been on her way in the silent films, but then those damn talkies came. Hollywood changed overnight, and she couldn't find work.

Eddie came back in holding a bridle and smiling like a leprechaun. Sally jumped straight up and the cape fell again.

"What the hell, Eddie!"

She stared at the tall, white horse. Eddie gestured to the beast, his randy eyes not leaving her loins.

"You are going to the party, babe."

Sally Rand sat sidesaddle on the horse and stared at the dock coming closer. Where Eddie had got the boat, she had no idea, but it was the only way in. There were plenty of rumrunners at the docks, and Eddie probably owned a few. There were no fences walling off Lake Michigan, and so, like an army approaching by sea, she and Eddie were floating directly toward the main fairgrounds that led to the Streets of Paris, where the party was taking place on a stage. Sally could smell dead fish and the rumrunner's diesel exhaust. She saw the lighthouse out beyond Navy Pier flashing red. Eddie knew the bootleggers, with their long, sleek boats that kept Chicago speakeasies in gin and beer. So it didn't surprise Sally that he came up with a boat when she pointed out that they still couldn't get into the party.

"We aren't going in the front gate; we're going in the back," he answered.

Sally Rand looked at the stubby Irishman.

"Eddie . . . that's the fricking lake!"

"Yeah. And that's the way we are going in, babe. From the water."

She had rolled her eyes, but then he disappeared again, and sure enough, half an hour later, she heard a boat rumble up. And now the boat was bobbing, and Eddie was guiding it down the dock. Sally had ridden horses in Missouri a long time ago. She remembered her mother taking her to theaters in Kansas to get her start and how she had tried to not talk like her. She couldn't afford to be some hick from Missouri, and her mother cried when she hit the road with no real destination but Hollywood. "I don't know how I'm going to do it, Ma," Harriet Beck had said before becoming Sally Rand. "But I'm going to be a star."

She thought about falling off the horse, but now was not the time to worry. Now was the time to show the world who Sally Rand was. The bow bumped against the bleached and rickety dock, which hadn't been used for a long time. Eddie snugged the boat as close to the shore as he could. Then he jumped out into the shallow water and guided the horse off the boat.

Eddie looked up with his hard, bright eyes and handed her the harness. "Go get 'em, babe."

Sally leaned down against the horse's mane and dug her bare heels into his sides. The horse jumped, and they galloped up the shore through the warm night, with the smell of rich food cooking and a soft breeze of perfume and cologne and cigars. Her long, blond hair flew back as the white horse clattered down the cobblestone lanes of Paris. Sally was homing in on the smell of the rich, with a nose for what would benefit her, the same way she had homed in on Eddie and made him her unofficial promoter. Her heart beat so hard she could hear it.

Now she was galloping down the streets of the Left Bank, constructed three days before to look just like Paris, with cafés and shows. The lights ahead told her where the real show was, and the twenty-three-year-old hugged the warm mane, turned the corner, and saw the stage. It wasn't high and had a ramp made for a woman charging in on a white horse.

Sally felt her cape fly behind her, and now she was a naked, painted blond of exceptional beauty with long legs astride her mount. Lady Godiva had nothing on her, and riding a horse in the nude had worked well for Lady Godiva, so why wouldn't it work for Sally Rand? She leaned in and heard the people shouting. She saw a policeman raise his hand, and then she hit the ramp with the iron horseshoes clattering on wood as the horse carried her onto the stage. The lights warmed her, and Sally heard people screaming and the music stopping. Then she reined in hard, and the white horse reared back perfectly, as photographers froze the moment.

Sally squinted into the glare and saw the matrons in jewels and long heavy dresses, the men in tuxedos and mustaches, the police, and then the blessed photographers. She sat straight up on the horse with her breasts firm and high while her white steed pranced, and she heard more shouts as she raised her hand and waved, and then people began to clap. They stood up and began to shout. This was the World's Fair of 1933! *A Century of Progress*! Of course a naked woman would gallop in on a white horse, then pull up in front of the cream of Chicago society and wave with all her womanhood on display! It was shocking, rude, outlandish, insulting, brilliant—it was Chicago! Just what the Rainbow City said to the world: To hell with the Depression and to hell with the gangsters. I Will! I Will! Chicago's second world's fair was going to break all the molds, and that included sex.

Sally Rand trotted from one side of the stage to the other, and the horse stood again on his back legs. Flashes flew like rose petals. There must have been a hundred photographers while the audience applauded like mad. This beautiful naked woman on a white horse had just opened the Chicago World's Fair of 1933, *A Century of Progress*, and there was no turning back. She was promptly arrested for lewd conduct, but it didn't matter. The star Arcturus had nothing on Sally Rand.

CHAPTER FORTY-FIVE

Death of the Untouchables

ELLIOT NESS WOULD NEVER TOP THE HIGH OF HIS TIME WITH THE Untouchables—a book, then a television series, and eventually a movie immortalized his name. But in real life he ended up as Cleveland's public safety director. He attacked corruption in the Cleveland Police Department, but stories of his drinking and infidelities followed him, and he wrapped his car around a tree in 1942 after a bender. A mayoral race in Cleveland didn't pan out, and, as with all alcoholics, the drinking began to take a heavy toll. A series of jobs outside law enforcement led to his selling frozen food to restaurant chains. A heart attack touched the untouchable in 1957 and kept him from ever seeing his life immortalized on the screen.

A different gangster drove out the rest of the Untouchables: the Great Depression. Chicago was hit the hardest, with thirty-eight banks closing in one month in 1932. While the Rainbow City was rising, Chicago teetered on the edge of bankruptcy during 1930, 1931, and 1932. "At one point Chicago was in debt $300,000. . . . [O]ne month after Capone had been convicted, the president of the First National Bank of Chicago said, 'we are busted in the United States.'" Chicago had no credit left to pay "school teachers, fireman, or police."[1]

The Secret Six fell apart. Samuel Insull, one of the group's main backers, was destroyed when his utilities empire crumbled and investors lost $785 million. He fled to Paris, and the battle to extradite him was front-page news. He was tried for mail fraud and embezzlement and acquitted. He died in 1938 with a debt of $14 million. Two other members of the Six also died: Julius Rosenwald in 1932 and Edward Gore in 1935. A scandal involving state's attorney John Swanson over alleged wiretapping by the Secret Six in 1932 all but finished the group. In 1933, "the Chicago Association of Commerce disbanded the Secret Six."[2]

Robert Isham Randolph continued on and was appointed director of operations during the Chicago World's Fair. The title allowed him some vigilante freedom, and he exercised it one night on June 8, 1934, when he took one final swipe at the Capone gang. Joseph Fusco, Matthew Capone, Dennis Cooney, and Ralph Capone went to the Old Mexico exhibit to watch Rosalia, a fan dancer. "Just before Rosalia made her appearance, Randolph and twenty-five fair police officers escorted Fusco, Cooney, and the two Capone brothers to jail. The hoodlums were not doing anything but munching on sandwiches and drinking beer when Randolph had them arrested. He later explained the arrests of the gangsters by saying, 'the reputation of the fair must be protected.'"[3]

Randolph was nominated as the Republican candidate to serve as Illinois's representative to the US Congress but lost to a Democrat. When World War II broke out, he enlisted, but the army discharged him in 1943. He was sixty and would die eight years later.

While Capone sat in jail, Franklin Roosevelt trounced Herbert Hoover in a landslide, pushed though the New Deal, and got the booze flowing again in 1933. He went to the world's fair and asked that it continue another year. Roosevelt saw it as an engine to get Americans buying again, and, being a sunny optimist, he related to the futuristic fair of bright colors along the wide, blue lake. In one hundred days, he had enacted the "Emergency Banking Relief Act, The Public Works Administration, the Civilian Conservation Corps, the Tennessee Valley Authority, the National Industrial Recovery Act and the Federal Deposit Insurance Corporation."[4]

The president knew that Americans must start spending again, and *A Century of Progress* showed that consumerism would save the economy, the country, and maybe the world. Even though the fair was a blazing success by all standards, the Great Depression wouldn't end until America became the world's supplier of tanks, weapons, and troops. World War II would do what *A Century of Progress* could not. The Great Depression ended when the Japanese bombed Pearl Harbor on December 7, 1941.

CHAPTER FORTY-SIX

A Day at the Fair

VERNON CISKE WAS ELEVEN YEARS OLD IN 1933 WHEN HE WALKED TO the world's fair from Sagamore and Madison on Chicago's West Side. Like most people in the city, he hadn't ventured more than a few miles from his city block. Vern arrived at the fair and passed Sally Rand on life-size posters, her feathers just covering her loins and breasts. He was alone but knew better than to go into that tent. "My mother would have worn me out with a switch," he remarked eighty-one years later. "I wanted to go on the Sky Ride and take a boat ride."[1]

He didn't pay the admission price at the front gate of fifty cents for adults and a quarter for kids. He couldn't. "I didn't have two nickels to rub together. You just walked in with the people in line. It wasn't hard. I must have gone a half dozen times."[2] Riding on a streetcar cost three cents at the time. The electricity in the cold-water flat Vern's family lived in had been shut off for nonpayment and would stay off for a year. The family got its lighting from old gas fixtures, a common practice during the Great Depression.

Children flocked to the world's fair and would overwhelm the gate on the designated "Children's Day." There was no youth culture in America and less for kids to do during the Great Depression. Many children went to work right after high school, if not before. But here was a child's mecca built on the lakeshore of Chicago. As the *Chicago Tribune* reported, "In spite of the broiling heat, the happy invaders surged upon the grounds by the thousands."[3] When the turnstile tabulators became jammed, the gates were thrown open, and kids like Vern Ciske entered for free.

Once inside, Vern noticed people had dressed up for the fair. Women were in dresses and heels. Some men wore suits; others wore spats with open white shirts. Some sported sunglasses. Most people didn't have the money for such luxuries in 1933. The crowd was middle-class and white. There were no African Americans. The world's fair was a convention of white people, and fair planners would concede to hold "Negro Day" to pacify black leaders.

Vern headed for the Sky Ride, took the elevator up, and rode a cable car two hundred feet in the air out to Northerly Island in the lake. The world unfolded below the eleven-year-old. He then ascended in the elevator to the top of the 625-foot tower and looked out. He had never been that high before, and the experience changed his view of the world. "I never knew what Chicago looked like from above before that," the ninety-two-year-old engineer recalled. "I never knew buildings looked like blocks."[4] Vern wouldn't get a bird's-eye view of the earth again until 1941, when he served as a navigator in a B17 bomber.

Afterward, the boy headed over for a speedboat ride out on the lake. There were gondolas there as well, and Vern availed himself of a pole-driven ride across the lagoon. He passed the Century of Progress Exposition Fountain, the world's largest, stretching one thousand feet into the water. Lagoon boats ferried people out to Northerly Island. In 1933 Chicagoans didn't ride in lagoon boats, speedboats, or gondolas. They walked or took electric streetcars run by a gloved man turning a wheel that reversed current in a transformer to go forward or backward. Vern had only ridden in a car twice, once with a delivery man who had driven him to Austin Avenue, the city's western boundary. So for a boy in 1933, riding in a boat with the wind whipping back his hair was an amazing experience.

Of course, the whole fair was amazing. Held on 427 acres along the south end of the lakefront on landfill from the Great Chicago Fire, the fair stretched along the lakefront from Roosevelt Road to 39th Street. Captain Frank Hawkes had just landed his plane and broken the transcontinental record. Men assembled cars in twenty minutes in the Chrysler Building as people watched. The 140-foot-long Goodyear blimp, *The Puritan*, hummed overhead, filled with people looking down on the boy who would shortly marvel at a man in the Hall of Science exhaling liquid oxygen.

Another very different person also had her eye on the fair. Sally Rand would pull in $6,000 a week by updating Fahreda Mahzur's belly dance, which had been a hit at the Columbian Exposition forty years before. The police would arrest the ex–movie actress many times for lewd behavior and bust other girls at the peep shows for having sex with men who paid for a dance, but popular modern culture was taking hold in America, and the urban fair of 1933 codified this in one of the largest displays of sex through the fantasy of striptease and burlesque. *A Century of Progress* celebrated not only technological but also sexual advancement, where for $1.75 people could sit in the darkness and forget about bread lines and soup kitchens while Sally Rand showed them another reality, if only for a little while.

In the end, 48 million people would pass through the Rainbow City on the lake, and 39 million would be paying customers. The fair would run from 1933 to 1934, bringing $400 million into Chicago's department stores, hotels, and restaurants and creating 22,000 jobs in construction and fair-related businesses. There would be 1,476 meetings at convention centers because of the fair, and, astonishingly, in the depths of the Great Depression, American businesses would invest $32 million as exhibitors. Not only did the fair save Chicago, but American business also saw it as an opportunity to showcase the benefits of capitalism versus communism, whose takeover was a very real possibility at the time.

The Dawes brothers, Rufus and Charles, found financing when Chicago was bankrupt and persuaded American businesses that displaying their ingenuity would convince consumers to spend again. The architects known as the "gang of eight" were pushed to come up with innovative ways of building inexpensively that became standard practice. Eight architects would put differences aside and pioneer building on a budget, while famed architect Frank Lloyd Wright put forth three radical plans that, never to be acted on, would languish in obscurity.

Vern walked through the Midway and saw the Streets of Paris, with its randy burlesque shows and Uncle Buck's Jungle Camp. He hummed the Pepsi Cola jingle from the fair: "Twice as much for a nickel too,

Pepsi Cola is the drink for you." He knew the song, but he didn't have a nickel. Pepsi was trying to move in on Coca-Cola's market by doubling the six-ounce bottle to twelve ounces. A deal for fairgoers, but a nickel could buy three donuts and a coffee at the restaurant around the corner from his house.

A cigarette girl with a box of Old Golds around her neck gave him a free pack of ten souvenir cigarettes. Vern took them to smoke on the way home. Like a lot of boys from the West Side, he had been smoking since he was nine. Somewhere he picked up a wallet embossed in gold with the words "Century of Progress 1933." Decades later he couldn't remember how he got it.

It was getting dark, and Vern had to walk home. In his neighborhood few cars passed down the street. "Nobody had cars then. . . . [W]e played in the street all the time. There were still blacksmiths on the corners. So you walked everywhere," he explained almost a century later. "I would have taken my bike I had built from spare parts at the Good Will, but I didn't have the money for a chain."[5]

It was dark, and Vern lit up one of his world's fair cigarettes and headed for home. He thought about the Italian aviator who had landed after a transatlantic crossing and wondered how he had enough gas. Vern had two pairs of pants and three shirts to his name and was returning to a cold flat without electricity. But the eleven-year-old's day at the world's fair was not bounded by money.

The Westinghouse show of a man creating an electrical arc, the house of the future, the Sky Ride, the Goodyear blimp—all had sparked his imagination. Perhaps they led Vern to become an engineer one day and build candy factories all over Chicago. The 1933 World's Fair was simply the promise that times would get better and a brighter world was waiting.

CHAPTER FORTY-SEVEN

Sex at the Fair

THE COPS ROLLED UP TO THE CHICAGO THEATRE TO ARREST SALLY FOR the fourth time that day. She just wouldn't stop taking off her clothes. And why should she? Sally Rand was one of the biggest draws of the 1933 Chicago World's Fair. Rand finished up her dance and allowed the sergeant and policewoman to escort her to the station. She was booked and then went to her regular show at the Streets of Paris. The arrests, while a nuisance, worked in her favor. Each garnered headlines and brought more people to her shows.

It came down to Judge Erwin J. Hasten to decide whether Sally Rand's show was lewd. The judge smiled at the diminutive defendant as he heard the arguments for her dance. It was art, not "lascivious burlesque."[1] The attorneys interrogated the arresting officers who had seen the dance. They admitted to their passions being aroused and their pulses quickened. The judge had also seen the show and thought she was a beautiful dancer.

Sally Rand took the stand and explained, "My dance is art. . . . [M]y public wants me. There is nothing vulgar, lewd, or obscene about my dancing."[2] She further explained that her dance came to her after she had watched a swan. She covered her body with "thick white cream"[3] and, in lifting her arms, created an illusion of that graceful bird. The judge wanted to know if her breasts and loins were covered. Sally replied that they were except for one moment. "In the middle of the dance, without ostentation, my gown is removed at the side of the stage. After that I open my fans."[4]

The judge fined her $25 for indecent exhibition and required some mesh under the grease paint. The newspapers proclaimed that the judge saw the dance as art and featured many photographs of Rand with members of the court. At the Chicago Theatre admission fees topped $79,000 in one week, at the fair revenues soared, and Rand's salary climbed to $1,000 a week during the worst year of the Great Depression.

"The Streets of Paris took in so much cash that a Century of Progress had to establish a separate banking operation."[5] Revenues for the Streets of Paris in general hit $100,000 a day, with $500 of that going to the peep shows. There were many dancers at *A Century of Progress* besides Sally Rand, but she was the most sensational. Faith Bacon, who claimed to have originated the fan dance, said any kind of clothing took away from it. "Long legs, long hair, a small waist, full breasts, and two fans were required to create this ethereal art."[6] Bacon added that getting arrested was key, because that brought publicity, which brought people. "Be sure you spell your name right to the reporters," she admonished.

Sally Rand was a headliner at the Streets of Paris, but for a cheaper thrill people could pay a dime or a quarter at the peep shows and maybe see a dancer. The peep shows were part hoax, part lurid, part stupid. In a small dark space for a couple of minutes the patron viewed a woman, a man, or a clown. No one knew in advance what he or she'd see, and many surely felt ripped off. But the truth was that Sally Rand performed with a very seedy element of the fair.

In Life Class, people paid a quarter for a crayon and a piece of paper and sketched a mostly naked woman sitting on a chair. In Visions of Light, three topless women danced to flashing lights and music.[7] In another show three baseballs thrown at a target might bring a mostly naked woman rolling out of a bed. The fair allowed nudity but balked at prostitution. At the Dance Ship a man could dance with a woman who "wiggled her body up and down,"[8] and then a date was arranged for a price in an annexed room. Sex was rampant.

The fact that everyone was drinking in public for the first time in ten years perfected the recipe for lust unbounded. Major Lenox Lohr's assistant, Martha McGrew, shut down the Dance Ship after several attempts to prove prostitution was going on. She had considerable power over the fair's operations and enacted a 1:30 a.m. curfew "to reduce the problems of drunken unescorted women who might take a notion to fall into the lagoon."[9] The Dance Ship changed its name to the Pirate Ship and brought in Texas Guinan and her nightclub revue, under the new name "A Century of Whoopee,"[10] to compete directly with Sally Rand.

But some people just were prudes. Mary Belle Spencer, a lawyer and mother of two, filed an injunction against nudity at the Streets of Paris. She contended that nudity "represented a cess pool of iniquity, a condition of depravity and total disregard of purity and display of the most disgraceful lewdness and abandon ever publicly shown in any institution of the character such as this Century of Progress purports to represent."[11] Spencer claimed that Sally Rand and her like would harm property values, as families would not want to come to Chicago after going to the fair and businesses were less likely to settle in a town that promoted such lewd displays.

The suit ended up in the lap of superior court judge Joseph B. David, who did not really want to hear the case. He made his pronouncement: "They are just a lot of boobs to come to see a woman wiggle with a fan or without fig leaves. But we have the boobs and we have a right to cater to them."[12] Attorney Jay McCarthy fought an uphill battle to show that nudity corrupted the public. Judge David dismissed his argument, saying, "Some people want to put pants on a horse. . . . If a woman wiggles about with a fan, it is not the business of the court. . . . I would be the last person to cast a blotch upon A Century of Progress."[13] Mary Belle Spencer would later admit that she was trying to gin up business for her law practice, but nudity did irritate her.

Still, the fair was cognizant of the nudity problem. President Rufus Dawes got involved and told concessionaires they had to "modify nudity in their shows."[14] Frank Bell, who headed up operations and maintenance, dictated that, at a minimum, women must wear something over their loins and breasts. Major Lohr, who took his wife to the fair, as well as other dignitaries, saw what was going on but did little about it. The Streets of Paris was a cash cow, and you don't shoot the cow before you have milked it of all the cash.

Then, in July 1933, Mayor Edward Kelly and state's attorney Thomas J. Courtney visited the Streets of Paris and deemed some of the shows "cheap, tawdry, and downright suggestive."[15] The mayor summoned Lohr and George Donoghue, superintendent of the parks, to his office and told them to clean up the sideshows or shut them down. The major was in a quandary. He personally saw nothing wrong with the shows and noted that most of the patrons went home satisfied. Still, something had to be done.

From now on, Lohr and others decreed, dancers had to wear bras and panties. Sally Rand improvised with a piece of gauze. Several dancers began to wear "invisible clothing."[16] With the use of special lighting that "masked the invisible clothing," police couldn't be sure what the dancers had on. In frustration, a policewoman named Hazel Ward forced Sally Rand to dance in a long nightgown one night.

Lohr later commented on the nudity problems of the Streets of Paris: by getting arrested and going to court, "fan dancers and oriental dancers presented a serious dilemma."[17] They became the fair's most lucrative attraction. He never mentioned Sally Rand or the extraordinary amount of money generated by sex at the fair. Even Hollywood took note, and William Hays, president of the Motion Picture Producers and Distributors of America, issued a special ban on the fan dance in movies.

The truth is, *A Century of Progress* allowed working-class women with little education to make money in the worst times of the Great Depression. The dancers at the 1933 World's Fair in Chicago were not middle class. Like Sally Rand, they had taken their shows on the road to find freedom, money, and maybe fame. Inadvertently they pushed the sexual revolution from the bottom up and made it a part of *A Century of Progress*.

A rags-to-riches story in her own right, Sally Rand inadvertently pushed sexual liberation for women by celebrating the body but also by leading by example, insisting on a woman's right to make money from her body. As Cheryl Ganz writes in *The 1933 Chicago World's Fair*, "Singled out by the media as the fan dancer extraordinaire, Sally Rand became the popular heroine of sexual service work. . . . Rand defied those who would define public morality by banning nude dancing, and in doing so she represented those who enjoyed a bit of sex and vice in films, tabloids, magazines and on stage."[18]

Sally Rand was ahead of her time, but this was the theme, after all, of *A Century of Progress*.

CHAPTER FORTY-EIGHT

A Century of Progress

A CENTURY OF PROGRESS TECHNICALLY CELEBRATED THE HUNDRED-YEAR anniversary of the village of Chicago's incorporation. This was an era of progress, and the people who viewed the dream homes and cars of the future didn't have enough money in their pockets for souvenirs. Whereas the Columbian Exposition had asked fairgoers to believe in humanity, the 1933 fair asked them to put their faith in science and technology to make their lives better. The fair was a secular celebration that provided a beacon of hope after the carnage of World War I, the hedonism of the 1920s, and the collapse of the American economic system.

The fair would ultimately cost $100 million, paid for entirely by private enterprise. In this way it was the first "corporate fair,"[1] financed, pushed, and produced by executives who believed the best way out of the Great Depression was to get the American public back on the road to consumerism. It was the grandest commercial ever produced and would serve as an economic catalyst for Chicago and the nation.

The same time constraints applied that had dogged the 1893 fair, with many believing that organizers could never finish it within the allotted five years. Louis Sullivan had criticized the architectural plan of the first fair, and Frank Lloyd Wright would be a thorn in the side of planners of the 1933 event. But the fair planners of the Columbian Exposition hadn't had to contend with Al Capone.

The connection between the Columbian Exhibition of 1893 and the 1933 World's Fair couldn't be any clearer. Daniel Burnham had laid out the first fair, and now his son, Daniel Burnham Jr., was secretary of the second. Burnham Sr.'s 1909 Plan of Chicago had called for creation of a series of five islands as parks for the people of Chicago. Only Northerly Island would be built, and not until 1925. Mayor William Thompson had envisioned an airport as its primary use, but the Great Depression had blasted away any such future plans. The vacant land composed of landfill dredged from the lake bottom and debris from the Great Chicago Fire served no real purpose until the 1933 World's Fair.

Planners had wracked their brains for an attraction to top the Ferris wheel, the Columbian Exposition's response to the 1889 Paris fair's Eiffel Tower. The Ferris wheel had pushed the limits of technology at the time. To come up with something even more sensational than carrying people aloft on a giant wheel would take all the skill and resources the fair planners possessed.

The answer would take eighteen months of work and 1,652 men at a cost of $1.4 million during the Depression. For forty cents people could ascend in a double-decker elevator a third of the way up two twin, 625-foot steel towers, then board an airship and travel at six miles an hour over the lagoon along with thirty-six other people. A rocket car loaded with 40,000 pounds of wet sand and sent across the lagoon assured engineers the Sky Ride was safe.

A reporter for the *Chicago Tribune* who rode in the Sky Ride summed it up this way: "They seal you in and start you off, bumping slightly, for a ride across the lagoon to the tower on the other side. It costs you forty cents a head to see this sky view of the fair and another forty to go to the top of the tower. A clear day in the towers gives you an idea of the spreading city below you."[2] For a population that hadn't seen earth from the window of a plane, this had the same wondrous appeal as going into space.

Corn kernels would be popped with invisible microwaves. People could get their hand x-rayed and see their own bones for the first time or talk to a robot smoking a cigarette. Visitors could enter a theater at the Hall of Science and be televised onto a screen. For people born at the turn of the century, watching television was akin to flying to another planet.

Masonite, vinyl, Sheetrock, asbestos, plywood, and Formica used in construction were introduced to the public, along with the floating, cantilevered roof. The modernist movement in architecture would be on display and represent a clear break with the past, when form had taken precedence over function. Prefabricated structures, defined for people as "Houses of Tomorrow," were bolted together in days.[3] The entire *Century of Progress* exhibition was designed to last just one year. The technology it employed would later fuel the building boom after World War II, when suburban houses were mass-produced for returning GIs. Today's suburban sprawl harkens back to innovations pioneered during the 1933 World's Fair.

Visitors in the darkest year of the Great Depression could see a glass man light up and talk about his own organs. The first Major League Baseball All Star Game was played in Comiskey Park. People could make a long-distance call to fifty-four cities and for the first time talk to a faraway relative or friend. People cried, laughed, or listened with reverence as Aunt Mildred or Uncle George spoke to them from thousands of miles away.

Yet the most popular exhibits involved mass production. A canning machine that produced a souvenir can after a person pushed a button proved so overwhelming that one in forty couldn't operate it. Americans in 1933 had never seen a large machine with moving parts produce one item after another. Technology, especially industrial technology, had been invisible to people in the third decade of the century. Some were simply too scared to even touch the button.

An actual car assembly line in the Chrysler Building was another extremely popular exhibit. People watched two hundred workers put Chevrolets together and then drive them away. Transportation was held out as a marvel when the *Pioneer Zephyr* steam locomotive pulled up to the fair after making a Denver-to-Chicago dawn-to-dusk speed record. The *Graf Zeppelin*, complete with swastikas recently painted on the side, landed on the fairgrounds, and an Italian aviator landed his planes after a transatlantic crossing. A giant 218-foot thermometer would tell the temperature with neon tubes. Judy Garland would sing. Sally Rand would dance.

George Keck's House of Tomorrow featured synthetic building materials and forecast a future in which dishwashers and air-conditioning would be commonplace household items. Glass doors whisked open magically as people walked into bright, airy homes that faced the amazing teal of Lake Michigan. To Depression-era fairgoers, this was the same as telling their counterparts in the 1980s that they would one day have computers in their homes.

The Hall of Science itself was breathtaking, covering eight acres, with a 175-foot tower capped by a twenty-five-note carillon and constructed of innovative asbestos wallboard. The dazzling facade brought people to a standstill. At a time when life seemed bleak, the building's brilliant colors lifted downtrodden spirits, inviting people to escape, to play, to hope again. Twenty-four brilliant colors created contrast and variety, earning the fair the name "The Rainbow City."

Sally Rand created a special dance for the fair using a giant plastic bubble in place of the ostrich feathers. Her fame grew, and as Cheryl Ganz later wrote, "Many fairgoers carried her spirit and message home with them in the little Tru-Vue souvenir film strip that captured images of her bubble dance."[4] The next day, the next week, and through all the dark days of the Depression, any time they picked up the little plastic viewer, Sally Rand remained on the opening frame of the strip. "The bubble dance as created by Sally Rand is a poetic interpretation of life. Just as the bubble silently, gracefully rises, falls, and floats away and returns . . . so too our hopes, dreams, and ambitions move before us."[5]

CHAPTER FORTY-NINE

Rags to Riches

HORATIO ALGER REFLECTS BACK AT US FROM EVERY CORNER OF THE republic. The country was built, and continues to feed, on the notion that anyone in America can become as rich or as famous as they want. That promise had propelled the gangster and the nymph. It had propelled the 1933 World's Fair. It was the flip side of the Great Depression. Despair is the other side of optimism.

So, in the stew of *A Century of Progress* we find the poor girl from Missouri going out to find her fame and fortune in Hollywood, only to end up back in Chicago without a nickel to her name but in possession of a pair of ostrich feathers. She would then become world famous and find some fortune. We find the poor Italian in Brooklyn stealing from fruit stands for his family and then becoming the most powerful and richest gangster in American history.

And so they meet in Chicago as the nation teeters on the edge of the economic abyss and then falls in. A world's fair shifts into gear, denoting first the incorporation of Chicago as a village and then, with high irony, *A Century of Progress* during the worst gang war in history and then the Great Depression, which empties the city of its capital, its jobs, its very lifeblood. The stage is set for a very great fall or a very great comeback.

The story is the struggle to pull off a world's fair without public money, under the aegis of corporate money, corporate leadership, and a corporate effort to rid Chicago of Al Capone. Major Lenox Lohr immediately offered corporate America an opportunity to showcase its products as long as it paid for the building and exhibits. In this way he had corporations build many of the structures at *A Century of Progress* and advertise the fair to the public.

When the fair was still in the planning stages Chicago had been taken over by Al Capone and his outfit. Democracy might just be dialectic, and the fact that one man could take over a major American city is a cautionary tale. Just as the fair was promoted to bring back consumers with corporate products, the same money was found to rid the city of Al Capone. And it is interesting to note it was done with a financial device.

Gone was the first fair, with its celebration of the arts. Adolf Hitler would send over his dirigible and set off a firestorm in 1933. He would have done well to take note of the 1933 World's Fair. It represented a flexing of industrial muscle that would come to fruition in eight short years after American entry into World War II. Had he been so inclined, Hitler would have seen the Chrysler and Ford assembly lines slapping cars together in record time while people watched. He would have noted the resourcefulness and use of cutting-edge technology to build an entire city with running water, lights, and phones in less than three years.

Hitler would have noticed the mechanization of canning and the strange new beamed images of something called television. He would have noted the Sky Ride, spanning the lagoon and erected faster than the San Francisco Bridge, yet even taller. He would have noted the power of telecommunications, of lighting technology, of steam engines, planes, and cars, the smooth mechanization of moving 50 million people through a fair that generated a profit when the whole world was experiencing the worst times in modern history.

An industrial giant was just awakening, and an American century just beginning. *A Century of Progress* shows how corporate might had moved into the ascendancy and solved the crime problems of Chicago and then put on a fair that rivaled anything Europe could have achieved in scope, advancement, time, and money. America, while knocked to its knees in the nadir of the Great Depression, still had raw economic and industrial strength that would eventually outweigh that of Germany and the Axis powers combined. Hitler had dismissed Americans as a mongrel people, but he missed the power of a cohesive culture that held out amazing opportunity.

Of course, Adolf Hitler was oblivious, as were most people who doubted the fair would ever come off. The press roundly predicted *A Century of Progress* would be a financial and psychological disaster. But packing Al Capone off to prison generated a boost, and then, in a cultural vacuum, the Rainbow City came to life, and a fan dancer named Sally Rand, who had failed as a star in Hollywood, would become the number one draw of the fair and roll in a host of possibilities.

Judy Garland sang at the 1933 World's Fair, and Sally Rand danced, and both young women were emblematic of better times to come. Judy would give people hope in 1939 in *The Wizard of Oz*, proclaiming there was no place like home, and Sally Rand showed it by turning her one asset into a vehicle for fame and fortune. In this way she pulled herself up by the proverbial bootstraps at a time when it seemed impossible to do so.

Sally Rand reflected a future when even sex might be decriminalized and people could have pleasure without guilt—then anathema to the white Anglo-Saxon ethos that characterized most of the country. Sex was bad if not used for procreation, but Prohibition had pulled the lid off that one. Women were already drinking, smoking, and having sex behind closed doors; Sally Rand just brought it all out into the open.

Even Al Capone's demise is part of the story. He did pull himself up, but his fall from grace ensured that he would sink back down. Sally Rand pulled herself up, and some would say that her "profession" contributed to her later demise. American culture does add caveats to its Horatio Alger ethos, and, as from Gatsby in F. Scott Fitzgerald's classic, we demand a moral component when the rags turn to riches, which also speaks to our discomfort with real wealth. We all want it, but it is tainted, as in the Old Testament's admonishment that it is easier for a camel to go through the eye of a needle than for a rich man to get into heaven.

And so the triumph of the 1933 Chicago World's Fair, *A Century of Progress*, fits very nicely into our American story. It is always darkest before the dawn, and good does triumph over evil, and if we just work hard enough and long enough, we will get to where we want to go. These were all components in the intersection of hard times, Prohibition, gangsters, nymphs, fame, fortune, and a world's fair held on a lakefront in a city in 1933.

After World War II the country would break from small towns into vast suburban planes huddled around large cities. Televisions, movies, airlines, mobility, the completion of the interstate highway system, and eventually globalism would make world's fairs obsolete. The thrill of the fair was seeing the world in one place. The world would later come into people's homes as television antennas dotted the horizon and we became a country of watchers. The thrill of a provincial people who had never ridden in an airplane or made a long-distance call and who went to a fair where all was possible would be gone.

Gangsters and nymphs are gone as well, but it is a testament that Al Capone and Sally Rand survived as icons. Immortality is granted to the few, and, as with Sally Rand's fan dance glimmering at us from YouTube videos, we can only imagine those people in their time. As, one day, people will imagine us.

CHAPTER FIFTY

End of the Fair

THE GATES TURNED ALL DAY ON OCTOBER 31, 1934, THE FINAL DAY OF *A Century of Progress*. Schools and public offices were closed. The mayor came. "R. E. Wedgewood came one last time; a seventy-eight-year-old man who had attended more than any other fairgoer—314 times in two years. People toured the House of Tomorrow, observed premature babies in incubators, filled the cafes to capacity . . . searched the souvenir stands for keepsakes."[1]

Pins, jewelry, playing cards, token medals, bookends, ashtrays, canes, purses, and beer steins were snatched from vendors who discounted everything. Children coveted a "toy Radio Flyer Wagon, a cast iron Greyhound bus, a Fort Dearborn construction kit . . . or a world's fair brownie box camera."[2] President Rufus Dawes gave a closing speech in the Court of States: "Were we to live a thousand years, we would never forget it, for it lifted up our spirits, restored our souls and brought us hope."[3]

Then Dawes pressed a button at midnight and ignited the sky with fireworks. Celestial starlight had opened the parade, and gunpowder would close it. Then a bugler played taps over the loudspeaker, and people cried. The 1933 World's Fair, *A Century of Progress*, the great respite from the Great Depression, was really over. Some people began to leave, but some stayed. Then the rioting broke out. Major Lenox Lohr recorded what happened next with all the flair of a military engineer. Even through his stilted prose, one can feel his shock that the people had suddenly turned on him and the fairgrounds.

Until eleven thirty at night the enormous crowd packing the grounds had behaved just as they had all days preceding. Then, as if by magic, over three and a half miles of Fair front, pandemonium broke loose. Everything that could be moved was taken; signs, some with letters six feet tall, light fixtures, benches, chairs, ornamental facades, curtains, anything which they could pick up, reach or climb to. Of the sixty-five huge pennants along the Avenue of Flags, not a shred remained. . . . Hundreds of small trees and shrubs were pulled up by the roots and carried as far as the gates where they were reluctantly left. There was literally a small forest around each gate the next morning.[4]

Fireman turned hoses on the vandals to stop the looting. Items left behind covered an acre outside the gates. What to make of this? The people of Chicago had glimpsed the future and respectfully toured that world and then destroyed it at the end. Maybe poor people were grabbing what they could or young adults were taking advantage of a city left unguarded. When the fair ended, it seemingly became public property. These were hard times, and here were all these unobtainable things. Major Lohr could not bring himself to condemn the people who had frequented the fair. He saw the looting as people wanting to just take home "a souvenir, a memento, a keepsake of the Fair they loved so much and which in a few minutes would pass forever. So they literally began to take the fair apart. It was done without malice, it was not done by hoodlums, it was perfectly understandable, but the devastation was unbelievable."[5]

This seems naive wishful thinking. Could it be that Chicagoans in 1934 harbored ill will toward anyone who had more than they? Chicago was among the hardest hit of all cities during the Great Depression. *A Century of Progress* called out to people to embrace a future in which technology and science would produce a more perfect world, but were people ready for it? World War II would show the vicious underbelly of humanity in less than a decade, when industrial powers tried to annihilate each other with primal rage that still lurked just beneath the surface. The Secret Six and others had saved Chicago from Capone, but they could not save Chicagoans from themselves.

The fair was torn down quickly, leaving as a reminder only an ancient Roman column donated by Benito Mussolini. Many exhibits went to the Museum of Science and Industry, "including the Pioneer Zephyr train in which visitors experience a recreation of the streamliner's famous run from Denver to A Century of Progress."[6] The Sky Ride was special and a spectacle to the end. "The reverberating report of 120 pounds of dynamite blasting apart the connections of the two main cables with the anchorage to the west of the tower at 5:55 AM gave notice that the instant had come to crash the [625-foot west] tower." It wobbled and seemed to fight back; then "came a shrieking screaming chorus of rending steel"[7] as it fell to earth with a crash.

The public protested its noninvolvement in the demolition, and the bringing down of the second tower became a spectacle. It was the last show of the 1933 World's Fair, and the crowd that gathered at Lagoon Theater was not disappointed when the east tower thundered to the ground after Thermite burned through the steel and the tower fell in upon itself. Various buildings were sold or donated, and the rest were destroyed. Sally Rand's dressing room ended up in the richest enclave on the North Shore of Chicago. An estate in Lake Forest became probably the only shrine to the fan dancer of the world's fair. Sally Rand, who would find fame but not fortune, would have approved.

Epilogue

Chicago mayor Anton Cermak was shot on February 15, 1933, while shaking hands with President-elect Franklin D. Roosevelt. He died weeks later of his wounds. Many speculated that the assassination was Al Capone's payback for the mayor's efforts to clean up Chicago. Some thought Frank Nitti was behind it, after having experienced an attempt against his life by three Chicago cops. Actually, the shooter, Giuseppe Zangara, had wanted to shoot Roosevelt and missed when Lillian Cross hit his arm as he fired. Zangara's statement to police said he hated rich and powerful people. The truth is that Mayor Cermak was at the wrong place at the wrong time.

After the world's fair ended, Al Capone still popped up in the newspapers and peppered the courts with appeals. The federal government found him a rock in its shoe and moved him to a new maximum-security prison, Alcatraz, "a craggy thumb-shaped rock in the middle of San Francisco Bay . . . with dense fogs and chill winds blowing in from the Pacific."[1] Alcatraz was practically escape proof. Swimming to San Francisco through the rough, icy waters of the bay would result in certain death. Al Capone was truly cut off from the world.

The end of Prohibition deflated the Capone organization in Chicago. The convictions of Jake Guzik and the Capone brothers Al and Ralph had cut the head off the snake. Jack McGurn was gunned down on February 15, 1936. The target of the St. Valentine's Day Massacre, Bugs Moran, went to prison in 1946 and died there in 1957. Frank Nitti, who took over the organization after Capone went to jail, was shot by three policemen in 1932. He survived and ran what was left of the organization for a decade. After being indicted for extorting millions from movie executives, he committed suicide in Riverside, Illinois.

George Johnson continued to serve as US attorney for the Northern District. His legacy from the Capone conviction showed through when O. J. Simpson was found guilty of stealing sports memorabilia. Prosecutions of serious criminals for lesser crimes had become known as "Capone-style cases." George Johnson died in 1949, and the Chicago papers immortalized him: "He will be remembered as the man who fought and defeated the most ruthless crime syndicate of our day."[2]

Al Capone would be released from Alcatraz on January 6, 1939, a broken man. Syphilis had robbed him of his mind, and he could not do simple math. He went to a federal penitentiary on Terminal Island in Los Angeles to finish out a year on a misdemeanor charge. On November 16, 1939, Capone was set free. The rest of his life was a slow descent due to the ravages of venereal disease. After a stroke on January 18, 1947, Al Capone died. The *Chicago Tribune* gave him a bitter sendoff: "Al Capone was a vile influence on Chicago from the day he came here until he was finally rendered harmless by the occupational disease of his original disease of pandering."[3]

Sally Rand did very well after the world's fair. She was famous and, to some degree, rich. After a string of unsuccessful marriages and a Hollywood comeback that fizzled, she returned to her fan dance and stayed on the circuit for the rest of her life, living out of hotel rooms. She would perform all the way up until she was seventy, though she died in obscurity in 1974. Among her personal papers are multiple filings for bankruptcies and the dunning letters of creditors. Sally Rand's arc was that of most people who find and then lose fame. She had lived long enough to find obscurity but never quit working. When a photographer took an unflattering photograph of her at sixty doing her fan dance, it was probably one of the few times the power of illusion did not save her.

Rufus Dawes would continue as president of the Century of Progress Corporation and of the Museum of Science and Industry in Chicago until his death in 1940. Charles Dawes retired from banking and government and died in 1951. Lenox Lohr went on to head the National Broadcasting Company and then became president of the Field Museum. He would write several books, including one on the management of the 1933 fair. He then organized the 1948 and 1949 Chicago railroad fairs.

He just couldn't get enough. His final contribution was to give all his organizational papers to the University of Illinois, Chicago. Truly he was a world's fair man. He died in 1968.

If you walk on Northerly Island today, there is nothing left of the fair except for the one Roman column donated by the Italians. It sits there as a strange monolith to a people long gone. The bikers ride past along the lakefront on brightly colored bikes, wearing synthetic clothes that would have amazed people in 1933. But the fair gave them a glimpse of the future, and the column stands as a totem between past and present. One can touch the smooth column, blink, and for just a second see those people at the fair during the Great Depression, trying to find a moment of light in all that darkness.

They are not so different from ourselves.

NOTES

Forty Years Later
1. Mangum, *F. Scott Fitzgerald in Context*, 311.
2. Korom, *The American Skyscraper*, 93.
3. Pridmore, *Marshall Field's*, 24.

Chapter 2: Valentine's Day, 1929
1. Bergreen, *Capone*, 34.
2. Ibid., 35.
3. Ibid., 299.
4. Willbanks, *Machine Guns*, 183.
5. Ibid., 86.
6. Parr, *True and Complete Story of Machine Gun Jack McGurn*, 190.
7. Bergreen, *Capone*, 310.
8. Ibid., 311.
9. Jeffers, *History's Greatest Conspiracies*, 122.

Chapter 3: Chicago's Second World's Fair
1. Bergreen, *Capone*, 312.
2. Ibid.
3. Ibid., 313.
4. G. Phillips, *On This Day*, 81.
5. Bergreen, *Capone*, 313.

Chapter 4: WAMPAS Baby Star
1. Knox, *Sally Rand*, 4.
2. Ibid., 5.
3. Ibid., 7.
4. Ibid., 15.

Chapter 5: Public Enemy Number One
1. Bergreen, *Capone*, 315.
2. Eig, *Get Capone*, 133.
3. Adler, *Hollywood and the Mob*, 12.
4. Bergreen, *Capone*, 20.
5. Watson, *Crime and Justice*, 269.

Chapter 6: *The White City*
1. Larson, *Devil in the White City*, 238.
2. Ibid.
3. Ibid., 423n383.
4. Ibid., 33.
5. Ibid., 95.
6. Ibid., 185.
7. Ibid.
8. Ibid., 373.

Chapter 7: *Bootlegging*
1. Marryat, *A Diary in America*, 47.
2. Ibid., 43.
3. Minnick, *Whiskey Women*, 68.
4. Okrent, *Last Call*, 197.
5. Ibid., 206.
6. Ibid., 207.
7. Ibid., 211.
8. Bergreen, *Capone*, 262.

Chapter 8: *The Big Man*
1. Eig, *Get Capone*, 84.
2. Ibid., 191.
3. Ibid., 192.
4. Cray, Kotler, and Beller, *American Datelines*, 210.
5. Capone, *Uncle Al Capone*, 12.
6. Ibid., 13.
7. Eig, *Get Capone*, 203.
8. Ibid., 205.
9. Ibid., 206.
10. Ibid., 209.
11. Ibid., 219.
12. Ibid.

Chapter 9: *The Big Fellah Comes Home*
1. Eig, *Get Capone*, 213.
2. Ibid.
3. Ibid.
4. Ibid., 223.
5. Ibid., 228.
6. Ibid., 229.
7. Ibid.

Chapter 10: The Perfect Storm
1. Eig, *Get Capone*.
2. Ibid.
3. Ibid.
4. Ibid., 243.
5. Ibid.
6. Ibid.
7. Hafer and Hein, *Stock Market*, 27.
8. Lion, *Bix*, 234.
9. Roberts, *America's First Great Depression*.
10. Shannon, *Great Depression*, 36.
11. Ibid.
12. Eig, *Get Capone*, 245.
13. Krugman, Wells, and Graddy, *Essentials of Economics*, 293.

Chapter 11: Financing a Fair
1. Ganz, *1933 Chicago World's Fair*, 43.
2. Ibid., 40.
3. Ibid., 41.
4. As quoted in ibid., 41.
5. Ibid., 42.
6. Ibid., 42.
7. Lohr, *Fair Management*.
8. Ibid., 13.
9. Ibid., 32.
10. Ibid.
11. Ibid., 33.
12. Ibid.
13. Eig, *Get Capone*, 225.

Chapter 12: The Untouchables
1. Eig, *Get Capone*, 236.
2. Ibid., 239.
3. Ibid., 240.
4. Ibid., 241.
5. Ibid., 297.

Chapter 13: Birth of the Nymph
1. Ganz, *1933 Chicago World's Fair*, 13.
2. See Fitzgerald, *Collected Stories*.
3. Ganz, *1933 Chicago World's Fair*, 14.
4. Ibid.
5. Ibid., 13.

6. Ibid.
7. Ibid., 14.
8. Ibid.
9. Ibid.
10. Knox, *Sally Rand*, 20.
11. Ibid., 21.
12. Ibid., 22.
13. Ibid.
14. Ganz, *1933 Chicago World's Fair*, 8.

Chapter 14: Death in the Underground
1. Kobler, *Capone*, 262.
2. Hoffman, *Scarface Al and the Crime Crusaders*, 91.
3. Eig, *Get Capone*.
4. Hoffman, *Scarface Al and the Crime Crusaders*, 91.
5. Ibid.
6. Goodman, *Tracks to Murder*, 62.
7. Stuart, *The Twenty Incredible Years*, 416.

Chapter 15: Breaking Ground
1. Ganz, *1933 Chicago World's Fair*, 46.
2. Ibid.
3. Ibid.
4. Ibid., 47.
5. Lohr, *Fair Management*, 54.
6. Ibid., 58.
7. Ibid., 56.
8. Ibid.
9. Ibid.
10. Ibid., 57.
11. Ibid., 58.
12. Ibid., 59.

Chapter 16: The Secret Six
1. Eig, *Get Capone*, 256.
2. Ibid.
3. Ibid.
4. Ibid.
5. Hoffman, *Scarface Al and the Crime Crusaders*, 141.
6. Ibid., 142.
7. Ibid.
8. Ibid., 145.
9. Ibid.
10. Ibid.
11. Ibid.

Chapter 17: The Modernists
1. Lohr, *Fair Management*, 62.
2. Ibid., 60.
3. Lohr, *Fair Management*, 60; *The Inland Architect and News Record* 44: 30.
4. Lohr, *Fair Management*, 61.
5. Schrenk, *Building a Century of Progress*, 55.
6. Ibid.
7. Ibid.
8. Ibid., 59.
9. Ibid., 56.
10. Ibid.
11. Ibid., 57.
12. Ibid.
13. Ibid.
14. Ibid.
15. Ibid., 58.
16. Ibid.
17. Ibid., 59.
18. Larson, *Devil in the White City*, 26.

Chapter 18: Lady Godiva
1. Knox, *Sally Rand*, 23.
2. Ibid., 35.
3. Ibid.
4. Ibid., 37.
5. Ibid., 37.

Chapter 19: Horatio Alger Returns
1. Eig, *Get Capone*, 268.
2. Ibid., 266.
3. Ibid.
4. Ibid., 447.
5. Ibid., 273.
6. Ibid., 275.
7. Ibid., 276.
8. Hoffman, *Scarface Al and the Crime Crusaders*, 146.
9. Ibid.
10. Ibid., 147.
11. Ibid., 148.

Chapter 20: The Design
1. Florman, *Good Guys, Wise Guys, and Putting Up Buildings*, 149.
2. Lohr, *Fair Management*, 63.
3. Ibid.

4. Schrenk, *Building a Century of Progress*, 62.
5. Ibid., 63.
6. Lohr, *Fair Management*, 64.
7. Schrenk, *Building a Century of Progress*, 63.
8. Ibid., 66.
9. Lohr, *Fair Management*, 64.
10. Schrenk, *Building a Century of Progress*, 68.
11. Ibid.

Chapter 21: The Secret Six Get to Work
1. Estleman, *Confessions of Al Capone*, 254.
2. Hoffman, *Scarface Al and the Crime Crusaders*, 149.
3. Ibid., 150.
4. Ibid.
5. Ibid., 150–51.
6. Ibid., 151.
7. Ibid., 152.
8. Ibid.

Chapter 22: Beginning to Build the Rainbow City
1. Ganz, *1933 Chicago World's Fair*, 72.
2. Lohr, *Fair Management*, 188.
3. Ibid., 189.
4. Ibid., 182.
5. Ibid., 192.
6. Ibid., 193.
7. Ibid.
8. Ibid.
9. Ibid.

Chapter 23: Gold Diggers
1. Ganz, *1933 Chicago World's Fair*, 18.
2. Ibid.
3. Ibid.
4. Ibid.
5. Knox, *Sally Rand*, 30.

Chapter 24: Meeting Al Capone
1. Hoffman, *Scarface Al and the Crime Crusaders*, 1.
2. Ibid., 2–3.
3. Ibid., 155.
4. Ibid.
5. Ibid., 157.

Chapter 25: Water, Electric, and the Sky Ride
1. Lohr, *Fair Management*, 250.
2. Ibid.
3. Ibid., 107.
4. Ibid., 241.
5. Ibid., 242.

Chapter 26: One Hundred Thousand
1. Eig, *Get Capone*, 296.
2. Ibid., 296.
3. Ibid., 297.
4. Tully, *Treasury Agent*, 66.
5. Bergreen, *Capone*, 452.
6. Eig, *Get Capone*, 292.
7. Hoffman, *Scarface Al and the Crime Crusaders*, 159.

Chapter 27: The Depression Fair
1. Stillman, *Great Depression*.
2. Curry, Sproat, and Cramer, *The Shaping of America*, 524.
3. Eig, *Get Capone*, 301.
4. McNiff, *Values and Virtues*, 7.
5. Lohr, *Fair Management*, 34.
6. Ibid., 37.
7. Ibid., 37.
8. Ibid., 70.
9. Ibid., 71.

Chapter 29: Springtime in Chicago
1. G. Phillips, *Gangsters*, 6.

Chapter 30: The Sky Ride
1. *Chicago Tribune*, July 14, 1934.
2. Ganz, *1933 Chicago World's Fair*, 75.
3. Lohr, *Fair Management*, 233.
4. Ibid., 173.
5. Ibid.
6. Ganz, *1933 Chicago World's Fair*, 74.
7. Lohr, *Fair Management*, 172.

Chapter 31: The Trial of Al Capone
1. Hoffman, *Scarface Al and the Crime Crusaders*, 144.

Chapter 32: Color and Light
1. Schrenk, *Building a Century of Progress*, 101.
2. Ibid., 102.

3. Ibid.
4. Ibid.
5. Ibid., 103.
6. Blaszczyk, *Color Revolution*, 208.
7. Lohr, *Fair Management*, 61.
8. Ibid.
9. Schrenk, *Building a Century of Progress*, 104.
10. Ganz, *1933 Chicago World's Fair*, 62.

Chapter 33: The Plea Bargain
1. Eig, *Get Capone*, 330.
2. Ibid., 332–33.
3. Ibid., 333.

Chapter 34: The Temple of Womanhood
1. Ganz, *1933 Chicago World's Fair*, 98.
2. Ibid.
3. Ibid., 92.
4. Ibid., 90.
5. Ibid., 92.
6. Ibid.
7. Ibid., 93.
8. Ibid.
9. Ibid., 94.
10. Ibid., 95.
11. Ibid.
12. Ibid., 96.
13. Ibid.
14. Ibid., 97.
15. Ibid.

Chapter 35: The Bad Plea Bargain
1. Eig, *Get Capone*, 333.
2. Ibid., 334.
3. Ibid., 335.
4. Ibid., 336.
5. Ibid., 338.
6. Ibid.
7. Ibid., 340.
8. Ibid., 341.

Chapter 36: Frank Lloyd Wright's Fair
1. Schrenk, *Building a Century of Progress*, 188.
2. Ibid.
3. Ibid., 189.

4. Ibid.
5. Ibid.
6. Ibid.
7. Ibid.
8. Ibid., 190.
9. Ibid.
10. Ibid.
11. Ibid.
12. Ibid., 191.
13. Ibid., 192.
14. Ibid.
15. Ibid.
16. Ibid.
17. Ibid., 192.
18. Ibid.
19. Ibid., 193.
20. Ibid., 195.
21. *Time* 17 (1931): 63.
22. Schrenk, *Building a Century of Progress*, 197.

Chapter 37: Hayseeds
1. As quoted in Eig, *Get Capone*, 342.
2. Ibid.
3. Ibid., 345.
4. Ibid.
5. Ibid.
6. Ibid., 347.
7. Ibid.
8. Ibid.

Chapter 38: The Gaseous Tube
1. Schrenk, *Building a Century of Progress*, 108.
2. Lohr, *Fair Management*, 105.
3. Schrenk, *Building a Century of Progress*, 106.
4. Lohr, *Fair Management*, 106.
5. Schrenk, *Building a Century of Progress*, 109.
6. Ibid., 110.
7. Ibid.
8. Ibid., 109.

Chapter 39: The Trial of Al Capone
1. Eig, *Get Capone*, 350.
2. Ibid., 353.
3. Ibid.

4. Ibid., 161.
5. Ibid., 356.

Chapter 40: The Disposable Fair
1. Lohr, *Fair Management*, 227.
2. Ibid.
3. Ibid.
4. Schrenk, *Building a Century of Progress*, 130.
5. Ibid.
6. Ibid., 131.
7. Ibid.
8. Ibid., 134.
9. Ibid.
10. Lohr, *Fair Management*, 67.
11. Ibid.

Chapter 41: Verdict
1. Eig, *Get Capone*, 360.
2. Ibid.
3. Ibid.
4. Ibid.
5. Ibid.
6. Ibid.
7. Ibid., 365.
8. Ibid., 367.
9. Ibid.

Chapter 42: Racing the Clock
1. Lohr, *Fair Management*, 193.
2. Ibid., 82.
3. Ibid.
4. Ibid., 83.
5. Ibid., 84.
6. Ibid., 85.
7. Ibid., 86.

Chapter 43: Capone on Ice
1. As quoted in Eig, *Get Capone*, 370.
2. Ibid.
3. Ibid.
4. Ibid., 374.
5. Ibid., 375.
6. Ibid.

Chapter 44: Lady Godiva Again
1. Lohr, *Fair Management*, 197.

Chapter 45: Death of the Untouchables
1. Allsop, *Bootleggers*, 189.
2. Hoffman, *Scarface Al and the Crime Crusaders*, 171.
3. Ibid.
4. Ibid.

Chapter 46: A Day at the Fair
1. V. Ciske, personal interview.
2. Ibid.
3. *Chicago Tribune*, June 1, 1934.
4. Ciske, interview.
5. Ibid.

Chapter 47: Sex at the Fair
1. Ganz, *1933 Chicago World's Fair*, 19.
2. Ibid.
3. Ibid., 20.
4. Ibid.
5. Ibid.
6. Ibid., 21.
7. Ibid.
8. Ibid., 22.
9. Ibid.
10. Ibid., 23.
11. Ibid.
12. Ibid., 24.
13. Ibid.
14. Ibid., 23.
15. Ibid.
16. Ibid., 25.
17. Ibid., 26.
18. Ibid., 27.

Chapter 48: A Century of Progress
1. Ganz, *1933 Chicago World's Fair*, 75.
2. *Chicago Tribune, A Century of Progress*, 27.
3. Schrenk, *Building a Century of Progress*, 131.
4. Ganz, *1933 Chicago World's Fair*, 156.
5. Ibid., 157.

Chapter 50: End of the Fair

1. Ganz, *1933 Chicago World's Fair*, 151.
2. Ibid.
3. Ibid., 152.
4. Lohr, *Fair Management*, 261.
5. Ibid.
6. Ganz, *1933 Chicago World's Fair*, 153.
7. Ibid., 265.

Epilogue

1. Eig, *Get Capone*, 396.
2. Ibid., 388.
3. Ibid., 396.

Bibliography

Adler, Tim. *Hollywood and the Mob: Movies, Mafia, Sex and Death*. London: Blooms-bury, 2008.

Allsop, Kenneth. *The Bootleggers: The Story of Chicago's Prohibition Era*. London: True Crime Library, 1998.

Asbury, Herbet. *The Great Illusion: An Informal History of Prohibition*. New York: Green-wood Press, 1968.

Bergreen, Laurence. *Capone: The Man and the Era*. New York: Simon and Schuster, 1996.

Blaszczyk, Regina Lee. *The Color Revolution*. Cambridge, MA: Massachusetts Institute of Technology Press, 2012.

Burnham, Daniel, Jr. "How Chicago Finances Its Exposition." *Review of Reviews*, Octo-ber 1932.

Capone, Deirdre Marie. *Uncle Al Capone: The Untold Story from Inside His Family*. Fort Myers, FL: Recap Lodge Press, 2010.

Chicago Tribune. *A Century of Progress: A Photographic Tour of the 1933–34 Chicago World's Fair*. Chicago: Agate Digital, 2016.

Cotter, Bill. *Chicago's 1933–34 World's Fair: A Century of Progress*. Charleston, SC: Arcadia, 2015.

Cray, Ed, Jonathan Kotler, and Miles Beller, eds. *American Datelines: Major News Stories from Colonial Times to the Present*. Chicago: University of Illinois Press, 2003.

Curry, Richard, John G. Sproat, and Kenyon C. Cramer. *The Shaping of America*. New York: Holt, Rinehart and Winston, 1972.

Eig, Jonathan. *Get Capone: The Secret Plot That Captured America's Most Wanted Gangster*. New York: Simon and Schuster, 2010.

Engelmann, Larry. *Intemperance: The Lost War Against Liquor*. New York: Macmillan, 1979.

Estleman, Loren D. *The Confessions of Al Capone: A Novel*. New York: Forge Books, 2013.

F. Husum Publishing Company. *Chicago and the World's Fair*. Chicago: F. Husum Pub-lishing Company, 1933.

Findling, John. *Chicago's Great World's Fairs*. New York: Manchester University Press, 1994.

Fitzgerald, F. Scott. *Collected Stories of F. Scott Fitzgerald: Flappers and Philosophers/Tales of the Jazz Age*. New York: Barnes & Noble, 2007.

Florman, Sam. *Good Guys, Wise Guys, and Putting Up Buildings*. New York: Thomas Dunne, 2012.

Ganz, Cheryl. *The 1933 Chicago World's Fair: A Century of Progress*. Champaign: University of Illinois Press, 2008.

Goodman, Jonathan. *Tracks to Murder*. Kent, OH: Kent State University Press, 2005.

Hafer, Rick W., and Scott E. Hein. *The Stock Market*. Westport, CT: Greenwood Press, 2007.

Harvey, Corbett. "The Architecture of the World's Fair." *Journal of the Royal Architectural Institute of Canada* (June 1934).

Hines, Thomas. *Burnham of Chicago: Architect and Planner*. Chicago: University of Chicago, 1974.

Hoffman, Dennis. *Scarface Al and the Crime Crusaders: Chicago's Private War Against Capone*. Carbondale: Southern Illinois University Press, 1993.

Jeffers, H. Paul. *History's Greatest Conspiracies: One Hundred Plots, Real and Suspected, That Have Shocked, Fascinated, and Sometimes Changed the World*. Guilford, CT: Lyons Press, 2004.

Kilham, Walter H. *Raymond Hood, Architect: Form Through Function in the American Skyscraper*. New York: Taylor, 1973.

Knox, Holly. *Sally Rand: From Film to Fans*. Bend, OR: Maverick, 1988.

Kobler, John. *Capone: The Life and World of Al Capone*. New York: Da Capo Press, 2003.

Korom, Joseph, Jr. *The American Skyscraper, 1850–1940*. Boston: Branden Books, 2008.

Krugman, Paul, Robin Wells, and Kathryn Graddy. *Essentials of Economics*. 2nd edition. New York: Worth, 2009.

Larson, Eric. *The Devil in the White City*. New York: Crown, 2003.

Levin, Phyllis Lee. *Edith and Woodrow: The Wilson White House*. New York: Scribner, 2001.

Lion, Jean Pierre. *Bix: The Definitive Biography of a Jazz Legend*. New York: Continuum, 2005.

Literary Digest. "All Roads Lead to Chicago's Rainbow City." *Literary Digest* (June 1933).

Lohr, Lenox. *Fair Management: The Story of a Century of Progress*. Chicago: Cuneo Press, 1952.

Mangum, Bryant. *F. Scott Fitzgerald in Context*. Cambridge: Cambridge University Press, 2013.

Marryat, C. B. *A Diary in America*. 1923; rpt. San Bernadino, CA: Ulan Press, 2012.

McNiff, Jean. *Values and Virtues in Higher Education Research: Critical Perspectives*. New York: Routledge, 2016.

Minnick, Fred. *Whiskey Women: The Untold Story of How Women Saved Bourbon, Scotch, and Irish Whiskey*. Sterling, VA: Potomac, 2013.

Murray, George. *The Legacy of Al Capone*. New York: G. P. Putnam's Sons, 1975.

Okrent, Daniel. *Last Call: The Rise and Fall of Prohibition*. New York: Simon and Schuster, 2010.

Parr, Amanda J. *The True and Complete Story of Machine Gun Jack McGurn: Chief Bodyguard and Hit Man to Chicago's Most Infamous Crime Czar Al Capone and Mastermind of the St. Valentine's Day Massacre.* Leicester, UK: Matador, 2005.

Phillips, David. *On This Day.* iUniverse, 2007.

Phillips, Gene D. *Gangsters and G-Men on Screen.* New York: Rowman & Littlefield, 2014.

Pridmore, Jay. *Marshall Field's: A Building from the Chicago Architecture Foundation.* San Francisco: Pomegranate, 2002.

Roberts, Alasdair. *America's First Great Depression: Economic Crisis and Political Disorder After the Panic of 1837.* Ithaca, NY: Cornell University Press, 2012.

Rydell, Robert. *World of Fairs: The Century-of-Progress Expositions.* Chicago: University of Chicago Press, 1993.

Schrenk, Lisa. *Building a Century of Progress: The Architecture of Chicago's 1933–34 World's Fair.* Minneapolis: University of Minnesota Press, 2007.

Shannon, David A. *The Great Depression.* New York: Prentice Hall, 1960.

Stillman, Edmund O. *The Great Depression.* New York: New Word City, 2015.

Stuart, William. *The Twenty Incredible Years.* Chicago: M. A. Donahue, 1935.

Tully, Andrew. *Treasury Agent: The Inside Story.* New York: Simon and Schuster, 1958.

Watson, Carolyn Boyles. *Crime and Justice: Learning Through Cases.* 2nd ed. Lanham, MD: Rowman & Littlefield, 2013.

Willbanks, James. *Machine Guns: An Illustrated History of Their Impact.* Santa Barbara, CA: ABC-CLIO, 2004.

Wright, John Lloyd. *My Father, Frank Lloyd Wright.* London: Dover, 2012.

INDEX

About the Author

William Elliott Hazelgrove is the best-selling author of ten novels and four works of nonfiction: *Ripples*; *Tobacco Sticks*; *Mica Highways*; *Rocket Man*; *The Pitcher*; *Real Santa*; *Jackpine*; *My Best Year*; *The Bad Author*; *The Pitcher 2*; *Hemingway's Attic*; *Madam President: The Secret Presidency of Edith Wilson*; *Forging a President: How the Wild West Created Teddy Roosevelt*; and *Al Capone and the 1933 World's Fair: The End of the Gangster Era in Chicago*. His books have received starred reviews in *Publisher Weekly* and *Booklist*; been selected by Book of the Month, Literary Guild, History Book Club, and Junior Library Guild; received ALA Editors' Choice Awards; and been optioned for the movies. He was the Ernest Hemingway writer-in-residence, writing in the attic of Ernest Hemingway's birthplace. He has written articles and reviews for *USA Today* and other publications. He has been the subject of interviews on NPR's *All Things Considered* and featured in the *New York Times*, *Los Angeles Times*, *Chicago Tribune*, *Chicago Sun Times*, *Richmond Times Dispatch*, *USA Today*, and *People* and on NBC, WBEZ, and WGN. He runs a political-cultural blog, *The View from Hemingway's Attic*. Visit him at www.williamhazelgrove.com.